Hotel Management
and
Administrative Practices

Hotel Management and Administrative Practices

Devesh Bhushan

RANDOM PUBLICATIONS
NEW DELHI (INDIA)

Hotel Management and Administrative Practices

ISBN 978-93-5111-495-6

Published in 2015 in India by

RANDOM PUBLICATIONS

4376-A/4B, Gali Murari Lal, Ansari Road
New Delhi-110 002
Phone : +9111-43580356, 011-23289044, 011-43142548
e-mail: sales@randompublications.com,
info@randompublications.com, randomexports@gmail.com

Reprinted 2019

Type Setting by : Friends Media, Delhi-110089
Printed at : Thomson Press (India) Ltd.

Preface

There are many different industries all over the world. But there are few industries which are called successful business. There is a long way between business and successful business. Business becomes successful by a proper management system. So the management system is very important in the sector of development.

The management system that manages all things about hotel business is called hotel management. A hotel general manger has to look after all activities of the hotel including hotel administration, accounts, marketing, maintenance, housekeeping, food and beverage management and catering. This management system runs the hotel properly and manages every single thing according to the way it should be. Mistakes are banned in this type of management system. Because proper management depends on how perfectly it managed. So each and every person related to this hotel management system should be careful and should be aware of responsibility. That's way the management board needs professionals for their management system.

Today many universities and educational institutions prefer hotel management as a subject to their students. They provide the environment and training opportunities to their students. After completing the course of hotel management, they can apply to various and luxurious hotels all over the world.

Describing in great depth and detail all areas of hotel management and administration, this book provides an up-to-date and comprehensive examination of the responsibilities of a hotel general manager. It shares with readers the procedures effective managers use to ensure their hotel's and their own success. It will be an ideal book for university hospitality programs and management training programs within the hotel industry.

Author

Contents

1

Hotel Organizational Structure

Lodging is an important component of the tourism industry, providing accommodation to travelers while away from home. Lodging operations are diverse, ranging from small bed-andbreakfast properties in rural locations to large hotels with several thousand rooms in major cities.

In addition to generally having higher occupancy and average daily rate, chain properties tend to be more profitable, delivering trading profit per room seven times more than their independent counterparts. As a result, the industry is expected to continue to consolidate, with an increasing number of mergers and acquisitions resulting in a small number of large companies dominating the marketplace. A differentiation must be made between hotel ownership, hotel branding, and hotel operations. Historical developments with Real Estate Investment Trusts (REITs) in the United States gave rise to a situation where many owners could not operate their own hotels.

Instead they must use a separate management company to oversee day-to-day operations, resulting in a split between hotel ownership and hotel operations.The situation is further complicated by the widespread use of both franchises and marketing agreements that provide a consumer brand and require compliance with brand standards.

At any one time there may be up to three parties holding a stake in the operations of a particular property:

(1) the owner, who holds title to the assets, is responsible for mortgage payments and provides the capital for the operation;

(2) the brand, which brands the property and provides standards, distribution services, marketing, technology, and other services; and

(3) the management company, which provides management talent and operates the property on a day-to-day basis.

Within each management company the brand portfolio is quite mixed, with each company operating under a variety of competing flags in different geographical markets. In the US lodging industry there are multiple stakeholders with, at times competing, interest in the operations of the property.

A working knowledge of the classifications used in the hotel industry is important to understanding its organization. The various types of properties, their market orientation and location, sales indicators, occupancy, and revenues as they relate to levels of service and various types of business affiliations are all means of classifying hotel properties.

Types of Lodging Facilities

Classification of hotel facilities is not based on rigid criteria. The definitions can change depending on market forces, legal criteria, location, function, and, in some cases, personal preference, but the definitions that follow are generally accepted.

Hotels

A hotel usually offers guests a full range of accommo-dations and services, which may include reservations, suites, public dining and banquet facilities, lounge and entertainment areas, room service, cable television, personal computers, business services, meeting rooms, specialty shops, personal services, valet, laundry, hair care, swimming pool and other recreational activities, gaming/casino operations, ground transportation to and from an airport, and concierge services. The size of the property can range from 20 to more than 2,000 rooms. Hotels are found in center-city, suburban, and airport locations. Guest stays can be overnight or long-term, as much as several weeks in length. Properties sometimes specialize in catering to particular markets, such as conventions or gambling. Casino hotels usually take a secondary role to the casino operation, where the emphasis is on profitable gaming operations. Marriott's hotels operated as JW Marriott Hotels & Resorts and Renaissance Hotels, as well as Hyatt Hotels & Resorts brands operated as Hyatt Regency, Grand Hyatt, and Park Hyatt Hotels, are examples in this category.

Motels

Motels offer guests a limited range of services, which may include reservations, vending machines, swimming pools, and cable television. The size of these properties averages from 10 to 50 units. Motels are usually in suburban highway and airport locations. Guests typically stay overnight or for a few days. Motels may be located near a freestanding restaurant.

All-Suites

The all-suites concept was developed in the 1980s as a separate marketing concept. These hotels offer guests a wide range of services that may include reservations, living room and separate bedroom, kitchenette, optional public dining room and room service, cable television, videocassette players and recorders, specialty shops, personal services, valet and laundry, swimming pool, and ground transportation to and from an airport. The size of the operation can range from 50 to more than 100 units. This type of property is usually found in center-city, suburban, and airport locations. The length of guest stay can be overnight, several days, or long term. Although this type of hotel may seem new, many downtown, center-city hotels have offered accommodations with in-room kitchenette and sitting room since the early 1900s. Now with mass marketing—advertising products and services through mass communications such as television, radio, and the Internet—this type of hotel is considered "new." Examples of the all-suite concept include Hilton's Embassy Suites and InterContinental's Candlewood Suites.

Limited-Service Hotels

Limited-service hotels appeared in the mid-1980s. Hampton Inn and Marriott were among the first organizations to offer limited-service properties. The concept of limited service was developed for a specific segment of the market: business and cost-conscious travelers. The range of accommodations and services may include reservations, minimal public dining and meeting facilities, cable television, personal computers, personal services (valet and laundry), and ground transportation to and from an airport. The size of the property can range from 100 to more than 200 rooms. Limited-service hotels are found in center-city, suburban, and airport locations. They are usually located near restaurants for guest convenience. Guest stays can be overnight or long term. These properties sometimes specialize in catering to the business traveler and offer special business technology centers. Limited-service hotel properties include Holiday InnExpress, operated by InterContinetal Hotels Group; Comfort Inn, by Choice Hotels International; and Marriott's Fairfield Inn.

Extended-Stay Hotels

Extended-stay properties were designed to offer guests a home-away-from-home atmosphere over long stays precipitated by business, leisure, or personal necessity. For example, a person may have to attend to a business project for several days or weeks; another may want to visit with relatives whose home does not have adequate accommodations for visitors; a third may be accom-panying a relative or friend receiving an extended health treatment at a medical center and require overnight accommodations. The patient himself may appreciate the homelike atmosphere of the extended-stay hotel in which to recover between treatments.

Types of Hotels

Hotel is an establishment selling service-food, drink and shelter. The value and the potentiality of a hotel is assessed by the size, location, the number of rooms and other revenues earning points it possesses. The classification of hotels with in the industry is a complicated task. Hotel can be classified on different basis. Followings are some of the basis of classification:

Most of the hotels generally run on plan system. There are various types of plan, which are internationally recognised. Hoteliers according to their convenience or the policy of the management can adopt these. The list in which the prices of hotel services are incorporated is known as hotel tariff. On the basis of tariff pattern hotel are divided as follows:

— *European Plan*: In this case only the lodging i.e. bed is offered. Thus the charges are made for lodging only. The client is free to take or not to take teas, breakfast, and meals in the hotel. He has a choice of eating at any other good restaurant. The guest is booked to pay for lodging only and is charged separately for all other things or services he enjoys or consumes. This system is generally followed by youth hostels or hotels which are situated in metropolitan cities. European plan hotels fix the prices of rooms separately so that guest may either have their meals in the hotel dinning at its regular prices or go to the other restaurant. In India most of the hotels are being run on European Plan. Almost all the public sector hotels are run on this basis.

— *Continental Plan:* In the case of continental plan bed and breakfast are included in the charges. Thus bed is offered along with breakfast and the client is, however, free to take his meal and tea as he likes. Thus the guest tariff includes lodging and breakfast and for other he is separately billed.

— *American Plan*: Hotel where American plan is prevalent, board lodging is provided in the charge. The tariff fixed includes board and lodging. It is an all inclusive full board tariff. Accommodation and three meals daily are included in the price of the room. It includes bed, breakfast and two principal meals and evening tea. It does not include EMT nor coffee after lunch, or dinner. The needs are usually 'table d' hote'. It is also known as 'full pension'.This means that guests day ends about 24 hours after his arrival that is, the guest arriving between lunch and dinner is entitled to retain his room until the next afternoon and to have dinner the first night and breakfast and lunch the following day for the fixed rate. This analysis is mostly used at those tourist resorts, which are not situated in big cities. Most of the tourists who do not want to carry too much, has go for all inclusive accommodation so that the entire amount is paid at the starting point. These terms are supposed to be sold to the guest, though for internal record, a clear apportionment of charges between accommodation and meal is made. This is particularly important where some guests stay on inclusive terms and others not.

— *Modified American Plan (MAP):* The tourists mostly prefer this plan, as it is comparatively flexible. It is offered in most of the good hotels and is normally by arrangement. It includes hotel accommodation, breakfast and either lunch or dinner in the price of the room. Thus, in this type of accommodation bed and breakfast and along with it one principal meal, lunch or dinner, at the discretion of the client is also included. It generally includes continental breakfast and either 'table d' hotel' lunch or dinner in the room rates. It is also known as demi-pension. It has been observed that the Indian style hote Is in India follow the European plan, and the western style hotels which cater the foreign tourists, operate the American plan. In the past foreign tourists used to visit India for pleasure and leisure trips. They had plenty of time to travel and stay. Nowadays, we have typical tourists, businessmen or travelers, who would like to visit the country for a week and the city for a day. They do not have time and desire to return back to their hotels again and again.

International Hotels

There are modem western style hotels in all large cities as well as important tourist centers. These have been classified on the internationally accepted star ranging from 5 star to 1 star hotels. These are the hotels of international repute having more than 200 rooms with their counter parts in all the large cities. These establishments provide accommodations, restaurant facilities, grillrooms, banqueting suites and bars as an integral part of their businesses. There normal activities are often 'supplemented by shops' of diverse kinds, garages, laundry and similar services. Also, in many instances, residential, furnished and unfurnished flats equally belong to the over all operating company.

Hotels in the international grouping are mostly owned by public companies and controlled by a Board of Directors. The President/Chairman of the Board is usually a prominent figure of the industry, the secretary, a chartered accountant, and the managing director, a leading personality in the hotel industry. The overall operational responsibility of the company's affairs falls to the managing director. These hotels are generally divided into various departments under a resident/general manager who is, directly responsible to the managing director. The relationship and responsibilities of the departmental heads, general manager and. Managing director should be clearly defined and understood. The general manager manages the hotel through his departmental heads and all immediate operational data are his responsibility. The managing director takes charge of the broad operational and financial policies of the company.

Apart from the profitable lettable accommodation—the suites, flat lets, and studio rooms:-a considerable revenue is extracted from catering. There is a restaurant, which opens for luncheons and where also there are tea dances, and evening dinner dances. Good band and international fame cabarret artists are employed. The cliental dances to famous bands and are entertained by well-known cabaret artists. True to tradition the restaurant specialises in entertainment, the grillroom caters for the epicures and the banqueting suites, large and small, handle all the special and functional catering. The new thought in maximum revenue promotion from catering advocates three main regular activities over and above the banqueting business and the room service on the floors a large restaurant for entertainment operating a moderate "allin" tariff, a popular priced cafe complete with snack-bar and a small, select grillroom, a rendezvous of the gourmet working on a high price allocate service in return for the finest fare that money can purchase.

Residential Hotels

A purely residential hotel is not a hotel in the legal sense of the word since its tenants are not transients. Its methods of operation are quite similar to those of residential hotels. They serve a few rooms for visiting friends of their tenants, and most of them are glad to accommodate other transients in order to fill rooms that may be vacant. Example of such hotels is Oberoi Apartments, Qutab Hotel, and Oberoi Maiden etc. These are the largest group of all. They meet great need that of the resident. An endless mixture of varied sizes of residential establishments exists ranging from a few exclusive hotels to boarding houses of all kinds. Many of the quieter residential towns, large cities abound with these establishments. This group can be classified by the wealth of their patrons. The guests are drawn from different walk of life, people of independent means, from retired folk living on investments or pensions and from-men women wage earners. The residential hotel is the development of USA, evolving after people discovered that permanent living in hotels offer many advantages. A residential hotel usually apartment building with the service of a hotel, maid and linen services, dinning room and room services with board and possibly a cocktail lounge. Some are luxurious, and offer full suites, whereas others are moderate and feature single rooms. Although they are few in numbers, they usually let a room for a long period of time. In some of the cases their terms are weekly. They have fixed hours for breakfast lunch tea, dinner etc. These hotels are generally in the hands of private operators. Services and amenities provided are comparable to that of average well regulated home. The food is more or like a home style. As the residents are having fixed income, therefore it arises a number of economic problem for the owner.

The revenue of residential are more or less fixed where as the operating cost is increasing day by day. There are some advantages. The rent from room is fixed although most of the times these people are away from their rooms and secondly they are much less trouble some than any other residential. These types of hotels are the product individualistic family system. These hotels are found in USA. Terms are weekly. The turnover of residential is very slow, especially in good houses, although the more enterprising of residential housekeepers frequently set rooms aside for regular short stay visitors. The general standard of comforts of establishment can be described as adequate and resembles that of the average well regulated home. There are set hours to rise, to breakfast, lunch, and dinner. Though public rooms are provided the guest spends much of their time in their bed sitting studio type rooms. These hotels are usually privately owned owner operated. The staff consists of one or more waitresses or waiters, cook, kitchen and floor maid etc. The food is more home style. The economic of residential establishment has its problems.

The future of the residential establishments relies upon the service flat Service flats range from great block to smaller houses letting out one room letting out one room flat lets. The block of flats has its own restaurant, catering for residents and chance customers alike, and operates a room catering service. Experience has shown, that with this type of restaurant unless there is a possibility of strong and regular chance trade, both luncheon dinner and functional, the venture can prove very precious. Small one room flat both furnished and unfurnished are always good propositions. The latest thought advocates the equipping of small kitchen units comprising cooker, freezer and wash-up for those who find for themselves. Sometimes a room service is available in the form of room trays. The flats are centrally heated and serviced. Apartment houses of this nature are more reasonable to live in than guest houses, offering a fuller and more personal service. Residential premises equipped to be operated in the self-help idiom with a much labour—saving equipment as possible and the entire outfit designed to warrant the minimum of maintenance is the answer to high costs will become the guest house of the future for people of limited means.

Commercial Hotels

Commercial hotels depend mainly on executives and on the individual traveling for pleasure. Thus these hotels mainly cater for the commercial traveler and they are not found in all the larger provincial towns. As the hotel caters primarily to business people, it is generally convenient to establish these hotels near to office buildings, restaurant and entertainment outlets. All firms with connexions upon a nation wide scale send out their representatives on the road. Some 'reps', hilly an area to cover, others range the whole country, some travel with a display of goods, other travel light all have travel and lodging allowances.

Commercial travelers, with their set and often-limited expenses require in expensive accommodation. But being for the most men from good homes, they require a certain standard of comfort. These businessmen like company and enjoy getting together with their fellow travelers. For these reasons there are commercial hotels catering for their needs. The commercial requires good, plain, home-style food, a comfortable bed, clean surroundings and a place where they may read or write in peace. Stock rooms, let at a rental for displays, are usually available at these hotels. Facilities typically include small meeting and conference room, a medium sized restaurant and lounge and a swimming pool. Since occupancy at there hotels usually declines on weekends, many hotels have installed elaborate recreational amenities, health club, tennis court, all-year-round swimming pools.

Commercial hotels are normally owner run and a successful business depends upon their operating on a friendly and comfortable use. A good name is a sound asset with the 'knights of the road', who, amongst their community will recommend the good and warn against the not so good house. Success again depends upon the building of a consistent and regular business. The commercial is certainly a regular caller and will always patronise and remain faithful to a house where he is known and where a warm and comfortable welcome is guaranteed. The number of rooms in these hotels varies around the fifteen mark. The average guest stay is of short duration, though some have a wide area to cover and make the hotel their headquarters.

In some of the big industrial towns largely fully licensed commercial hotels exist complete with grill room, functional accommodation and garage, It must be emphasised that the commercial hotel is not and should never be taken for a poor type of lodging house. Neither should a bad concept be formed of the traveler. The modern commercial is an important businessman, a representative carefully selected by his firm. Marked attention is paid by the sales director to engage the right type—a man of education and integrity, because its representative knows a firm and obviously he must be carefully selected. Hoteliers who make a specialisation of catering for the commercial traveler not only find a regular and remunerative business, but a pleasant task as well.

Star Hotels

The hotel on completion is inspected as a functioning establishment or approval and placement in the appropriate star category. There are five such categories ranging from 5 star for hotels which offer luxury features, to one star for hotels which offer adequate standard of comfort and cleanliness. There are no uniform criteria at international level for grading and classification of hotels. When inquired the reaction of the tourists, it was pointed out that it is more important to list facilities alone with the rates fixed, thereby giving them the choice to select. Quality is more important to them than the physical aspects of a hotel.

The star system creates an impression of luxury and waste—an artificial label with unwanted connotations. Material criteria's are unsatisfactory. These criteria's 30 not contain any built in guarantees. Facility wise, a luxury hotel will not merit any consideration of, for instance, it does not employ sufficient personnel. Quality of service is very important consideration. After all, hotels constitute a service industry. The standard for gradation of hotels in India are laid down by the government of India from the points of view of the suitability of the hotel for foreign tourists. All hotels which are approved get worldwide publicity through tourist literature published by the government and distributed in India as well as abroad/overseas and are eligible for foreign exchange for their essential imports of equipment and provision and for their advertising, publicity and promotion abroad, from the government's special quota of foreign exchange for tourist promotion.

There are certain general features, facilities and services expected of establishments in each category. For example, hotels in the category of four, five star, and five star deluxe should be completely air-conditioned, three star hotels need have airconditioning in only 50% of rooms; two star hotels need not serve continental cuisine and one star hotels need have only 25 attached baths.According to the regulatory conditions for approved hotels, the officials of the government or any other officer deputed by it to inspect hotel premises from time to time will be allowed free access with or without prior notice. In the event of breach of any of the conditions by the hotels, the government shall have the right to withdraw the approval. The characteristics of star hotels of different categories are described below.

— *One star hotels*. The general construction of the building of one star category hotels should be good and the locality and environs including immediate approach should be suitable. The hotel should have at least

10 lettable bedrooms of which at least 25% should have attached bathroom with a bathroom for every 4 of the remaining rooms. All bathrooms should have modern sanitation and running cold water with adequate supply of hot water, soap and toilet paper. The rooms should be properly ventilated and should have clean and comfortable beds and furniture. There should be a reception counter with a telephone and a telephone for the use of guests and visitors. There should be a clean and moderately well equipped dining room/restaurant serving clean wholesome food, and there should be a clean, wellequipped kitchen and pantry.

— *Two star hotels*. The building of two star category hotel should be well constructed and the locality and environs including the approach should be suitable for a good hotel. The hotel should have at least 10 lettable bed room of which at least 75% should have attached bath rooms with showers and a bath room for every four of the remaining rooms and should be with modern sanitation and running cold water with an adequate supply of hot water, soap and toilet paper. 25% of the rooms should be air-conditioned,and all rooms must be properly ventilated, clean and comfortable, with all the necessary items of furniture. There should be a well-furnished lounge.There should be a reception counter with a telephone. There should be a telephone or call ball in each room and there should be a telephone on each floor unless each room has a separate telephone.

— *Three star hotels*. The architectural features and general construction of the building of three star category hotels should be of a very good standard and the locality including the immediate approach and environs should be suitable for a very good hotel and there should be adequate parking facilities for cars. The hotel should have at least 20 lettable bed rooms, all with attached bath room with bath tubs and/or showers and should be modem in design and equipped with fittings of a good standard, with hot and cold running water. At least 50 per cent of the rooms should be airconditioned and the furniture and furnishings such as carpets, curtains etc., should be of a very good standard and design. There should be adequate number of lifts in buildings with more than two stories including the ground floor. There should be a well appointed lounge and separate ladies' and gentlemen's cloak rooms equipped with fittings of a good standard.

— *Four star hotels*. The facade, architectural feature and general construction of the building of four-star category hotel should be distinctive and the locality including the immediate approach and the environs should be suitable for a hotel of this category. There should be adequate parking facilities for cars. The hotel should have at least 25 lettable bedrooms, all with attached bathrooms. At least 50% of the bathrooms must have long baths or the most modern shower chambers, with 24 hours service of hot and cold running water. All public rooms and private rooms should be fully airconditioned and should be well furnished with carpets, curtains, furniture, fittings, etc. in good taste. It would be advisable to employ the services of professionally qualified and experienced interior designers of repute for this purpose. There should be an adequate number of efficient lifts in buildings of more than 2 storeys including the ground floor. There should be a well-appointed lobby and ladies' and gentleman's cloaks room equipped with fittings of a standard befitting a hotel of this category.

— *Five star hotels*. The facade, architectural features and general construction of the building of five star and five star deluxe hotels should have the distinctive qualities of a luxury hotel of this category. Five star deluxe category hotels are a qualitative extension of the five star categories, while quantitatively, the basic features are as of a five star category. In a five star deluxe hotel, the comparative all around standard of service and amenities are of very superior quality and high standard. The locality including the immediate approach and environs should be suitable for a luxury hotel this category, and there should be adequate parking space for cars. The hotel should have at least 25 lettable bedrooms, all with well appointed, attached bathrooms with long baths or the most modern shower chambers, with 24 hours service of hot and cold running water. All public rooms and private rooms should be fully air-conditioned and should be well appointed with superior quality carpets, curtains, furniture, fittings, etc. in good taste.

Organizational Structure of a Hotel

A hotel is an establishment that provides lodging, usually on a short-term basis. Hotels often provide a number of additional guest services such as a restaurant, a swimming pool or childcare. Some hotels have conference services and encourage groups to hold conventions and meetings at their location. Hotels differ from motels in that most motels have drive-up, exterior entrances to the rooms, while hotels tend to have interior entrances to the rooms The cost and quality of hotels are usually indicative of the range and type of services available. Due to the enormous increase in tourism worldwide during the last decades of the 20th century, standards, especially those of smaller establishments, have improved considerably.

All hotels are organized around the following functions:

1. Front desk operation
2. Housekeeping
3. Building maintenance/engineering, and
4. Security.

Beyond these common services, hotels and their departments can vary tremendously. For example, most luxury hotels include a restaurant and beverage department, while most budget facilities do not. The performance of these functions can also vary widely among different types of hotels. Business guests of a convention centre may expect hi-tech front desk operations, and guests at a resort may prefer a more personal approach. At any rate, all hotels carry out these functions both behind the scenes and at the front of the house.

There are two approaches to classify departments in typical hotels:

— *Revenue generating versus cost centers*: The first approach is trying to differentiate between departments revenue-wise. In fact, this approach entitles that if a department generates revenue to the hotel (eg., rooms division department, food and beverage department), it is called a revenue generator. On the other hands, if a department incurs costs without directly contributing to hotel profitability, it is called a cost or support centre (eg., accounting department, maintenance and engineering department).

— *Front of the house versus back of house*: This approach classifies departments according to department staff's frequency of communication with guests. If communication between staff and guest is frequent, then the department is said to be a front of the house department. On the other hand, if the communication between department staff and guests in nonexistent or on occasions, then the department is said to be back of the house department.

Following are some important departments of a hotel:

Rooms Division Department

The majority of hotels revenues (60.2 %) is generated from Rooms Division Department under the form of room sales. This very department provides the services guests expect during their stay in the Hotel. It is typically composed of five different departments:

a) Front office:

- Sell guestrooms; register guests and design guestrooms
- Coordinate guest services
- Provide information
- Maintain accurate room statistics, and room key inventories
- Maintain guest account statements and complete proper financial settlements

b) Reservation:

- Receive and process reservation requests for future overnight accommodations.
- With technology development, the Reservation Department can, on real time, access the number and types of rooms available, various room rates, and furnishings, along with the various facilities existing in the hotel
- There should be close relationships with Sales and Marketing Division concerning Large Group Reservations

c) Housekeeping:

- Inspects rooms before they are available for sale
- Cleans occupied and vacant rooms
- Communicates the status of guestrooms to the Front Office Department
- Cleans and presses the property's linens, towels, and guest clothing (if equipped to do so, free of charge or for a pre-determined fee)
- Maintains recycled and non-recycled inventory items

d) Uniformed services:

- *Bell attendants:* Ensure baggage service between the lobby area and guestrooms

- *Door attendants*: Ensure baggage service and traffic control at hotel entrance(s)
- *Valet parking attendants*: Ensure parking services for guest's automobiles
- *Transportation personnel:* Ensure transportation services for guests from and to the hotel
- *Concierge:* Assists guests by making restaurant reservations, arranging for transportation, and getting tickets for theater, sporting, or any other special events

Responsibilities of the rooms department include reservations, guest reception, room assignment, tracking the status of rooms, prompt forwarding of mail and phone messages, security, housekeeping of guest rooms and public spaces such as lobbies, and answering guests' questions. To perform these many duties effectively, the rooms department may be divided into a number of specialized subunits. To complicate matters, in many instances these subunits are also referred to as departments. The laundry department is responsible for cleaning and pressing all the hotel's linens and employee uniforms as well as guest laundry. Because of its specialized function, little of the knowledge and skills required to manage a laundry operation is transferable to other areas of hotel operations. The front office is one of the most important departments in a hotel, as it often offers the only contact between guests and staff. A hotel's front office is where guests are greeted when they arrive, where they are registered and assigned to a room, and where they check out.

The reservations department takes and tracks the hotel's future bookings. The housekeeping department is responsible for cleaning guest rooms and public spaces. Because of their specialized nature, the security and engineering departments are discussed in separate sections. A great deal of interdependence exists among the subunits of the rooms department. The front office must let reservations know whenever walk-in guests register. A similar level of cooperation is required between the front office and housekeeping. When a guest checks out, the front office must inform housekeeping so that the room may be cleaned. Once a room is cleaned, housekeeping must inform the front office so that the room may be sold. Certain tasks within the rooms department must occur in a specific order.

Housekeeping cannot properly provision a guest room if the laundry does not supply enough clean towels or bed sheets. Engineering cannot replace a defective light switch in a guest room if housekeeping does not report the problem. Effective management of this busy department calls for standardized plans, procedures, schedules, and deadlines, as well as frequent direct communication between the executives who manage the key operating units of the rooms department.

The hotel and lodging business is vulnerable to security and safety problems. Problems can be created by guests, employees, or intruders. Security breaches can result in embezzlement, theft, arson, robbery, and even terrorism. Depending on the size of a hotel or a lodging establishment, the security function may be handled by a fully staffed department on site, contracted to an outside security company, or assigned to designated staff members sonnel in the rooms department. In a larger, full-service hotel, the director of security may report directly to the general manager. In smaller hotels, the security function might become a task of the rooms department. Engineering department's responsibilities include preventive maintenance; repair; replacement; improvement and modification to furniture, fixtures, and equipment (FFE); and ensuring uninterrupted provision of utilities (gas, electricity, water).Preventive maintenance involves routine checks and inspection of the key components of all equipment.

Maintenance of recreational facilities may be part of the engineering department's responsibilities. In particular, swimming pools require extensive maintenance to ensure proper filtration and to prevent the accumulation of algae and other conditions unsuitable for swimming. Prompt repair minimizes loss of productivity in other hotel operating departments and inconvenience to hotel guests. When a particular FFE has reached the end of its useful life and repair is no longer cost-effective, replacement is indicated. Improvement projects enhance the existing operation or reduce operating costs of the facility.

Modification projects alter the existing operation to accommodate one or more new functions. One hotel might have a large engineering staff that includes plumbers, carpenters, painters, electricians, and other technicians. Another might have maintenance personnel who have general knowledge and understanding of the hotel's operations but rely on outside contractors for specialized jobs. In larger, full-service hotels, engineering may be a separate department, with a director who reports directly to the resident manager.

Food and Beverage Department

Food and beverage department constitutes the second largest revenue generator of a typical hotel with an average of 23.1 for Food sales, and 8.6 % for Beverage sales. In a five-star hotel, Food and Beverage outlets might have the following forms:

— Quick service
— Table service
— Specialty restaurants
— Coffee shops
— Bars
— Lounges
— Clubs
— Banquets
— Catering functions
— Wedding, birthdays, etc.

The primary function of the food and beverage department is to provide food and drink to a hotel's guests. In earlier times, when an inn had a single dining room that could hold a limited number of guests, this was a fairly simple task. Today, however, providing food and drink is much more complicated. A large hotel might well have a coffee shop, a gourmet restaurant, a poolside snack bar, room service, two banquet halls, and ten function rooms where food and beverages are served. It might also have a lounge, a nightclub, and a lobby bar. On a busy day, it's quite likely that functions will be booked in many outlets at the same time. In addition, some outlets may have multiple events scheduled for a single day. As you can see, there is great diversity in the types of activities performed by a food and beverage department, requiring a significant variety of skills on the part of its workers. Because of the diversity of services provided, the food and beverage department is typically split into subunits. The executive chef, a person of considerable importance and authority in any full-service hotel, runs the food production, or kitchen, department.

A variety of culinary specialists who are responsible for different aspects of food preparation report to the executive chef. The actual serving of food in a large hotel's restaurants is usually the responsibility of a separate department, headed by the assistant food and beverage director. The food service department is composed of the individual restaurant and outlet managers, maitre d's, waiters, waitresses, and bus help. Because of their special duties and concerns, many large hotels have a separate subunit that is responsible only for room service. Because of the high value and profit margins associated with the sale of alcoholic beverages, some hotels have a separate department that assumes responsibility for all outlets where alcoholic beverages are sold.

The person responsible for this department is the beverage manager. Most full-service hotels also do a considerable convention and catering business. The typical convention uses small function rooms for meetings and larger rooms for general sessions, trade shows, exhibits, and banquets. As a hotel or lodging business increases the use of its facilities for conventions and meetings, it may form a separate convention services department. The convention services department and its personnel are introduced to the client, a meeting planner, or an association executive by the marketing and sales department. The convention services department then handles all of the client's meeting and catering requirements. Individually catered events include parties, wedding receptions, business meetings, and other functions held by groups. To provide for the unique needs of these types of customers, hotels often organize separate catering and convention departments. Depending on the size of the hotel, the job of cleaning the food and beverage outlets themselves as well as of washing pots and pans, dishes, glasses, and utensils is often delegated to a subunit known as the stewarding department. It is only through continuous cooperation and coordination that a hotel's food service function can be carried out effectively.

Sales and Marketing Department

A hotel, usually have sales and marketing division. However, if the staff size, volume business, hotel size, expected group arrivals is low enough, the hotel might have marketing staff placed under the reservation department. A typical sales and marketing division is composed of four different departments:

a) Sales
b) Convention services
c) Advertising
d) Public relations

The marketing and sales department is removed from most of the day-to-day operational problems faced by other departments. The division of work among the sales managers is based on the type of customers a hotel is attempting to attract. Individual sales managers often specialize in corporate accounts, conventions, or tour and travel markets. Sales managers' accounts are sometimes subdivided along geographical lines into regional or national accounts.

Accounting division

The accounting department is responsible for recording financial transactions, preparing and interpreting financial statements, and providing the managers of other departments with timely reports of operating results. Some of the activities that are undertaken in the accounting division are listed below:

a) Pays outstanding invoices
b) Distributes unpaid statements
c) Collects amounts owed
d) Processes payroll
e) Accumulates operating data
f) Compiles financial reports
g) Makes bank deposits
h) Secures cash loans
i) Performs other control and processing functions

The accounting department combines staff functions and line functions, or those functions directly responsible for servicing guests. Other responsibilities, carried out by the assistant controller for finance, include payroll preparation, accounts receivable, and accounts payable. Another dimension of the accounting department's responsibilities deals with various aspects of hotel operations, cost accounting, and cost control throughout the hotel. The two areas of central concern to the accounting department are rooms and food and beverage.

The accounting department's front office cashier is responsible for tracking all charges to guest accounts. At the close of each business day, which varies by hotel but typically occurs at midnight or after the bulk of guests' transactions have been completed, the night auditor is responsible for reconciling all guest bills with the charges from the various hotel departments. Although the front office cashier and the night auditor physically work at the front desk and, in the case of the cashier, have direct contact with guests, they are members of the accounting department and report to the assistant controller of operations.

The accounting department is anything but a passive staff unit contending with routine recordkeeping. The accounting department is also responsible for collecting and reporting most of a hotel's operational and financial statistics, which provide important data for decision making and budget preparation purposes. The head of the accounting department may report not only to the hotel's general manager but also to the hotel chain's financial vice president or to the hotel's owner. The reason for this dual responsibility and reporting relationship is to afford the hotel corporation an independent verification of the financial and operating results of the hotel.

Human Resources Division

The three functions of the human resources department are employee recruitment, benefits administration, and training. The director of human resources is also expected to be an expert on federal and state labor laws and to advise managers in other departments on these topics. The human resources department's major challenge is in its interactions with other hotel departments.

Although the human resources department recruits, interviews, and screens prospective employees, the final hiring decision rests within the department in which the potential employee will be working. The same is true of promotion and disciplinary decisions; the human resources department's input is, in most cases, limited to advice and interpretation of legal questions. The human resources department's effectiveness depends on its manager's ability to form effective working relationships with managers of other departments.

Security Department

Security department personnel are usually screened from inhouse personnel, security officers or retired police officers, across certain physical skills, and prior experience. The functions of the security division mainly include:

a) Patrols the property

b) Monitors supervision equipment

c) Ensures safety and security of guests, visitors, and employees.

Maintenance Division

This very department maintains the property's structure and grounds as well as electrical and mechanical equipment. Some hotels might have this very division under different names, such as maintenance division, property operation and maintenance department.

Organizational Control

Organizational control is a multilevel control approach in which explicit organizational goals, roles, and responsibilities are dynamically developed, distributed, and maintained to serve as guidelines for making detailed operational control decisions by the individual agents. By restricting the scope of local control decisions and communication actions, these organizational guidelines lower the cost of distributed resource allocation and agent coordination, help limit inappropriate agent behavior, and reduce communication requirements.

The factors determine the most appropriate span of organizational are:

1. task similarity,
2. training and professionalism,
3. task certainty,
4. frequency of interaction,
5. task integration, and
6. physical dispersion.

When a large number of employees perform similar tasks, the span of control can be increased. When the employees perform very different tasks, the supervisor must give each subordinate more individual attention in order to keep in touch with the different types of tasks; this requires a narrower span of control. For example, the rooms department manager might easily manage the front desk agents and housekeepers until the brand standards for check-in or checkout of a guest increase in complexity and the standards for the various types of rooms and their cleaning procedure increase in detail. At this time, the rooms department manager's span of control must be narrowed.

The better trained and more skilled a subordinate is, the less supervision is required. For example, a front desk agent might require a higher level of training and skill than a room service waiter. Thus, a front desk supervisor can supervise more employees than the room service supervisor. Task certainty refers to the predictability of a task. Routine tasks allow management to devise standard procedures for subordinates to follow, minimizing questions about the job and widening the span of control. On the other hand, close supervision is called for when tasks are ambiguous and uncertainty is great.

For example, the task of checking a guest in or out of the hotel can be documented and standard procedures can be created, so the front desk manager can have a rel-atively wide span of control over the front desk agents. However, because of the diversity of customers the sales manager encounters, the tasks of a hotel sales manager are less certain. The director of sales is responsible for coaching the sales managers, observing sales calls, and ensuring deal closings; these tasks require a hands-on approach that limits the number of employees the director of sales can handle, narrowing the span of control.

If the supervisor-subordinate relationship requires frequent interaction, the span of control must be narrow. If interaction is infrequent, the span of control can be wide. For example, the hotel controller must review regularly the status of collections and payments with staff. In contrast, the frequency of interaction between the chief engineer and his or her subordinates is directed by written work orders in most circumstances and thus requires less direct communication, enabling a wider span of control. If the supervisor must integrate and coordinate the tasks of subordinates, the span of control narrows. For example, in the production of a meal for one table of four guests with different appetizers, salads, and entrées, the chef must have a narrow span of control to ensure that each component of the meal is assembled correctly and delivered to service personnel on a timely basis. The span of control of the executive housekeeper can be much wider because the procedure for cleaning and preparing each guest room is similar, if not exactly the same, for every room.

One of the most important strength of a functional organizational design is efficiency. The performance of common tasks allows for work specialization, which increases overall productivity. Workers develop specialized skills and knowledge more rapidly. Training is easier because of the similarity of tasks and the resulting opportunities for inexperienced workers to learn from experienced workers. This helps new employees quickly learn the kinds of behavior that lead to success and promotion. Coordination of activities within functional departments is easier than in more broadly based organizations. A functional organization fosters efficiency, teamwork, and coordination of activities within individual units. However, the functional organization's most important strength is also the source of its great-est shortcoming. The success of a hotel as a business is measured by its overall performance and not by the performance of any one department.

A hotel with spotless guest rooms will not be successful if guests' front desk experiences are not up to par. Even if guests' dining experiences are superb, the hotel will fall flat on its face if its rooms are dismal. It is sometimes difficult for each department to fully appreciate its role in the overall success of the organization. It is vital that each department keep in mind the hotel-wide goals of customer service and profitability rather than focus narrowly on its own concerns. Some means must be found to coordinate the activities of functional departments and to set hotel-wide strategies and goals. A hotel's functional organization demands strong leadership. New initiatives in hotels often require cooperation and coordination between functional departments. New ideas tend to be stillborn if department heads lack a hotel-wide perspective or have difficulty coordinating their activities. The tendency to concentrate on doing things right often overshadows the organization's ability to do the right thing.

The GM, as the chief executive of the hotel, emerges as the single person capable of providing the overall organizational direction, decision making, coordination, and arbitration needed to make a hotel's functional departments work together effectively. A hotel simply cannot run itself from the departmental level. Thus, the GM must be a strong leader to be effective.

The executive operating committee (EOC) of a hotel, made up of the general manager and senior executives from each department, is designed to increase the level of coordination between departments. There is no standard membership for this committee, but it usually comprises those executives who report directly to the general manager. The EOC is also responsible for a hotel's major budgetary units, such as the food and beverage and housekeeping units. EOC functions depend on how the hotel GM chooses to use the group, the GM's style, and the structure of other management meetings in the hotel.

Distribution of Authority

Authority can be distributed throughout an organization or held in the hands of a few select employees. The delegation of authority creates a chain of command, the formal channel that defines the lines of authority from the top to the bottom of an organization. The chain of command specifies a clear reporting relationship for each person in the organization and should be followed in both downward and upward communication. Following the chain of command enables each new employee, no matter what his or her position, to know exactly for whom and to whom he or she is responsible. When designing an organizational structure, managers must consider the distribution of authority. Decentralization is the process of distributing authority throughout an organization. In a decentralized organization, an organization member has the right to make a decision without obtaining approval from a higher-level manager. Centralization is the retention of decision-making authority by a high-level manager. Traditionally, hotel and lodging management has been very centralized, probably due to its roots in small, owner-operated lodging.

As the hotel and lodging industry has expanded, decentralization has become a more frequent style of operation. Decentralization has several advantages. Managers are encouraged to develop decision-making skills, which help them advance in their careers. The autonomy afforded by this style of operation also increases job satisfaction and motivation. When employees are encouraged to perform well, the profitability of the organization increases. Many hotel and lodging organizations have begun to empower employees and supervisors to make decisions that typically have been made by managers.

Staff Meetings

Big hotels increase communications through an elaborate structure of additional committees and meetings, including some or all of the following: operations, staff, sales forecast and marketing, departmental, subdepartmental, credit, safety, energy conservation, and employee meetings. The operations committee comprises the general manager, department heads, front office manager, manager on duty, and representatives from housekeeping, security, engineering, and food and beverage. The staff committee might include the GM, department heads, and all subdepartment heads who report to the department heads. The sales forecast and marketing committee might meet one to four times per month for several hours so the GM and department heads can review room demand for the coming 90 days and devise strategies to increase room nights (and thus bring in more revenue) and to increase average daily rates by up-selling potential guests to higher-rated rooms with perhaps more amenities or services. The departmental committee consists of the department head and his or her subdepartment heads, managers, and supervisors.

Meeting once or twice per month for an hour or so, the group reviews departmental issues.Similarly, subdepartment committees meet monthly for about an hour so the subdepartment head, managers, and supervisors can address issues unique to their subdepartment, such as the selection of a new type of floor cleaner by the housekeeping department or a more energy-efficient light bulb by the engineering department. The credit committee includes the general manager, the controller, sales, the front office, reservations, catering, and the credit manager. Meeting monthly for an hour, the committee reviews those guests and clients of the hotel who were granted credit but have not settled their account. The safety committee typically comprises representatives from human resources, food and beverage, housekeeping, and engineering. Meeting monthly for an hour or so, the committee reviews safety programs and safety records, addresses problems, and discusses the implementation of new safety regulations.

The future success of a hotel will be driven in large part by the ability to foresee and capitalize on change. As we go through global transitions, the successful hotel will examine the key factors that will not only define success but also the ability to survive in coming years. These key organizational trends must be acknowledged by the successful hotel organization: visionary leadership, globalization, diversity, flexibility, flat structure, customer focus, zero defects, network orientation, and being in the information fast lane. The organization must be able to respond to increasingly globalized sales, the movement to maintaining sales offices in many countries and hotel properties across the globe, and an increasingly globalized labor market.

Flexibility in the modern hotel organization means assuring that systems, processes, and people can respond differently to different situations; fewer detailed rules and procedures; greater autonomy and encouragement of initiative; customizing employment relationships to include telecommuting and job-sharing; and lifetime employability rather than lifetime employment. The trend toward flatness in hotel organizations means fewer levels of management, workers empowered to make decisions, and fewer differences in responsibility. The organization's employees need to believe in a sense of entrepreneurship that reacts proactively to market diversity. Traditional organizations that follow well-documented rules must give way to leaders who can balance a sense of discipline with one of flexibility. If the customer is king or queen in the 21st century, hotel organizaions will be best served by focusing less on their hotel assets as measures of success and more on their customers. This involves a fundamental shift from viewing the real estate asset as the wealth creator to seeing the customer as the key to building shareholder wealth.

A failing hotel organization is overmanaged and underled. The networked hotel organization can facilitate direct communication across unit and property boundaries, ignoring the chain of command; cross-unit team structures; outsourcing and downsizing; strategic alliances with competitors and others; customization; and decentralization. Being in the information fast lane is critical. The traditional role of information technology as a back office support for accounting and bookkeeping has clearly moved to front and center stage. Information technology today influences all aspects of business from corporate strategies to organizational structure. Technology was once viewed as a way to reduce costs by replacing people. That attitude has been firmly supplanted by the idea of seeking information technology support for the creative work all organizations must pursue. Information technology must enable organizations to react more speedily to market needs and, of course, produce the fulfillment of customer demands both quickly and accurately.

Technological advances and Organizational Changes

The organization and business operations of hotel companies will be reshaped to satisfy the changing needs of constituents. This is due in part to rapid technological advances in information and communications, as well as a transformation of the capital base of the hotel industry. Customers and stakeholders will demand seamless access to hotel company business information and processes. Heightened business interdependencies between hotel companies, their suppliers, and marketing and service representatives, will undoubtedly blur corporate lines. Major changes will take place in the way the hotel industry accesses and deploys financing and venture capital.

Nearly every business and most individuals in the United States have already entered the electronic age of information and communications. Laptop computers, cellular telephones, beepers and interactive communication devices have all become commonplace tools are heavily. Within the next few years, consumers will have unlimited direct access to most channels of market and business information and distribution. Consumers will want to handle daily activities and business transactions without leaving their homes or offices using their own personal computers.

Buying and selling goods and services, paying bills, researching topics of interest, handling banking transactions, and planning daily personal and business activities are all part of this change. What implications does this have for the hotel industry? Well, for starters, many individuals will want to book personally-tailored vacation packages and business itineraries using direct links through their own personal computers. This will require full access to on-line facility data bases and vacation catalogues, as well as price lists. Also, they will need direct access to hotel and airline rooms and seat inventory control systems. This alone could revolutionise the marketing and sales paradigm for the hotel industry.

Technological advances in information and communication will cause hotels to make dramatic chances in the way they serve and physically accommodate guests. Count on it, interactive computing and multimedia devices will be as commonplace in hotel rooms of the future as present-day remote control televisions and touch-tone telephones. Guests will want the option of avoiding interaction with hotel service and clerical personnel by using these devices. Just think, no more waiting in line to check in or out of your hotel room. No delay while waiting for the hotel operator or some other service clerk to answer the telephone to schedule your wake-up call, take your room service order or book your restaurant reservation. No need to call for additional towels, or to order a shoe shine or dirty laundry pick-up. You can do all of this by touching a few icons on your television screen.

Technological advancements may alter the physical design and space allocation of hotels in the future. Quite possibly, a computing and multimedia room will be required on every floor of every full-service hotel. Possibly, the amount and size of meeting rooms and auditoriums will change as guests wishing to participate in large conferences from the comfort and convenience of their guest rooms, may wish to use interactive video conferencing devices and remote response terminals, to participate. Another possibility is that the front desk area could be cut hack to a small greeting kiosk and the remainder of the space put to more productive use such as retail space.

Many new sources of revenues could result from these changes. Direct guest room linkups to a wide variety of online entertainment and informational networks will be a standard requirement in the future. This could mean large access fees for hotels. Rental or usage charges for peripheral devices could also mean big business. A number of hotel companies presently are focusing their attention on redesigning or participating in new global distribution systems. These will better link hotel companies, airlines, travel companies, and rental car companies to each other--but not directly to the consumer. Just think of the marketing opportunities that exist today for hotel companies to reach customers directly using international computer networks, on-line bulletin boards, and direct "E-mail" advertising. A few innovative hotel companies have already seized this opportunity.

Owners, investors, lenders and suppliers all want and are demanding more timely information on which to base their business decisions and monitor their business interests. Many hotel companies are finding that stakeholders particularly owners and lenders- want to check-in directly to the flow of business and financial information. Think about demands for information that might come up in the future. Hotel lenders may want on-line access to hotel treasury and cash management systems to daily sweep bank accounts and monitor compliance with covenants of loan agreements. Investors may want up-to-the-minute financial statement information to gauge investment performance and make daily investment decisions. Suppliers may want on-line access to perpetual inventory records to automatically trigger purchase orders and shipments. Already, travel agents, meeting planners and tour wholesalers want on-line access to room inventories and pricing information. To accommodate these needs, major changes in the business and accounting information systems of hotels and hotel companies will have to be implemented.

Sweeping organizational and operational changes will occur in the hotel industry. The need for large headquarters facilities with multiple departments and large technical support staffs will greatly diminish because of technological advancements in information and communications. In marketing and sales, huge competitive advantages can result from setting up state-of-the-art" customer databases with interactive communication linkups.

Through the use of wide area networks and other linkages, individuals will be able to share information and experiences between locations rapidly and set up multi-location workgroups to facilitate problem-solving. This will significantly reduce the need to cluster technical support staffs under one roof. The ability exists to link suppliers seamlessly with hotel companies using "E-mail" and knowledge management software. For the first time, outsourcing for a wide variety of technical and business support functions, such as payroll and personnel management, purchasing and new business development, is a viable option for most hotel companies. For hotels, the entire organizational and operational structure may change as a result of technological innovation. Front-office functions could be minimised or eliminated. Universal service representatives could tend to virtually every guest need from a single work station. Guests will likely be able to initiate many service functions directly using interactive guest room devices. This could change the service staffing requirements and mechanical resources to more productive activities such as better execution of guest requests. This also holds true for many back-office functions. Through better uses of technology, many hotels can approach elimination of many of the clerical functions presently performed in the back offices of hotels.

The shift in capital is expected to have a dramatic effect on the future underwriting of hotel loans and investments. No longer will the game be to convince the lender's credit committee or the investor's capital committee to do the deal. Now the game will be to convince the independent agencies rating the securities that the deal is good, since they are the ones that Wall Street investors rely on to rate the underlying securities. Underwriting parameters will continue to be tough in the future since virtually all loans will ultimately be sold in pools to investors as securities. Lenders will want to be sure that every loan meets the minimum underwriting criteria set by the investment bankers who sell the loans to investors. After the loan is made, a far greater amount of periodic business and financial information will be required from the borrower.

Future of Hotel Organization

No hotel company operating today can be unaware of the swift pace of global change and its impact on every facet of the hospitality industry. With just five years left in this century, we can expect change to be the only constant. New business practices are evolving virtually as fast as our technologies, while resistance to change has become one of the primary causes of business failure. The specter of constant change raises fundamental questions as to the creation of shareholder wealth in a capital-constrained, highly competitive environment. How will hotel organizations build shareholder wealth, and what key drivers will result in success? What future products and services will be essential in a technology-driven, global environment marked by rising customer expectations? Moreover, what alternative approaches and skills must organizations develop to ensure market success?

The future success of hotel organizations will be driven in large part by the ability to foresee — and capitalize — on change. Beyond this truism, however, there is an urgent need to identify what will be required in the competitive environment of the future with its intense focus on serving customer needs. The hospitality industry — as is the case with business generally — is subject to deep currents of change set in motion as economic and social systems shaped in the industrial era evolve to a knowledge-based era driven by technology advances.

Recognizing that the hotel industry has a somewhat split personality reflecting the inherent conflicts between its real estate and operational aspects, it is important to understand the industry's real estate origins and how they are shaping the challenges ahead.

The origins of the industry's real estate persona are embodied in the classic theory of location - "if we build it, they will come." As a result of this "building" complex, the industry has tended to have a real estate and asset orientation, rather than a customer focus. From the hotel company perspective — especially that of the brand-oriented "chain" — the varied interests of a diffused property ownership group can be quite different than the singular interest of the chain that operates and markets the properties.

Even when the ownership of geographically dispersed hotel properties is controlled by a single hotel organization, the financial structuring tends to be property-specific. Corporate financial strategies are frequently subjugated to the needs of the last property deal brought into the company's fold. Each property in a so-called "chain," is frequently the subject of a unique and distinctive ownership and financial structure. This phenomenon — quite common in the real estate sector, but unusual for business enterprises generally — makes for elusive economies of scale in the structuring and financing of property-driven expansion.

In today's changed environment, the hotel organization must deal with a number of new realities. Investors in our industry are no longer satisfied with long-term capital appreciation and psychic income that heretofore were often the justification for otherwise seemingly uneconomic investments in hotel property or, indeed, hotel chains. The first reality is that there is a very specific and identifiable relationship between bottom line performance and value. Improvements in business operations raises values. It is not surprising, therefore, that the new owners attracted to this industry in recent years have new sets of demands. This transformation from an old-guard group of investors and owners to income and return-driven newcomers has meant that the once "quiet enjoyment" of operators in their management of hotels for third parties is being disturbed, interrupted and overturned.

These challenges all take place in an environment where capital has become extremely selective in markets that have little stability. A global shortage of capital will not remain a short-term problem, and future hotel organizations must have a stronger alignment to capital providers — a critical "customer" group. Hotel companies will need to compete by offering better returns and performance than in the past. Hotel chains have found their development timetables quashed in recent years, making it difficult to achieve goals of critical mass often required to improve performance. These factors are driving consolidation in the brand "sweepstakes." Capital markets, therefore, continue to favor well-established companies, a reality that must drive entrepreneurial organizations to meet the future now by planning for an evolving corporate context in which to operate.

Key Success Factors

Within this broad context, hotel developers, owners and management companies will all need to develop new strategies, skills and processes that look forward to the competitive demands of the future. These ultimately must address issues related to vision and planning, as well as organizational skill sets and processes to attract and retain customers. To stake a claim in the future, current business practices should be examined in light of what can be expected to be the key success factors.

As the information age produces greater worldwide integration of business activities, a global knowledge base will become invaluable. Success in local and regional hotel markets will be shaped decisively by a global business environment that defines capital movement, customer expectations and applications of new technologies.

If the customer is "king" in the 21st century, hotel organizations will be best served by focusing less on their hotel assets as measures of success, and more on their customers. This involves a fundamental shift in viewing the real estate asset as the wealth creator — to the customer as the key to building shareholder wealth. A customer focus must imbue business decisions at all levels of developing and operating a hotel organization. Pursuing such a course will inevitably impact shareholder wealth. To accomplish this, however, customers need to participate in the product development process.

Fully realizing a customer focus in the industry poses a significant challenge. The hotel industry must confront problems due to conflicts between operational needs and real estate goals. Quite simply, an operator must remain customer-focused, but the short-term strategies to meet these needs may be inconsistent with the long-term objectives of property owners. Balancing those goals will be essential. A customer. focus implies a significant shift in what drives hotel development — placing primary emphasis on the customer with the locations to follow. Nevertheless, a hotel organization with its large investment in fixed assets — the real estate — can never be as nimble as a consumer products company in adjusting products and services to match rapid shifts in the marketplace.

The Japanese taught us that the concept of "zero defects" in products and services can yield tremendous benefits. But today an even more rigorous standard dominates — quality that surprises. In practical terms, the hotel industry finds it extremely difficult to meet the standard of zero defects in service. Hotel services are based primarily on people, not computers or other equipment. Quality that surprises takes the concept of zero defects a step further. Yesterday's surprising product or service is today's status quo. Twenty years ago, a business executive did not expect a consistent and predictable level of service wherever he or she traveled in the world. Today that is a standard — not the exception — as is the expectation for sophisticated technology in hotel rooms to support business needs. With customer discrimination so acute, it is not surprising that brand loyalty is a diminishing "commodity" in the hotel industry.

Find the ingredients for visionary leadership. Today's hotel organizations need to recognize the need for visionary leadership. The ability to forecast the future — to anticipate change rather than react to it — will be one of the single greatest determinants of market dominance in the years ahead. The old "command and control" model of leadership is giving way to a focus on leadership in ideas, information, inspiration, vision and teamwork. Warren Bennis, an authority on leadership in the U.S., puts it this way — "For the most part, failing organizations tend to be over-managed and under-led. The leader sets the tone for the moral character, the vision, the corporate culture and the fiber of the institution."

While visionary leadership is essential, it must be linked to business operations and foster a risk bias, rather than a procedural bias. This will allow the organization to stretch and, in turn, change. And it must be shared by empowered professionals and staff throughout the organization, including those who meet the customer. Overcoming the resistance to change can be a daunting task, particularly in large hotel organizations in which diversions from the status quo may threaten established management lines. It suggests that a culture based on conformance may need to be replaced by an emphasis on flexibility, learning and cooperation. Management competencies will need to be aligned in order to achieve the desired result. For many organizations, this may mean a shift from traditional hierarchies typical of companies in an industrial era to a flatter organization with a more transparent interface between leadership, organizational functions and employees.

Empower Management

For many of the industry's leaders, vision is driven by the strategic planning process, a function which has become critical for success. Strategic planning, however, has at times been a step-child in the hotel industry, and it is often the first to be cut when organizations are downsized. It is clearly in transition. There also has been a tendency to decentralize and simplify this function — both actions of potential benefit. Strategic planning must be led by the top people in the organization — the CEO and COO. On the other hand, it should be close enough to the customer to ensure that planners can "listen" to and be influenced by customer needs.

Beyond the ability to envision the future, core management capabilities will make the difference — they are essential. A clear vision without the management skills to support it cannot be a recipe for success. First and foremost, hotel management must have strategic development skills and the ability to integrate complex factors affecting success. Market volatility has become the norm, in part caused by the rapidly changing tastes of customers. Customers are increasingly approaching the hotel industry with widely different social, economic and political backgrounds, to say nothing of employees. Being able to deal with these diversities in a positive and constructive fashion that capitalizes on the differences, rather than working to find ways to mitigate them, is the clear path for successful management in the future.

The organization will also need to be imbued with a sense of entrepreneurship that reacts proactively to the market's diversity. Traditional organizations that follow well-documented rules must give way to leaders who can balance a sense of discipline with that of flexibility. Talent and resources must be marshaled and leveraged. In an industry with high fixed costs and labor intensity, the concept of leverage in the hotel business is an all-important one. Improving labor productivity through technology must be a goal for today's forward-looking hotel organization. Management must also be able to narrow the gap between the employer and the employee, forcing a flatter organization in the process. This will put management closer to the customer and speed the two-way communication process up and down the organization.

References

Boni, G. de and Frederick Francis Sharles. *Hotel organization, management and accountancy. Hotel organization and management.* London New York: Sir I. Pitman, 1926.

Boomer, Lucius Messenger. *Hotel management; principles and practice.* New York: Harper, 1931.

Hitz, Ralph and National Hotel Management Co. *Standard practice manuals for hotel operation.* New York: Harper, 1936.

Hotel Management Clipping Bureau of Good Ideas. *Hotel Management Clipping Bureau of Good Ideas.* New York: Ahrens Pub. Co., 1931.

Tellman, John. *The practical hotel steward.* Chicago: The Hotel monthly, 1913.

2

Front Office Management

Regardless of the class or type of the hotel, front office is the most visible and essential focal-point of a hotel. The focal point of activity within the front office is the reception desk, which is located in the front lobby of a hotel and dispenses all front-of-the-house activities of the hotel. It is the communication centre of the hotel with great amount of guest contact. Guests interact with the hotel for the first time by interacting with the staff of the front office, and they form the first impression about the hotel based on the efficiency, competency and behaviour of the front office staff.

The reception desk performs the functions like the sale of rooms, guest registration, room assignments, handling of guest requests, maintenance of the guest accounts, cashiering along with handling mail and providing information. The financial tasks usually handled by the front desk personnel include receiving cash payments, handling guest folios, verifying cheques and handling foreign currency and credit cards. In this Unit, you will be familiarised with all these aspects of the front office management.

Function of the Front Office

The primary function of the front office is that of a facilitator between the guest and other departments of the hotel. Another job of Front office desk is also to support and help in providing services to the guests. The number of interactions and transactions between the guest and the hotel during a guest stay, determine the type and nature of front office operations. The stages of guest stay are:

- pre-arrival,
- arrival,
- occupancy, and
- departure.

Various trans actions between the guest and the hotel, therefore, depend upon the stage of the guest stay. The transactions can be best understood by going through the guest cycle (Figure 1).

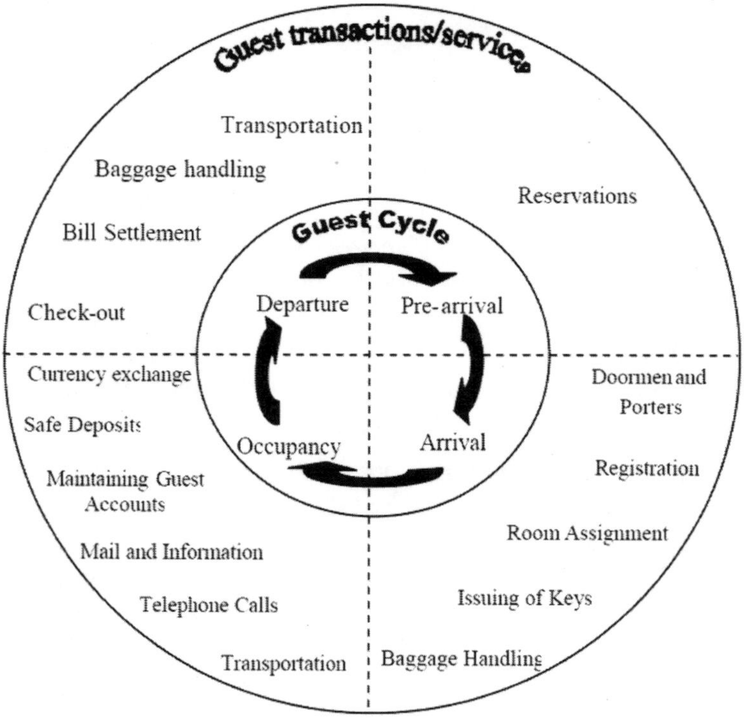

Figure 1: The Guest Cycle

The following transactions and exchange of services occur between a guest and the hotel:

- reservations,
- check-in and registration,
- mail and information,

- uniformed service and baggage handling,
- telephone calls and messages,
- handling guest accounts, and
- check-out and bill settlement.

All these services and transactions are handled by the front office department. The functions and services of the front office department can be differentiated depending upon the area where they are being performed. Some of the functions are performed by the reception desk as front-of-the-house operations and rest are performed as back-of-the-house operations.

Front-of-the-House Operations

Front-of-the-House operations are known so because these operations take place in front of the guests. Thus, these operations are related either to direct interaction with the guest or they are being conducted in front of the guest. The front office activities start from the time a guest calls or sends in a request for reservation/ accommodation. Staff of the front office department starts interacting with guest by taking in guest information and reservation request, leading to confirmation of reservation and finally to the handling of guest on arrival and guest check-in.

Check-in activity is a must for both, a guest with reservation or a walk-in -guest, i.e., one without prior reservation. The reservation system of hotels varies but nowadays since it is mostly computerised, therefore, features are the same. Check-in procedures require the collection of a lot of information. This is because information helps in building guest record data and serves the purposes of a ready reckoner in case of any emergency involving the guest. Front office takes in the guest information for future use and provides the guest with information about the hotel and its various services and thus, becomes the connecting link between the guest and the hotel. The pivotal role played by the front office is quite apparent from this very fact that it is the centre of all activities connected with guests in the hotel.

Therefore, decisions regarding the sale of a room to a particular guest, availability and allocation of a room, maintaining guest account by coordinating with the housekeeping and room service are the major front-of-the-house activities. Finally, the account settlement or deciding on the time of account settlement is generally a part of check-out process, performed by front office. Thus in short we can say that front office is the first and last place (as in check-in and check-out), wherein a guest interacts with the hotel.

Back -of-the -House Operations

As the name suggests these operations involve the activities which do not take place in front of the guests. The front office activities start the moment an enquiry or request regarding accommodation is made. This enquiry is answered keeping in view converting it into a reservation request. Although reservation is an activity of front office, major hotel lines/chain of hotels have centralised reservation system, operational 24 hours a day 365 days a year. (Reservation and its various intricacies will be discussed in the later sections).

A confirmed reservation leads to browsing of information, i.e., guest-record to det ermine whether this is a repeat guest and if yes what are the personal information and preferences of the guest. This helps you giving personal touch to guest's stay with the hotel.

When the guest checks -in, his or her account gets activated. This account keeps track of the guest's financial interaction with the hotel. These financial interactions involve room rent, room services, laundry, food and beverage at the hotel's outlet and any other facility used by the guest during his or her stay. For instance, these financial transactions begin the moment when he/she while waiting for allocation of a room start making phone calls to his/her associates to inform them the arrival or order for something in the lobby itself.

The daily night auditors help the back of the office department in the hotel in maintaining the guest accounts. Many hotels have a credit line extended to their guests or to the companies which they represent. The credit limit is predetermined and the hotel allows the guest to accumulate the amount before asking for either a full or partial payment. Many a times a guest is asked to provide his/her credit card during check-in while cash is expected mode of payment during checkout with multinational brands coming into India the concept of property management system has emerged which allows night auditors to flash guest's folio on day to day basis on their T.V. monitors. This kind of arrangement saves lot of guest's time at the time of checkout.

It also co-ordinates with housekeeping and room sales to maintain the status of occupied as well as unoccupied rooms. Finally, the guest record or personal data is maintained by the front office, which is essentially a back-of-the-house activity. Thus, the Guest cycle which started by taking guest booking, receiving guests, providing for their stay and billing them on departure gets completed.

Structure of the Front Office

The department of the front office performs quite a few functions/operations. It becomes necessary to have a well-defined organizational structure for smooth operations. The organizational structure of the front office depends on factors such as:

- *Size of the Hotel*: Bigger the hotel, the more specialised the staff is required to be. Whereas in the smaller hotels, one employee/staff member may perform a wide variety of duties.
- *Standard of Service*: High-class hotels usually provide more personal services for guests and, therefore, they expect greater specialisation from their staff.
- *Type of Guests*: The needs of Guests usually differ on the basis of their purpose of visit, i.e., business client prefers less time to be spent on checking-in and checking-out, and it is quite possible they won't mind carrying their own luggage. So the emphasis is more on staff in the front desk section than at the concierge.
- *Type of Hotel*: A hotel situated in the airport area knows that a guest may check-in or check-out at any time during the 24 hours of a day. So more emphasis needs to be there on front desk as a full team is needed to be on duty at all times.

Even though the organizational structure of a hotel depends on the above stated factors, typically all the hotels follow somewhat similar organizational structure. Figure 2 gives the uniform structure of the organization structure followed by a large hotel. The figure makes it clear that the department of front office is divided into many sub-divisions or functional/operational areas. In the figure a broken line joins the front office manager to the cashiering section. This is so, as in large hotels the cashier's department reports directly to the accounts department, with the financial controller taking overall responsibility. Thus, the sketch of the front office department remains the same but it takes different structure depending on the hotel or hotel culture.

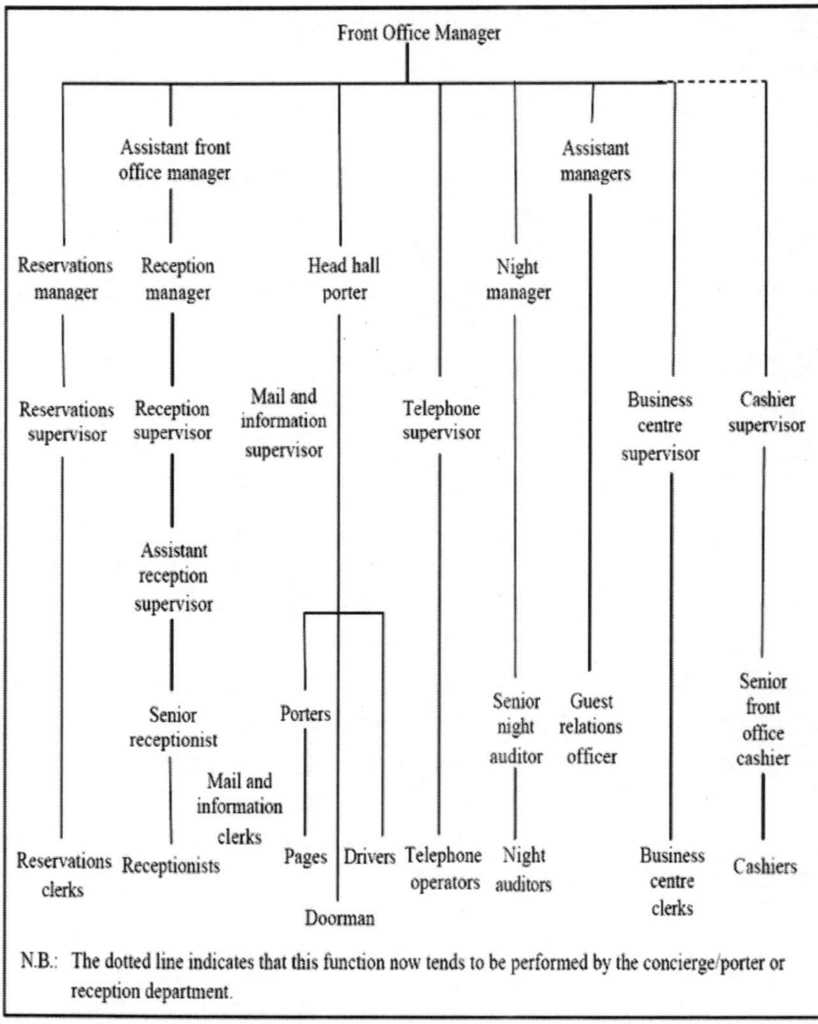

Figure 2. Organizational Chart of the Front Office

Hotel Operation Systems and Guest Cycle

Until the 1960's, nearly all hotels were operating under the manual system. At late 70's, with the introduction of computers, hotels shifted to semi-automated systems. Nowadays, most of the five-star hotels operate under the fully automated system. Below is a brief description of the three different systems under which hotels might operate.

— *Non-automated [manual] systems*: This very system is the one characterised by the sole usage of hands. In fact, all formats, procedures, and different kinds of calculations are done manually.

— *Semi-automated [Electro-mechanical] systems*: This system gets use of some Electro-mechanical equipment. In fact, under the semi-automated system, each department might have its own computer system under which it handles all its operations.

— *Fully automated [computer based] systems*: That's the best system ever used in the hotel industry. In fact, it is characterised by the excessive use of departmental software package programs integrated and connected to a main frame or terminal situated at the front office department.

Guest Cycle under Three Different Systems: Following stages of the guest cycle under the three different systems do not conflict with each other. In fact, the only differences are due to the nature of the system use. Therefore, what will be discussed above is not the repetition of the sequence; rather only differences will be highlighted.

Non-automated Systems

Pre-arrival activities: At the pre-arrival stage, reservation requests should be introduced in a loose-leaf notebook or index card. Moreover, only reservations up to 6 months horizons shall be honoured. Lastly, it is not practical, under this very system, to issue reservation confirmation numbers, initiate pre-registration activities (at the exception of VIP and groups) and prepare occupancy forecasts. The reason is, time and money loss along with insufficient labour force to manually conduct all the above mentioned activities.

Arrival activities: At the arrival stage, guests shall either sign a page in the registration book or fill manually a registration record. Under this very system, the most widely used front office equipment is the room rack, in which registration records are inserted to serve as room rack slips. Moreover, registration books and records shall be time stamped as an internal control proving when the guest exactly came, who registered him/her. Lastly, guest folios shall be opened for each registered guest.

Occupancy activities: Under the occupancy activities, registration records shall be prepared with multi-copies. In fact, one copy shall be distributed to room rack, another stamped to the guest folio, another given to switchboard operators, and a final copy handed to the uniformed service personnel. Lastly, guests with charge privileges charges and payments shall be posted to respective guest folios.

Departure activities: At departure stage, cashiers should settle each guest account's outstanding balance and get room keys back from guests. Moreover, cashiers shall notify the housekeeping department that the room is no more occupied (i.e. room status change) to let this very department clean the room and prepare it for new arrivals. In addition, cashiers shall remove room rack slips from room racks to indicate departure. Lastly, these very rack slips of departed guests shall be filed in a cardboard box to serve as a guest history record

Semi-automated Systems

This very system is less common in small and middle size hotels. For, these very hotels, financially wise, might not afford the huge investments associated with the installation of different hardware and software. The main advantage of this very system over manual system is that various reports can automatically be generated. However, the major disadvantages associated with this system are various complexities of operating and controlling devices due to the fact that these equipment are not integrated with other systems and are subject to frequent maintenance problems.

Pre-arrival activities: At this very stage, guests can either call a national reservation network or directly contact the hotel. Moreover, reservation clerks can prepare pre-registration records, guest folios, and information rack slips.

Arrival activities: At this very stage, already reserved guests shall verify their pre-registration forms and have only to sign it. On the other hand, walk-ins shall complete a multiple copy registration record from the beginning.

Occupancy activities: At the occupancy stage, in order to track the different guest charge expenditures and all other possible guest transactions, hotels get an intensive use of various kinds of vouchers. Moreover, the most widely used equipment, under this very stage, is the mechanical cash registers and front office posting machines. Lastly, under this very stage, night auditor shall continuously resolve any discrepancy in guest accounts and efficiently reconcile guest folios.

Departure activities: At this very stage, cashiers shall relay room status information to the housekeeping department. Moreover, they should place registration records of departed guests in property's guest history files.

Fully Automated Systems

Pre-arrival activities: Under this stage, the reservation department is equipped with a software package, which is interfaced and connected with one or more central reservation office(s). Moreover, the reservation department can automatically generate letters of confirmation, produce requests for guest deposits and handle pre-registration activities for all types of guests and generate daily expected arrival lists, occupancy and revenue forecast list.

Arrival activities: At this stage, various reservation records can be transferred to front office department. Moreover, hotels might be equipped with an on-line credit authorisation terminals for timely Credit Card Approval, self check-in/check-out terminals. Lastly, all guest charges and payments are saved in electronic guest folios. As far as walk-ins are concerned, all registration activities should be initiated from the very beginning.

Occupancy activities: Under this very stage, guest purchases at different revenue outlets are electronically transferred and posted to appropriate guest accounts. Moreover, the front office department can run and process continuous trial balances and, therefore, eliminate the tedious work for the Night Auditor.

Departure activities: At this very stage, cashiers can automatically produce bills to be sent to various guests with direct billing privileges and create electronic guest history records.

Front Office Forms

At different stages of the guest cycle different forms are used depending on which operating system a hotel chooses. Below are some of the common forms used:

- Pre-arrival activities:
  - Reservation record or a reservation file

  - Letter of confirmation
  - Reservation rack and reservation rack slips
- Arrival activities:
  - Registration card (or record) or registration file
  - Room rack and room rack slips
- Occupancy activities:
  - *Guest folio*: shall be of duplicate forms and pre-numbered for cross-indexing control purposes
  - *Vouchers*: support documents detailing facts of a transaction, but does not replace the source document (i.e. the invoice). Examples of vouchers might include charge vouchers, allowance vouchers, paid-out voucher, and correction vouchers.
  - Information rack slips
- Departure activities:
  - Credit card vouchers
  - Cash vouchers
  - Personal check vouchers
  - Transfer vouchers
  - Guest history records

Whatsoever system and setting the hotel might use, it should reflect easy access to the equipment, forms, and supplies necessary. Moreover, the setting shall reflect position flexibility. Moreover, nowadays trend shows that traditional mail, message, and key racks are unnecessary at the Front Desk. Rather, they shall be stored in drawers or slots located under or away from the Front Desk. For, this would ensure security and safety of guests.

Front Desk designed alternatives:

- *Circular or semi-circular structure*: this very structure provides an effective service to more guests and appears more modern and innovative but since guests will approach the Front Desk from all angles, more staff is needed.
- *Traditional straight desk*: Under this very design, fewer staff is needed, but fewer guests can be served at the same time.
- *Deskless environment*: Under this design, there is no Front Desk at all. This is usually replaced by a hostess, or steward welcoming the guest,

seating him or her on a chair/sofa, and conduct registration activities there while, for example, having a cocktail or a drink.

Duties of Front Office Manager

The front office of a hotel is responsible fotr the following management functions.

Planning

At the planning stage, the front office manager shall determine the department's goals. Later, the front office manager shall use these goals as a guide for planning more specific and measurable objectives. Lastly, the front office manager shall determine the strategies and tactics to reach these objectives.

Organization

The front office manager shall organize the work to be done through dividing it among staff members. While doing so, the work shall be distributed fairly and shall be completed in a timely manner.

Coordination

Involves bringing together and using the available resources to attain planned goals. In its most basic form, a hotel is two or more people working together to reach a goal. Whether a hotel is highly bureaucratic or changing and self-organizing, the organization must exist for some reason, some purpose, some mission — or it isn't a hotel at all. The hotel must have some goal. Identifying this goal requires some form of planning, informal or formal. Reaching the goal means identifying some strategies, formal or informal. These strategies are agreed upon by members of the hotel through some form of communication, formal or informal. Then members set about to act in accordance with what they agreed to do. They may change their minds, fine. But they need to recognize and acknowledge that they're changing their minds. This form of ongoing communication to reach a goal, tracking activities toward the goal and then subsequent decisions about what to do is the essence of management coordination. It needs to exist in some manner — formal or informal.

Staffing

Staffing involves finding the right people, with the right skills, abilities, and fit, who may be hired or already working for the hotel.

Leadership

Involves overseeing, motivating, training, disciplining, and setting an example for the front office. One can categorize the exercise of leadership as either actual or potential:

— *actual* - giving guidance or direction, as in the phrase "the emperor has provided satisfactory leadership".

— *potential* - the capacity or ability to lead, as in the phrase "she could have exercised effective leadership"; or in the concept "born to lead".

In both cases, as a result of the constancy of change some people detect within the late 20th and early 21st centuries, the act of learning appears fundamental to certain types of leading and leadership. When learning and leadership coalesce, one could characterize this as "learnership". Leadership can have a formal aspect (as in most political or business leadership) or an informal one (as in most friendships). Speaking of "leadership" (the abstract term) rather than of "leading" (the action) usually implies that the entities doing the leading have some "leadership skills" or competencies.

Controlling

Control in one of the managerial functions like planning, organizing, staffing and directing. It is an important function because it helps to check the errors and to take the corrective action so that deviation from standards are minimised and stated goals of the organization are achieved in desired manner. According to modern concepts, control is a foreseeing action whereas earlier concept of control was used only when errors were detected. Control in management means setting standards, measuring actual performance and taking corrective action.

Evaluation

Determines the extent to which planned goals are, in fact, attained. Moreover, it involves reviewing and, when necessary, revising or helping to revise front office goals. Evaluation is carefully collecting and analyzing information in order to make decisions. There are many types of evaluations in organizations, for example, evaluation of marketing efforts, evaluation of employee performance, program evaluations, etc. Evaluations can focus on many aspects of an organization and its processes, for example, its goals, processes, outcomes, etc.

Room Rates Establishment

The front office manager shall assign to each room category a rack rate. In accordance, front office employees are expected to sell rooms at rack unless a guest qualifies for an alternative room rate. While establishing room rates, management shall be careful about its operating costs, inflationary factors, and competition. Generally, there are three popular approaches to pricing rooms:

Market condition approach

Under this very approach, management shall look at comparable hotels in the geographical market, see what they are charging for the same product, and "charge only what the market will accept". Some drawbacks of this approach are that it does not take into consideration the value of the property, and what a strong sales effort may accomplish.

Rule of thumb approach

In this very approach, the rate of a room shall be \$ 1 for each \$ 1,000 of construction and furnishing cost per room, assuming a 70% occupancy rate. This approach, however, fails to take into consideration the inflation term, the contribution of other facilities and services towards the hotel's desired profitability, and assumes a certain level of occupancy rate.

Hubbart formula approach

This very approach considers operating costs, desired profits, and expected number of rooms sold (i.e. demand). The procedure of calculating a room rate is as follows:

- Calculate the hotel's desired profit by multiplying the desired rate of return (ROI) by the owner's investment.
- Calculate pre-tax profits by dividing the desired profit by 1 minus hotel's tax rate.
- Calculate fixed charges and management fees. This calculation includes estimating depreciation, interest expense, property taxes, insurance, amortisation, building mortgage, land, rent, and management fees.
- Calculate undistributed operating expenses. This includes estimating administrative and general expenses, data processing expenses, human resources expenses, transportation expenses, marketing expenses, property operation and maintenance expenses, and energy costs.

— Estimate non-room operating department income or loss, that is, F&B department income or loss, telephone department income or loss.

— Calculate the required room department income which is the sum of pre-tax profits, fixed charges and management fees, undistributed operating expenses, and other operating department losses less other department incomes.

— Determine the rooms department revenue which is the required room department income, plus other room department direct expenses of payroll and related expenses, plus other direct operating expenses.

— Calculate the average room rate by dividing rooms department revenue by the expected number of rooms to be sold.

Forecasting Room Availability

Forecasting room availability is forecasting the number of rooms available for sale on any future date. This type of forecasting helps manage the reservation process, guides the front office staff for an effective rooms management, and can be used as an occupancy forecast, which is, further, useful in attempting to schedule the necessary number of employees for an expected volume of business. In order to forecast room availability, the following data are needed:

Number of expected

1. room arrivals
2. room walk-ins
3. room stayovers
4. room no-shows
5. room understays
6. room check-outs
7. room overstays

These data help the front office in conduct various daily operational ratios such as:

— No-shows percentage = (number of no-show rooms)/ (number of rooms reserved)

— Walk-ins percentage = (number of walk-in rooms)/ (total number of rooms arrivals)

— Overstays percentage = (number of overstay rooms)/ (number of expected check-outs)

— Understays percentage = (number of understay rooms)/(number of expected check-outs)

The forecasted number of rooms available for sale for any future date can be tracked using the following formula:

> Forecasted number of rooms available for sale = total number of guest rooms - number of out of order rooms - number of stayovers rooms - number of reserved rooms + number of no-show rooms + number of understay rooms - number of overstay rooms

Under non-automated and semi-automated systems, number of rooms available for sale forecasts are calculated upon demand and need and vary from three-day to ten-day forecasts. However, under fully automated systems, forecasts can be done at any moment for any future period of time. For, computers run forecasts on a room count considerations, hence eliminating tedious labour work and human error margins.

Budgeting

At least once per year, hotels shall prepare annual budgets, which are profit plans that address all revenue sources and expense items for the following calendar year. Moreover, the hotel annual operating budget represents standards against which management can evaluate actual results of operations. In the annual budget preparation process, close coordination efforts of all management personnel is vital. The hotel's annual operation budget is commonly divided into monthly plans, which in turn are divided into weekly and even daily plans, for better control over actual results. While preparing the front office department annual budget, the front office manager shall coordinate with the accounting department as to estimate only rooms revenue and related direct expenses. The hotel controller and the general manager, then, shall revise this very budget.

— *Forecasting room revenue*: In order to forecast room revenue, the front office manager might consult historical financial information such as past room revenue, past number of rooms sold, past average daily rate, and past occupancy rates.

— *Forecasting direct expenses*: Due to the fact front office manager is responsible only for his/her department direct expenses, the front office manager can, also, consult historical financial data depicting variable cost to room revenue ratios, in order to estimate department expenses.

— *Refining budget plans*: Sometimes, if external uncontrollable factors change significantly, in an unexpected way, then the actual operating budgeted figures shall be revised.

Room Reservation

The term "reservation" used in the context of a hotel, means the booking or reserving of a room (accommodation) by a guest. Reservations lead to reserving of a particular type of room fo r a particular guest for a given period of time. Reserving a room ensures or guarantees the guest the availability of a room on arrival at the hotel, as reservation is a commitment made by the hotel, when the hotel has accepted the reservation request.

A great deal of importance is attached with the reservation system because it helps in:

- selling the primary product of the hotel, i.e., lodging or accommodation,
- building a good first impression on the prospective client,
- generating customers for the other departments of the hotel, and
- generating and providing information to the other departments of the hotel.

Prior to computerization era, the main function of the reservation process is only to determine basic room availability. That is to say, the reservation clerk can only tell the potential guest that a room is reserved for him/her. However, the reservation clerk can not tell you the type of the room, rate honored. Nowadays, with the wide use of reservation software package programmes, it is now possible to reserve a room by room type, rate, and to accommodate all the possible special requests of the guest. Therefore, the selling function shifted from the front office to the reservation department. Hence, projections of room revenues and profitability analysis became one of the basic functions of the reservation department. In parallel, reservation department and reservation agents should have sales goals to achieve which might focus on number of room nights, average room rate, and/or booked room revenue.

Types of Reservations

The reservation system comes into action once a request for reservation comes to the hotel. It can be a direct query from the guest, or from a travel agent or tour operator among others sources. An effective and efficient reservation system is essential for maximising a hotel's profitability. Reference has already been made to the reservation systems of a hotel in MTM-4. The type of reservation system depends on the type and size of hotel. Many small hotels and motels use a booking dairy to keep track of reservation and resident guests. The front desk manager can double up as the reservation supervisor and the front desk clerk as reservation clerk. In a very small establishment (as in case of Bed and Breakfast lodges) you may see owners performing the task of reservation supervisor.

The most common manual system used by hotels of any type or size is known as Whitney System, devised by Whitney Paper Corporation of New York in the 1940s. In this system each reservation is recorded on a small, multipart piece of paper mounted in a metal frame, which, in turn, is filled in date and alphabetical order on a metal rack. The slips are usually colour coded to denote the type of guest. Usually there is one rack for every day over say, the next three months, and fewer racks for future periods. Copies of the slip, also on racks, may be sent to other departments such as reception or telephones when the guest arrives. This system gave rise to the expression "rack rate", which is how hoteliers often refer to the price for rooms.

Whitney System, though very efficient, generates lots of paperwork. This problem, however, is solved by computerised reservation system. The computerised system can perform all the tasks of Whitney System and organizes the guest data more efficiently. The guest's record is maintained in the hard disk of the computer. This not only helps in matching the guest information, but also provides information about the importance of the guest which can be judged from the data available on computer. This kind of information compiled on computer based reservation systems not only provides their credit standing and the reliability of the booking done through the agent but it also makes searching for data very easy.

The large group/chain of hotels have Central Reservation Systems which handle the reservation of the various properties of a single group atoned to centralised reservation office. For example, a hotel may have central reservation number, i.e., 24-7-365- symbolising availability 24 hours a day 7 days a week and 365 days a year. Nowadays, many single hotels have come together to form their own Central Reservation System serving these individually owned establishments. The use of computers in reservations has simplified check-in and checkout process. The hotel does not need much information during these operations as data is fed simult aneously.

Though computerised reservation systems are proved to be of a great help to hoteliers, it is up to a particular hotel to choose and use a system most suitable to their requirements. The most recent and most used way of making reservations accessible at far-flung locations is via internet. In such operations direct bookings and reservations requests can be made over the internet by just a click on the website of the hotels concerned. In some cases the reservation is directly upgraded but mostly the reservation staff reconfirms the request via e-mail or telephone before making official reservations.

Guaranteed reservation insures that the hotel will hold a room for the guest until a specific time following the guest's scheduled arrival date. On return, the guest shall guarantee his/her reservation of room unless reservation is properly canceled. In order to guarantee a reservation, guests might opt for one of the following methods:

a) Prepayment guaranteed reservation
b) Credit card guaranteed reservation
c) Advance deposit or partial payment
d) Travel agent guaranteed reservation
e) Voucher or Miscellaneous Charge Order [MCO]
f) Corporate guaranteed reservation

Non-guaranteed reservation insures that the hotel agrees to hold a room for the guest until a stated reservation cancellation hour (Usually 6 p.m.) on the day of arrival. Reservation agents shall make sure to encourage their guests to guarantee their reservations especially in the high season.

Central Reservation Systems

The majority of lodging properties belongs to one or more central reservation systems. A central reservation system is composed of a central reservation office, member hotels connected together via communication devices, and potential guests. Central Reservation Office [CRO] offers its services via a 24-hours toll free telephone numbers. Hotel members of the central reservation system shall provide and exchange accurate room availability data to central reservation offices. To illustrate, central reservation offices and member hotels shall communicate (on real time) any reservation transaction. This is possible, nowadays, with the sophisticated communication equipment available. These very equipment shall be provided by central reservation offices to its member hotels. Such equipment may range from Teletype, telex, facsimile machines, to personal computers, Internet connections. On return, central reservation offices charges a fee for the utilization of its services which might take the form of a flat fee and a variable fee, or a flat percentage of potential room revenue, actual room revenue, and/or rooms division gross profit.

Central reservation offices are divided into two:

a) *Affiliate reservation network*: This very network is referred to as the hotel chain's reservation system. In fact, it is composed of a CRO, and hotels, which are members of the same chain. The main advantages of affiliate reservation network are:
   a) Streamline the process of reservation
   b) Reduce overall system costs
   c) Attract business for or refer business to another chain property
   d) Affiliate reservation networks might serve, in addition to its main function, other duties like:
      — Serve as an inter property communication network
      — Serve as an accounting transfer tool
      — Serve as a destination information center
      — Serve as a connection with Global Distribution Systems

b) *Non-affiliate reservation network*: A non-affiliate reservation network is composed of a central reservation office, potential guests, and member independent hotels.

Intersell agencies are special types of central reservation offices contracting to handle reservation for more than one Product line.

Group Reservations

Conducting a reservation request for a group shall be treated differently than accommodating a reservation of individual guests. The main reason, is that individual reservation requests are treated by the reservation department, while group reservations are initiated by the sales and marketing division, and finalized through a careful coordination of the reservation from one hand

and the marketing from the other.Below is a detailed procedure of how group reservation, in a typical hotel, is conducted:

1. A group representative, a member of the travel agency or the tour operator, not individuals, shall communicate group reservations' request to the hotel's marketing department
2. Upon availability, the hotel's reservation department shall block the requested number of rooms for this very group
3. The Hotel shall give a deadline for the group, in order to receive their final list. That deadline is called cut-off date
4. After receiving the final list, the reservation department shall change the desired number of rooms' status from blocked to booked (or reserved) rooms, and release the remaining rooms (if any left) as vacant
5. If the hotel did not receive the final list by the cut-off date, then the reservation department has all the right to cancel the group reservation and release all the initially booked rooms into vacant rooms.

Reservation Availability

After receiving a reservation request, the hotel might accept it, as it is, if there is room availability. If not, the reservation department should suggest alternative room types, dates, and/or rates, to the potential guest. If, however, the potential guest insists on his/her previous request, the hotel should suggest an alternative hotel. That's one of the main reasons why we need to maintain good relation-ships with nearby competing hotels.The reservation department should always compare historical reservation volumes against actual arrivals. The main reason is to cope with overbooking, which a situation occurring when the total number of rooms reserved for a certain period of time exceeds the total number of rooms available for sale, for the same period of time. In order to cope with the overbooking problem, some statistical and historical data should be stored and processed by the hotel and should be continuously updated. Such data should include:

a) Number of rooms reserved for a specific date
b) Number of rooms occupied by stayovers
c) Forecasted no-shows percentage
d) Forecasted understays percentage
e) Forecasted overstays percentage

f) Forecasted cancellation percentage

g) Number of out of order rooms for a specific date

In order to function properly, the reservation department shall maintain control books, wall charts, and/or a computerized system. Whatsoever system chosen, the reservation department shall maintain and update that system to include any reservation transaction. Below is a description of the three commonly used sets of equipment to track room availability under the manual, semi-automated and fullyautomated systems:

— *Control books*: Control books are standard three-ring, loose-leaf binders with a tally Page assigned to each day of the year. Under this very system, when a potential guest calls to have a reservation, the reservation clerk shall check the cells corresponding to rooms.

— *Wall charts*: These are charts stapled on the wall depicting days of the month versus hotel rooms. Moreover, upon need and convenience, these charts might be customized to track appropriate room Numbers, rates, and codes, hence, is advantageous to control books. Moreover, in this very system, different colors are used to differentiate between different reservation transactions, types of guest reserving. Lastly, wall charts eliminates the erasures and rewriting associated with control book, hence lees errors might occur.

— *Computerized systems:* Computerized systems are by far the best systems that track room availability. In fact, these very systems control room availability data and automatically generate many reservation-related reports in an accurate manner. Moreover, computerized systems can itemize room availability for future periods by open dates, closed dates, versus special event dates. Lastly, this very system can forecast room availability for any reservation horizon needed in the future.

Reservation Recording

Each reservation department shall prepare a reservation record, which depicts the various personal and financial data of guests, for each reservation transaction. The aim is to identify guests and their occupancy needs before guest's arrival. Moreover, the hotel can personalize or customize guest services and better schedule staff accordingly. In order to create a reservation record, the following items are needed:

a) Guest name

b) Guest's home or billing address
c) Guest's telephone number, including area code
d) Name, address, and telephone number of guest's company, if appropriate
e) Name of and pertinent information about the person making the reservation, if not the guest
f) Number of people in the group, and perhaps ages of any children
g) Arrival date and time
h) Number of nights required or expected departure date, depending on how the system is programmed
i) Reservation type
j) Special requirements
k) Additional information, if needed

At the reservation process, reservation agents shall keep in mind that a rate quoted and confirmed must be honored. Moreover, reservation clerks should be aware of the following:

a) Supplementary charges for extra services or amenities
b) Minimum stay requirements in effect for dates requested
c) Special promotions in effect for dates requested
d) Applicable currency exchange rates, if quoting rates to an international tourist
e) Applicable room tax percentages
f) Applicable service charges or gratuities

The hotel should communicate guests by telephone, telex, mail, or e-mail a letter of confirmation, which confirms the important points of the reservation agreement. This very letter might be shown at the registration process in order to accelerate the pace of registration and prove that the guest has the right to have a room at the hotel.

The hotel shall send a confirmation letter to all reserved potential guests, whether their reservations are guaranteed or non-guaranteed. Below are the main points that should be communicated in a confirmation letter:

a) Name and address of the guest
b) Date and time of arrival

c) Room type and rate
d) Length of stay
e) Number of persons in a group, if any
f) Reservation type
g) Reservation confirmation number
h) Special requests, if any.

Hotels shall communicate meaningful confirmation numbers to their potential guests. These numbers shall have statistical meanings, which might help the hotel in maintaining an efficient historical database. Here is an example: 32 02 G JC 63

a) 32: Guest's scheduled arrival date on Julian dates calendar.
b) 02: Group reservation. In this very system, 01 might mean Frequent Independent Traveler.
c) G: means that the reservation is guaranteed. If N is written, it means non-guaranteed.
d) JC: are the initials of the reservation agent who processed the reservation.
e) 63: Consecutive numbering of all reservation confirmation numbers issued in the current year.

Registration Activities

In the semi and fully automated systems, most of the registration activities are handled at the pre-arrival stage while in the manual system they are conducted at the arrival stage. Registration encompasses the following major activities:

1. Creating the registration record
2. Assigning the room & rate
3. Fulfilling special requests

Pre-registration Activities

At the semi and fully automated systems, guests with reservations experience experience a more rapid check-in due to the information collected by reservation clerks during the reservation process. However, at the manual system, it is inconvenient to pre-register guests at the exception of VIP's and groups. For, VIP's, even under the manual system, need to feel different than other guests. Moreover, group reservations, even though time consuming, might create time benefits at the arrival stage. Lastly, whatsoever operating system the hotel opts for, all walk-ins shall be registered at the arrival stage of the guest cycle.

Registration Record

The registration record is a collection of important personal and financial guest information. A typical registration record includes:

a) Guest name and surname
b) Guest address and telephone number
c) Company affiliation
d) Expected arrival date
e) Planned departure date or length of stay
f) Required room rate
g) Required room type
h) Room number
i) Method of payment
j) Special requests
k) Signature

Rate Assignment

The hotel shall identify and allocate an available room from a specific required room category. That's why, under semi and fully automated systems, reservation and check-in clerks shall be sales minded while negotiating room and rate assignment with guests. This fact applies for registration clerks under the manual system. Moreover, while assigning rooms, check-in clerks shall keep an eye on hotel's future reservation commitments and not assign a room to a guest, while that very room is preassigned to some other guests at the same period of time.

While pricing rooms, the hotel shall keep in mind that rate should be between a minimum (determined by cost structure) and a maximum (determined by competition structure) boundary as depicted below:

Minimum (Hurdle Rate) < Room Rate < Maximum (Rack Rate)

Cost Structure < Room Rate < Competition Structure

Front office department shall finalize room rates with guests during the registration process. Moreover, rack rates shall only be applicable for walk-ins especially during the high season. Lastly, room rates might be affected by:

a) Seasonality

b) Variations in the number of guests assigned to rooms

c) Service level

d) Room location

e) Type of Guest and/or usage.

At registration, check-in clerks shall contact the housekeeping department to be informed about the last status of hotel rooms so that they can assign only clean and available for sale rooms to their guests. That's why, the Front office, Housekeeping and Reservation department shall maintain a high degree of collaboration between them. In order to be sales minded and convince potential guests to accept the highest priced rooms, the front office clerk shall be aware of the characteristics of each room type, the differences within the same room category.

Method of Payment

Guests, at the registration stage, shall communicate or confirm their intended method of payment. Below are the common methods of payments accepted by hotels:

— *Cash*: Guests intending to settle their accounts by cash shall have no in-house charge privileges and, hence, all their purchases should be paid in advance (i.e. PIA status), which means that as guests purchase any kind of service or product, they shall pay for it immediately. In accordance to cash payment, registration clerks shall prepare lists of PIA guests and communicate them to all Point of Sales outlets. On the other hand, paying immediately might not suit some guests, that's why hotels might give guest charge privileges, at the condition they provide an imprint of a valid card or an approved direct billing privilege at registration.

— *Personal checks*: Nowadays, very few hotels still accept personal checks as a method of payment due to the high probability of fraud associated with this method. In fact, in order to accept personal checks, most hotels necessitates that these very checks be supported by a credit card with a check-cashing guarantee, that the amount to be cashed against checks shall be within the hotel's established limit, and preferably accept personal checks only during standard business hours where banks are open. If personal checks are to be accepted, front office personnel shall imprint the credit card on the backside of the guest personal check and record the Guest ID card or driving license certificate along with the guest's address and telephone number on the face of the check.

— *Credit Cards*: Credit cards, nowadays, become a preferable method of payment for guests and hotels. In accordance to this very method of payment, front office clerks should check the following items before accepting the credit card as a method of payment:
  — Expiration date
  — *Invalid credit card*: This can be checked either by on-line authorization systems, or comparing the card across some cancellation bulletins
  — Credit card floor limit.

Some guests do not prefer to wait at checkout queues like other guests before departure. They, rather, prefer, only to sign their guest folios, go to their homes, later receive a certain invoice detailing their charges while they were staying at the hotel to be settled by payment to hotel bank accounts. In order to satisfy the needs of this category of guests, hotels created the direct billing process. To be eligible for a direct billing privilege, guests shall at pre-arrival stage or maximum at the arrival stage fill a hotel credit application form along with the provision of an imprint of a valid credit card. This very form is sent to the Front Office manager, or Rooms Division manager for approval. If not approved, guests are requested to pay with any of the other methods of payments.

Issuing Room Keys

With the issuing of room keys, the rooming process gets to an end. However, concerning room keys, front office clerks shall respect hotel's written policies governing guestroom key control. As an illustration, front desk agents shall only handle the room key to the guest without announcing and/ or spelling out the room number. This is a vital requirement to protect and ensure guest safety and privacy. After guest is handed his/her room key, front office clerks shall offer bellboy assistance.

Fulfilling Special Requests

The front office department shall watch for any guest special requests and try promptly to satisfy them. This way creates a good and professional relationship with the guests and increases the probability that the hotel will receive these guests for another time in the future (i.e. repeat guests). Guests' requests are usually grouped under the following categories:

a) Room type
b) Bed type
c) View
d) Location
e) Amenities

Some of the following innovations are nowadays commonly used while registering a guest:

a) Eliminating the front desk structure (i.e. deskless environment)
b) Having a hotel greeter register guests at a special lobby location
c) Creating a unique & separate registration area for VIP guests
d) Simplification of room process for corporate gatherings, tour , and convention groups Self registration (i.e. self check-in terminals)

Front Office Accounting

The front office accounting system is responsible for:

— Creating and maintaining an accurate accounting record for each guest or non-guest in the hotel
— Tracking all financial transactions throughout the guest cycle
— Ensuring internal control over cash and non-cash transactions
— Recording settlement for all goods & services provided

The front office accounting system shall be customised and tailored to track each hotel's needs. Therefore, no two hotels have exactly the same front office accounting systems.

Generally Accepted Accounting Principles (GAAP) are the following:

— *Unit of Measurement*: Companies operating in a specific country shall use that country's local currency as a unit of measurement.

— *Historical Cost*: The principle of historical cost states that the value of merchandise or services obtained through business transactions should be recorded in terms of actual costs, not current market values.

— *Going Concern*: The principle of going concern (also known as continuity of the business unit) requires financial statement to be prepared under the assumption that the business will continue indefinitely and thus carry out its commitments. Normally, a business is assumed to be a going concern unless there is objective evidence to the contrary.

— *Conservatism*: The principle of conservatism guides the decisions of accountants in areas that involve estimates and other areas that may call for professional judgement. Therefore, the principle of conservatism provides accountants with a practical alternative for situations that involve doubt. In these very situations, the solution or method shall be the one that does not overstate assets or income.

— *Objectivity*: This very principle states that all business transactions must be supported by objective evidence proving that the transactions did in fact occur.

— *Realisation*: Under the realisation principle, revenues resulting from business transactions are recorded only when a sale has been made and earned, when a hotel receives cash from a guest served in the dining room, for example.

— *Matching*: The matching principle states that all expenses must be recorded in the same accounting period as the revenue that they helped to generate. When expenses are matched with the revenue they helped to produce, external and internal users of financial statements can make better judgements about the financial position and operating performance of the hospitality business. There are two accounting methods for determining when to record results of a business transaction: cash accounting and accrual accounting.

— *Consistency*: The generally accepted accounting principle of consistency states that, once an accounting method has been adopted, it should be followed consistently from period to period. This way, accounting information can be comparable.

All guest folios shall be created during the pre-arrival or arrival stage of the guest cycle. Moreover, folios might be either placed in front desk folio tray [i.e. posting tray, folio well, or bucket] or stored as an electronic guest folios in fully automated systems. As far as walk-ins are concerned, all their guest folios are created at the arrival stage!

Record Keeping Systems

- *Non- automated systems*: Ensured through a series of columns listing individual debit and credit entries accumulated during the occupancy stage after which and establishment of an ending outstanding balance is needed.
- *Semi-automated systems*: Under this very system, all guest transactions should be printed sequentially on a machine-posted folio. Later, the front office clerk needs to come up with the folio outstanding balance. It is extremely important here to mention that, under this very system, each account's previous balance shall be re-entered each time a transaction is posted to the folio.
- *Fully-automated systems*: All guest charges are automatically posted to an electronic folio

Guest Charge Privileges

Potential guests who would like to have guest charge privileges shall present an imprint of an acceptable credit card or direct billing authorisation at registration. Failing to do so, guests would have to pay, in full, all their charges through cash, hence called Paid-in-Advance [PIA] guests and have, hence, have no post status.

Credit Monitoring

In order to monitor and control charge privileges, the front office clerk should check whether the total net purchases are less than the minimum of floor Limit (i.e.: credit card company's limit) and house limit (i.e. hotel's limit). At least, each day, lists of guests with high risk or high balance accounts shall be communicated to all point of sale outlets. This is vital since, failing to do so, will let point of sales outlets continue giving charge privileges to a point that eventually the credit card company refuses to pay the amount of money exceeding its limit. This will cause very serious financial losses to the hotel.

Tracking Transactions

Under the manual and semi-automated systems, tracking transactions is ensured through an intensive use of vouchers. On the other hand, Under fully automated systems, tracking transactions is ensured through on-line electronic transfer of transactional information from remote points of sale to the front office main frame terminal. In accounting, a transaction is an exchange of goods and services for cash or a promise to pay. Under this very assumption, "nothing happens until a transaction occurs". This means that front office clerks shall first of all have a transaction, its supporting documents to be able later to debit or credit certain accounts. In hotels transactions might have the form of:

— *Cash payment*: In this very transaction, front office clerks shall post cash payment as a credit in the guest folio. Moreover, cash vouchers shall be used as a transaction-supporting document.
— *Charge purchase*: Charge purchases represent deferred payment transactions that increase the outstanding balance of a folio account. In this transaction type, front office clerks shall use charge vouchers as a transaction-supporting document.
— *Account correction*: Account correction is used to resolve a posting error in a folio detected at the day the error is made (i.e. before the closing of the business day). In this transaction, front office clerks shall use correction vouchers as a transaction-supporting document.
— *Account allowance*: Account allowances occur because of two reasons:
  — Either as compensation of poor service, or as rebates for coupon discounts. That way, guest outstanding balance decreases.
  — As to correct a posting error detected after the closing of the business day.

Internal Control

In the hotel industry, the main purpose of internal control is to track transaction documentation, verify account entries and account balances, and to identify vulnerabilities in the accounting system. The keyword to internal control is auditing, which is the process of verifying front office accounting records for accuracy and completeness. Below are some forms that are of extreme importance to internally control, one of the most vital assets in the hotel:

— *Front office cash sheet*: The front office cash sheet lists each cash receipt or disbursement in order to reconcile cash on hand at the end of a cashier's shift with the documented transaction that occurred during the same shift.

— *Cash, house banks or petty cash*: Petty cash is the amount of cash assigned to a cashier so that he/she can handle the various transactions that occur in a particular work shift. At the beginning of each shift, all cashiers must sign their cash banks and at the end of the shift, shall deposit all cash, checks, and other negotiable instruments in the general cashier's safe deposit box. Moreover, at the end of each shift, cashiers should watch out for cash discrepancies.

Cash discrepancies might have the form of cash overages, shortages, or due backs. Lastly, cashiers might come up with the net cash receipt, which is: Amount of all cash, checks, and other negotiable instruments in cashier's drawer—amount of the initial cash bank + all paid outs

— *Audit control*: Along with the fact that hotels might employ internal control auditors, at least once in a year, to get use of external certified public accountants responsible for approving hotel's accounts.

Accounts Settlement

One of the responsibilities of front office clerks is to settle guest accounts, which means the eventual collection of payment for outstanding account balances. This is usually ensured either by full cash payment, transfer to an approved credit card, personal check, special programme, or direct billing account. Checkout and settlement describe the activities associated with the final stage of the guest cycle (i.e. departure). The major activities, which are conducted at departure, include:

— Resolving outstanding guest account balances

— Updating room status information

— Creating guest history records

Departure Procedures: At checkout, front office clerks shall:

— Check for mails, messages, and faxes

— Check for safe deposit box, or in-room safe keys

— Post all outstanding charges

— Verify account information

— Inquire about additional recent charges

— Present the guest folio for guest signature

— Verify the method of payment
— Process the account payment
— Update the room status

Methods of Settlement

— *Full cash payment*: the front office clerk shall destroy the guest's credit card voucher
— *Personal check payment*: the front office clerk shall shift the credit from guest ledger to personal check account, which is a sub-account of the city ledger and the guest shall only sign a personal check voucher
— *Credit card payment*: the front office clerk shall shift the credit from guest ledger to credit card account, which is a sub-account of the city ledger and the guest shall only sign a credit card voucher
— *Special programme payment*: the front office clerk shall shift the credit from guest ledger to special programme account, which is a sub-account of the city ledger and the guest shall only sign a special programme voucher
— *Direct billing payment*: the guest shall sign only his/her folio, and depart. Later, he/she, upon receipt of hotel invoice, shall deposit a certain amount of money in the hotel bank account.
— *Combined settlement method*: In this case, depending on which combination, front office clerk shall proceed by preparing different kinds of vouchers!

Sales minded cashiers: As guests tends to depart from the hotel, the cashiers shall approach them in the following way:

— Provide them comment cards and encourage them to use these very cards
— Thank the guest for choosing the hotel and wish him/her a safe trip
— Ask the guest whether he/she is considering returning to the property on any return trip to the area. Cashiers might sometimes accept future reservations!

Late check out: Late check out refers to the situation where guests check out after the hotel's established check out time. Late check out shall not be considered as a guest right, rather a privilege which might be honoured by the front office manager upon room availability whether free of charge or charged a late check out fee. There are a lot of innovative ways to check out apart from the traditional way. Below are two commonly used check out options:

— *Express check out*: This is usually convenient for guests who decide to check out very early in the morning. In fact, at night, bellboys (for example) shall slip the guest folio under the expected departed guestroom. When the guest wakes up, he/she shall sign the gust folio, and the credit card voucher, leave the room, give back the room key to the bellboy, and departs.

— *Self check out*: Guests might check out using self check out terminals situated at public areas or in their rooms if in-room check out systems are integrated with front office main frame.

Unpaid Account Balances: Unpaid account balances occur because of the following reasons, most of which are because hotels do not operate fully-automated systems:

— A departing guest honestly forgetting to settle his/her account

— Late charges

— Skippers

In order to minimise late charges, front office clerks shall:

— Post transactional vouchers as soon as they arrive at the front desk

— Survey front office equipment, voucher and folio racks for non-posted charges before the front office clerk checks a guest out

— Ask departing guests whether they have incurred any charge purchase or placed long distance telephone calls, which do not appear on their final folio

Account Collection

All unpaid account balances shall be transferred to city ledger accounts, which might have the form of:

— Credit card billing

— Direct billing

— Travel agency accounts

— Bad check accounts

— Skipper accounts

— Disputed bills accounts
— Guaranteed reservation accounts
— Late charge accounts
— House accounts

In order to receive all their city ledger accounts, hotels shall devise effective and efficient account receivables billing procedures.

Expense Accounting

In the accounting terminology, expense is an income statement account representing the cost of items consumed in the process of generating revenue or that expires due to the passage of time. Expense cannot be mixed with expenditure. For, Expenditure represents the purchase amount of a certain asset. In the hotel industry, expenses are divided into two main categories:

Direct expenses

These are the expenses that vary with the level of production. For example, in the Food and Beverage department, the Cost of Food Sales is a direct expense. For, the more dishes we serve, the more cost of Food Sales the Hotel incurs. Moreover, in the Telephone Department, the Cost of Calls is a direct expense. For, the more we connect guests to whatever destination wanted, the more cost of calls the hotel incurs. At this very stage a bracket would be opened to explain that there is a primordial difference between revenue generator departments.

In fact, revenue generator departments are classified into two: Service Type departments versus merchandising departments. Service type departments are revenue generators making money from solely providing services. On the other hand, merchandising departments ensure revenue by getting use of certain raw material, processing it, and than sell the final product. Therefore, only merchandising departments have a direct expense called Cost of Sales.

The various types of Rooms Division department direct expenses include:

— *Commissions expenses*: This account includes payments by the hotel to authorised agents that bring room business to the hotel. Usually at the end of each month, hotels sit with these agents in order to reconcile their monthly sales figures and authorise commission payment.

- *Reservation expenses*: This expense account represents any payment to various agents contracting to bring potential room revenue business to the hotel.
- *Contract cleaning expenses*: This expense account represents payment to contracting outside cleaning agencies. Some hotels might opt for contract cleaning because of its attractive financial implications. If this is the case, these hotels might not be forced to have a housekeeping department, or might keep house-keeping staff to minimum. Such expenses should be determined in light of the contract signed between both parties.
- *Laundry and dry cleaning expenses*: This cost applies to outside laundry and dry cleaning costs for the Rooms Division department. In most of the cases, such contracts are signed to benefit more than one revenue generator. In this case, the rooms division department shall report the laundry and dry cleaning expenses related only to the Rooms Division department.
- *Guest transportation expenses*: These expenses include the cost of transporting guests from and to the hotel via various means of transportation. If the guest transportation's volume business, staff, and costs are significantly high, then a separate department might be established.
- *Linen expenses*: This specific expense account includes the allocation of a portion of linen expenditure for a specific period of time. This practice goes along with one of the accounting principles: the matching principle. Some sub-accounts of linen expense might be:
    - Towels expenses
    - Blankets expenses
    - Facecloth expenses
    - heets expenses
    - Pillow expenses
- *Guest supplies expenses*: This account includes the various guest supplies provided free of charge to guests in their rooms. Some sub-accounts of guest supplies expenses might include:
    - Newspaper expenses
    - Guest stationary expenses

- Shoe cloth expenses
- Coffee expenses
- Writing supplies expenses
- Toilet requisites expenses
- Flowers expenses
- Hangers expenses
- Matches expenses
- Ice expenses
- Candy expenses

— *Cleaning supplies expenses*: Such an account includes the cost of Rooms Division's cleaning supplies. Some sub-accounts of guest supplies expenses might include:

- Brooms expenses
- Soaps and polishes expenses
- Cleaning cloths expenses
- Mops expenses
- Cleaning chemicals expenses
- Dusters expenses
- Brushes expenses
- Insecticides expenses
- Dustpans expenses
- Pail expenses
- Disinfectants expenses
- Cleaning accessories expense

— *Printing and stationary expenses*: This expense account includes printed formats, office supplies, printed manuals and guidelines for the use of the Rooms Division employees.

— *Uniforms expenses*: This expense account includes the allocation of a portion of uniforms asset for a certain period of time along with the expense of repairing, and cleaning them. If the hotel rents uniforms rather than purchasing them, then the uniform expense shall include the renting cost, usually predetermined in light of the contract linking the hotel and the uniform renting company.

Indirect expenses

These are the expenses that do not vary with the level of production, or variable costs that can not be feasibly distributed to various Financial Reporting Centers. In the hotel industry, indirect expenses are, hence, divided into two different categories:

Fixed Charges: Examples might include rent, insurance, property taxes, and interest expense. For, these very expenses are incurred for the benefit of the hotel as a whole not for the benefit of each single department. To illustrate, if a hotel insures itself against fire, theft and burglary, and one day some valuable equipment has been stolen, from any department whatsoever, the insurance company will indemnify the hotel.

Undistributed Expenses: Examples might include electricity, energy, and water expenses. For, usually the hotel receives a total energy bill to be paid. In the old days, some hotels went for allocating this amount according to certain factors. However, this practice proved to be misleading, since it might under-allocate energy expenses for some departments and over-allocate it for others.

Front Office Records

The major two front office records that are stored at departure are guest history records (which are stored alphabetically) and guest folios (stored numerically)

Guest History Records

Guest history records are collections of personal & financial data about guests who have stayed at the hotel. Maintaining guest history records helps the hotel better understand its clientele and determine guest trends when they develop. Moreover, these very records might serve as a source of mailing list or to identify guest characteristics that are important to strategic marketing. In addition, they serve as to develop and place advertisements that appeal to the types of clientele the hotel attempts to attract. Finally guest history records points out the need for a new, supplementary, or enhanced services.

Moreover, even though guest history records are stored in the front office department, they are handed to marketing department, whenever needed. In fact, marketing department might get use of guest history records as to create a programme to reward frequent guests with a free stay after a certain number of visits, or as an indicator to watch out for future repeat guest reservations in order to increase the hotel's repeat business market share. Guests tend to remember the friendliness, convenience, and special services that distinguish one property from another. This is called competitive advantage.

Night Audit

The major functions of the night audit is to:

— Verify posted entries to guest and non-guest accounts
— Balance all front office accounts
— Resolve room status and rate discrepancies
— Monitor guest credit limits
— Produce operational and managerial reports

The night audit requires attention to accounting detail, procedural controls, and guest credit restrictions. In this sense, the night auditor shall track room revenues, occupancy percentages, and other standard operating statistics. He/she shall, also, prepare a daily summary of cash, check, and credit card activities that occurred in the front office department on a daily basis. In night auditing, end of the business day is a vital time for the auditor. As far as the closing of business day is concerned, management shall determine the end of day, which is the time after which the night audit can prepare his/her daily Reports. This end of day is usually the time where the majority of outlets close or no more have frequent activity.

The night auditor shall always compare the data conveyed in different folios against points of sales outlets daily reports, housekeeping room status report. This is called cross-referencing, and is a vital procedure in the internal control. After comparing, the night auditor should come up with the guest, non-guest, and departmental accounts. This total should match the daily POS totals (i.e. in balance). If not, then the auditor is said to be out-of-balance, and the night auditor shall substantially review all account statements, vouchers, support documents, and departmental source of documentation in order to bring the audit to balance.

The night audit shall compare all credit limits of guests and non-guests accounts with credit card floor limits, hotel's house limit, guest's status and reputation. If high balance accounts are detected, the night auditor shall note and report this to management the following day. Under the manual, a daily transcript and a supplementary transcript are used to track daily transactions of guest and non-guest accounts respectively. Hotels operating under semi-automated systems use D-Cards for the same purpose.

Non-automated system: under this very system, 4 forms are widely used, which are:

— Daily and supplementary transcripts

— Guest and non-Guest folios

— Front office cash sheets

Semi-automated system: The audit of guest and non-guest accounts is ensured mostly through mechanical or electronic posting machines. The most important form obtained under this very system is the D Card.

Fully-automated system: This very system is the best compared to manual and semi-automated systems. In fact, this system can be interfaced with point of sale terminals, call accounting systems, and other revenue centers for quick, accurate and automatic postings to electronic guest and non-guest account folios. This very fact enables the night auditor to concentrate more on auditing transactions and analysing front office activities.

Night Audit Process: The night audit process focuses on two areas:

— Discovery and correction of front office accounting errors ensured through the cross-referencing process.

— Creation of accounting and managerial reports including audit balance, average rate, occupancy percentage, usage of package plans and other marketing programmes, and the number of group rooms and complementary rooms occupied.

Responsibilities of the Receptionist

The work of a receptionist involves spending a lot of time dealing with guest enquiries of all descriptions. The ability to answer guest enquiries accurately and promptly is the key to good customer service. While it may not be possible to know all the answers, to all questions, all the time, there are steps you can take to ensure that each guest enquiry is dealt with satisfactorily.

Enquiry

The type of enquiry you can expect to get on reception usually falls into three categories:

— *Reservation*: to deal with enquiries about reservations either over the telephone or in person, the receptionist must have on hand up-to-the-minute information of room status, the advance reservation chart, and the hotel directory and room rates/tariffs.

— *Information for the guest*: guests have come to expect reception staff to have all sorts of information at their fingertips. Enquiries can range from the cost of sending a postcard to Europe, to car rental facilities, to information on places of interest in the locality.

— *Information regarding guests:* enquiries about guests should be handled with caution and discretion. All guests are entitled to a measure of privacy and protection and any person requesting information about a guest, for example, the name and room number of a resident, should be referred to a supervisor or manager.

Receptionists are right if they believe that the customer expects them to know everything. Of course you cannot know everything, but it should be in your power to satisfy the guest's need, whatever the nature of the enquiry. As this is the service that is most likely to be in demand from reception or the information desk, you should build up your knowledge, particularly of the most frequently asked questions. These may include information on:

— the hotel facilities and services

— the locality—geographic location

— the locality—places of interest

— local services, e.g. transport, places of worship, airline offices, etc.

— entertainment—restaurants, theatre, etc

— additionally, foreign visitors may request information on local customs, cultural issues and language.

So while it may not be possible for the receptionist to have the answers to all questions, it is important to know where to get the answer and how. Every effort should be made to assist the guest with his enquiry. To do so promptly and accurately will require you having access to a range of information directories. You should have:

— a list of all the facilities and services in the hotel, with details such as opening times

— a list of names of members of staff, their job titles and telephone extensions

- details of what is happening from day-to-day throughout the hotel
- a good idea of what goes on in the locality so that you can inform guests looking for details of church services, entertainment and so on
- good reference sources to hand, such as local papers, telephone and trade directories, relevant street maps and so on
- timetables of local transport services
- tourist guide book of the region

Having the information on hand is of no use unless you know how to use the reference material you have. Make sure you find out how to use the reference books in the hotel to get the information you need—know how to use the index system, read timetables and interpret the postal tariffs. Adopt a simple general procedure to deal with standard enquiries:

- Greet the customer with a smile.
- Listen carefully to find out the requirements.
- Make a note of the relevant details if necessary.
- To avoid misunderstandings, repeat the main points back to the customer. Take special care if the enquiry is complicated, or the person has difficulty hearing.
- Ask further questions if you still are unclear.
- Deal with the enquiry immediately.

You should always try and deal with a guest enquiry yourself as it is very annoying for the guest if he has to ask several different staff members the same question. However there will be times when you cannot answer the enquiry and will have to direct the guest elsewhere. You should know what type of enquiries it is better not to try to answer but to pass on to the appropriate person. Some examples of these may include:

- What special discounts can be given to a group booking—refer to the front office manager or another senior manager
- Whether the hotel can accommodate a wedding on a particular day-refer to the banqueting manager
- Can the receptionist book an airline seat—refer to the local travel agent

Handling of Emergency Situations

You should be aware of enquiry situations, which could be regarded as emergencies, requiring an immediate and urgent response, for example, and a request for medical attention. Each hotel will have its own procedure for dealing with these situations and you should familiarise yourself with the practice in your hotel. Very often the principle will remain the same:

— Ascertain the facts
— Repeat and confirm the essential details
— Action immediately—it is usual in emergency situations to contact the supervisor or manager immediately
— Record the incident in the reception log book

In cases of emergency the essential points to remember are:

— *Remain calm and act immediately*: Remember that the most important part of the enquiry process is communication. Effective communication—with guest, colleagues and interdepartmental is essential to ensure a high level of customer service and guest satisfaction.

Keep this checklist with you as a useful reminder of what you should do not should not do when dealing with guest enquiries.

Handling Mail and Messages

When handling mail and messages it is important to process them promptly and efficiently. This is good customer relations practice where the principles of speed, accuracy and professionalism are all key to "getting the job done" to the highest possible standard. The range of mail and messages you are likely to be dealing with are:

— *Incoming mail*: Received via the postal system, mail may arrive for various departments in the hotel, hotel guests and staff. With the arrival of new technology it is now possible to receive "letters" by Facsimile (the fax machine) or via the computer terminal, which is known as electronic mail or e-mail.
— *Outgoing mail*: Letters and packages for posting.
— *Messages*: Telephone and personal messages for your own and other departments in the hotel and hotel guests.

It is necessary to have a procedure for receiving, recording and distributing all types of incoming mail both for guests and the hotel to ensure that the right message gets to the right person with the minimum delay. A simple and efficient procedure would involve:

- Time/date stamp all mail as soon as is received.
- Record in the mail register.
- Sort into appropriate batches—internal and guest.
- Distribute promptly.

Guest mail may fall into four categories and therefore it is important to know how to handle each type efficiently. The following procedures are suggested:

- Mail for guests in residence
  - Sort alphabetically.
  - Check against the alphabetical guest list and write the room number on the envelope.
  - Place in the appropriate pigeonhole in the letter rack. Large envelopes, packages, and registered mail will need to be stored in a separate place.
  - Notification may be sent to the guest to tell him that mail has arrived, for example, if the hotel has a telephone message light system this might be activated.
  - Alternatively, the hotel may operate a delivery system where standard mail is delivered to the guest room by the porter/bellboy.
  - A notification memo is placed in the pigeonhole in the letter rack asking the guest to collect it if a registered letter or package is received at the reception or information desk.
- *Mail for departed guests*: Many guests will leave a forwarding address, filling in a mail forwarding form. These are kept on file for a specified length of time. Once the expiration date passes, the cards should be removed. Any mail arriving after that date, or if no forwarding address was left, is returned to sender via the post office.
- *Mail for future guests*: Mail for guests yet to arrive is sorted into alphabetical order and kept to one side. The advance reservation list is checked for the guest's arrival date, a note made in the hotel diary that mail is being held, and on the appropriate date it is placed in the letter rack. Hotels with a computer system can check the guest records and leave a message on the computer for the guest at check-in.
- *Mail for which no record of a guest can be found*: This mail should be held over for a specified number of days and checked daily against the arrivals list in case a guest arrives who did not have a reservation

or there was a misspelling in the guest name originally. If after the specified number of days the name can still not be found then the mail is returned to sender via the post office.

Registered mail and special delivery services, for example DHL, must be signed for by the person accepting delivery and in turn must be signed for by the guest on collection. The recommended procedure for handling deliveries of this sort is:

— Enter into a logbook with date, time of arrival, and receipt number

— Place under lock and key or in a safe

— A notification memo is placed in the letter rack or the message light is switched on asking the guest to collect.

— The logbook is signed by the guest to confirm that they have taken delivery

However, you should always check the hotel policy and procedure regarding this and follow the guidelines accordingly.

If reception is responsible for dealing with any outgoing mail then a procedure is necessary to ensure that this mail is dispatched with the minimum delay. A standard procedure might be:

— Set a deadline for receipt of mail to be mailed that day.

— Make regular collections from the various departments throughout the day.

— Sort and weigh to ensure the correct postage is affixed.

— Post office receipts for registered mail should be attached in a special book kept for that purpose.

Handling messages

Messages are normally conveyed in writing or verbally. Many of which will need to be passed on by the receptionist to another person who may be:

— A member of staff

— A customer, guest, conference delegate, visitor, friend, relative or colleague of a customer

— A potential customer

If you receive a message for someone else verbally it is always a good idea to write it down rather than pass it on verbally, especially if the message is complicated or the person to receive it is not available straight away.

Procedure for taking messages:

- Establish who the message is for
- Write message down accurately with all the relevant details:
  - Make sure the facts are correct
  - Think what the recipient needs to know
  - Be concise

The most common mistakes when taking down messages over the phone are:

- Missing out a figure from a telephone number
- Forgetting to ask the caller's name
- Not taking the callers telephone number
- Repeat the message back to caller
- Pass on the message immediately or as soon as possible.
- Check if possible that the recipient has understood.

Messages may also be conveyed to guests via an in-house paging system. The system may vary in each hotel but the common methods are:

- *Paging board*: A page or bellboy walks through the lobby and public areas usually ringing a small bell to get the attention of guests, carrying a board with the name of the guest prominently displayed. This system alerts all guests that there is a message for someone and the onus is on the guest to check if the message is for him.
- *Public address*: An announcement can be made over a public address system requesting the guest by name to identify him for a message or telephone call.

Reception frequently sells postage stamps to guests as a service to them. It is important to be familiar with the postal rates and know how to look up postal charges on the postal tariff list. As this task involves the handling of cash, some form of control procedure should be in place to keep a record of sales and cash. Post cards may also be available and a similar control procedure should be in place.

Evaluation of Front Office Operations

A successful front office manager shall continuously evaluate the results of department activities on a daily, monthly, quarterly, and yearly basis. While evaluating, the following items and tools shall be used:

1. *Daily operations report*: It is also known as the manager's report, the daily report, and the daily revenue report. This very report contains a summary of the hotel's financial activities during a 24-Hour period. Moreover, it serves as to reconcile cash, bank accounts, 'and revenue and accounts receivable, and as an important data that must be input to link front and back office computer functions.
2. *Occupancy ratios*: Occupancy ratios measure the success of the front office in selling the hotel's primary product (i.e. guestrooms). Some common ratios used in the front office department are given below:
   — *Occupancy percentage* = (number of rooms occupied)/ (total number of rooms available for sale)
   — *Multiple occupancy percentage* = (number of rooms occupied by more than one guest) / (total number of rooms occupied)
   — *Average guests per rooms sold* = (total number of guests)/ (total number of rooms sold)
   — *Average daily rate* = (total rooms revenue) / (total number of rooms sold)
   — *Average rate per guest* = (total rooms revenue) / (total number of guests)
3. *Rooms revenue analysis*: One main report to enhance control over room revenue is the room rate variance report, which is the one that lists those rooms that have been sold at rates other than their rack rates.
4. *Hotel income statement*: This very statement provides important financial information about the results of hotel operations for a given period of time
5. *Rooms division income statement*: The rooms division income statement shall be referenced on the hotel's income statement. Moreover, the rooms division schedule shall be prepared by hotel's accounting division not the hotel's front office accounting staff.
6. *Rooms division budget reports*: These reports are monthly budget forms that compare actual revenue and expense figures against budgeted amounts depicted both in dollar values and percentage variances
7. *Operating ratios*: Operating ratios assist managers in evaluating the success of front office operations.

References

Beale, Joseph Henry. *The law of innkeepers and hotels: including other public houses, theatres, sleeping cars.* Boston: William J. Nagel, 1906.

Boni, G. de. *Hotel organization, management and accountancy.* London: Pitman, 1939.

Dicksee, Lawrence Robert. *Hotel accounts.* London: Gee & Co., 1905.

Hamilton, Francis Frazee. *Hotel front desk management, a treatise on the best methods and procedures in use in small hotels.* Miami, Fla.: Francis Frazee Hamilton, 1947.

O'Brien, Daniel J. and Charles Bennington Couchman. *Hotel administration, accounts and control.* New York: McGraw-Hill book company inc., 1927.

3

Human Resource Management in Hotels

In recent years, human resource management (HRM) has assumed greater importance in organizations, as it has been recognized as contributing to overall effectiveness. It is now widely acknowledged that human resources play an important role in the success of organizations. The human resource is almost always the key ingredient for organizational success. If the success of an organization depends on the calibre of its employees, then it is crucial that they be managed effectively, so that they can help the organization to achieve its objectives. Organizations need to utilize their human resources effectively to provide high-quality service to their customers, to improve pro- ductivity and hence profitability. In a labour-intensive industry such as hospitality, the effective utilization of human resources can give a hotel a competitive advantage.

In view of the growing importance of tourism, it is absolutely essential for hotels in both countries to develop efficient human resource management practices capable of providing excellent quality of service. Hotels must develop human resource practices which will enable them to recruit, select and retain competent employees who can contribute to the achievement of their objectives. Hotels have overseas guests who require high standards of service quality. To encourage tourists to stay in hotels, the hotels must meet the guests' expectations of service quality.

Over the last decade, human resource management has come to be viewed as the dominant paradigm within which analyses of the world of work have been located. Common perceptions of management practices in the hotel industry typically include work intensification, high labour turnover, lack of training and poor career prospects, and casualised terms and conditions of employment. Primary influences on managerial decision-making in the hotel industry are no different from the primary influences affecting decision-making elsewhere, countering the argument that mainstream management theories are inapplicable within the hotel industry. Furthermore, where hotels emphasise the importance of service quality enhancement and where they introduce HRM as an integrated, mutually supporting package of practices, a strong relationship between HRM and organizational performance is proposed.

The human resources management function includes a variety of activities, and key among them is deciding what staffing needs you have and whether to use independent contractors or hire employees to fill these needs, recruiting and training the best employees, ensuring they are high performers, dealing with performance issues, and ensuring your personnel and management practices conform to various regulations. Activities also include managing your approach to employee benefits and compensation, employee records and personnel policies. Usually small hotel managers have to carry out these activities themselves because they can't yet afford part- or full-time help. However, they should always ensure that employees have — and are aware of — personnel policies which conform to current regulations. These policies are often in the form of employee manuals, which all employees have.

Staffing

Staffing is one of a hotel's most important management functions, is an ongoing challenge because of the high rate of employee and manager turnover. Full-service hotels can experience annual turnover rates in excess of 100 percent in certain employee classifications. Some managers consider an annual employee turnover rate of 33 percent low. At this rate, the entire hotel must be completely restaffed every three years. The higher the turnover rate, the larger the number of employees who must be replaced. In an attempt to reduce employee turnover, hotel and lodging businesses are giving increasing attention to job design, seeking to enhance those job characteristics that give the employee the greatest satisfaction and motivation.

Good job design must take into account the needs of employees as well as the demands of the job. Well-thought-out job design begins when management conducts a job analysis-that is, a thorough evaluation of the specific tasks performed for a particular job and the time required to perform them. Job analysis is an ongoing process, as many jobs change with improvements in technology and pressure to improve product quality. The job analysis is the basis for the job description and job specification. A job description includes the job title, pay, a brief statement of duties and procedures, working conditions, and hours.

The job specification is an outline of the qualifications necessary for a particular job. In response to the limits of specialization, organizations can redesign jobs to improve coordination, productivity, and product quality while responding to an employee's needs for learning, challenge, variety, increased responsibility, and achievement. Such job redesign often involves job rotation, the systematic movement of employees from one job to another; job enlargement, an increase in the number of tasks an employee will do in the job; job enrichment, the attempt to give the employee more control over job-related activities; and flextime, a flexible work schedule that permits employee input in establishing work schedules. In team-driven job redesign, a concept similar to job rotation, employees can transfer back and forth among teams that provide different services or products.

Hotels recruit employees from a variety of sources. Newspapers and employee referrals are used to recruit nonskilled hourly employees. Supervisory and management employees generally are recruited through colleges and universities, promotions from within, professional associations, and management recruiters. Hotels that take more time in making their selections are more successful in retaining employees. Discussions of employee training and development often concentrate on training techniques without giving a full explanation of what a hotel is trying to accomplish. As training and development impart job skills and educate employees, supervisors, and managers, they also improve current and future employee performance, which affects the bottom line.

Effective training includes problem solving, problem analysis, quality measurement and feedback, and team building. Performance evaluation, also called performance appraisal, is the systematic review of the strengths and weaknesses of an employee's performance. The major difficulty in a performance appraisal is quantifying those strengths and weaknesses. The performance of some jobs is easy to quantify, while for others it is more difficult. An important part of the appraisal process is a well-established job description, so that the employee and the supervisor have similar expectations. Compensation includes the monetary and nonmonetary rewards that managers, supervisors, and employees receive for performing their jobs. In order to set compensation levels, the human resources department must periodically conduct job evaluations, which determine the value of the job to the hotel. Knowledge of the value of the job to the organization and of wage rates for each job classification allows the hotel to establish a fair compensation policy. There are several activities involved in staffing a housekeeping operation. Executive housekeepers must select and interview employees, participate in an orientation program, train newly hired employees, and develop employees for future growth.

Employee Selection

Each region has its own demographic situations that affect the availability of suitable employees for involvement in housekeeping or environmental service operations. For example, in one area, an exceptionally high response rate from people seeking food service work may occur and a low response rate from people seeking housekeeping positions may occur. In another area, the reverse may be true, and people interested in housekeeping work may far outnumber those interested in food service. Advertising campaigns that will reach these employees are the best method of locating suitable people. Major classified ads associated with mass hirings will specify the need for food service personnel, front desk clerks, food servers, housekeeping personnel, and maintenance people. Such ads may yield surprising results. If the volume of response for housekeeping personnel is insufficient to provide a suitable hiring base, the following sources may be investigated:

- Local employment agencies
- Flyers posted on community bulletin boards
- Local church organizations
- Neighborhood canvass for friends of recently hired employees
- Direct radio appeals to local homemakers
- Organizations for underprivileged ethnic minorities, and mentally disabled people

If these sources do not produce the volume of applicants necessary to develop a staff, it may become necessary to search for employees in distant areas and to provide regular transportation for them to and from work. If aliens are hired, the department manager must take great care to ensure that they are legal residents of this country and that their green cards are valid. More than one hotel department manager has had an entire staff swept away by the Department of Immigration after hiring people who were illegal aliens. Such unfortunate action has required the immediate assistance of all available employees to fill in. Whether you are involved in a mass hiring or in the recruiting of a single employee, a systematic and courteous procedure for processing applicants is essential.

The efficient handling of lines of employees, courteous attendance, personal concern for employee desires, and reference to suitable departments for those unfamiliar with what the hotel or hospital has to offer all become earmarks for how the company will treat its employees. The key to proper handling of applicants is the use of a control system whereby employees are conducted through the steps of application, prescreening, and if qualified, reference to a department for interview. Even though an employee may desire involvement in one classification of work, he or she may be hired for employment in a different department. Also, employees might not be aware of the possibilities available in a particular department at the time of application or may be unable to locate in desired departments at the time of mass hirings. Employees who perform well should therefore be given the opportunity to transfer to other departments when the opportunities arise. According to laws regulated by federal and state Fair Employment Practices Agencies (FEPA), no person may be denied the opportunity to submit application for employment for a position of his or her choosing. Not only is the law strict on this point, but companies in any way benefiting from interstate commerce may not discriminate in the hiring of people based on race, color, national origin, or religious preference. Although specific hours and days of the week may be specified, it is a generally accepted fact that hotels and hospitals must maintain personnel operations that provide the opportunity for people to submit applications without prejudice.

A carefully planned, concerned, and informational orientation program is significant to the first impressions that a new employee will have about the hospital or hotel in general and the housekeeping department in particular. Too often, a new employee is told where the work area and restroom are, given a cursory explanation of the job, then put to work. It is not uncommon to find managers putting employees to work who have not even been processed into the organization, an unfortunate situation that is usually discovered on payday when there is no paycheck for the new employee. Such blatant disregard for the concerns of the employee can only lead to a poor perception of the company. A planned orientation program will eliminate this type of activity and will bring the employee into the company with personal concern and with a greater possibility for a successful relationship. A good orientation program is usually made up of four phases: employee acquisition, receipt of an employee's handbook, tour of the facility, and an orientation meeting.

Once a person is accepted for employment, the applicant is told to report for work at a given time and place, and that place should be the personnel department. Preemployment procedures can take as much as one-half day, and department managers eager to start new employees to work should allow time for a proper employee acquisition into the organization. At this time it should be ensured that the application is complete and any additional information pertaining to employment history that may be necessary to obtain the necessary work permits and credentials is on hand. Usually the security department records the entry of a new employee into the staff and provides instructions regarding use of employee entrances, removing parcels from the premises, and employee parking areas. Application for work permits, and drug testing, will be scheduled where applicable. All documents required by the hotel's health and welfare insurer should be completed, and instructions should be given about immediately reporting accidents, no matter how slight, to supervisors.

For new facilities, access to the property should be gained within about one week before opening, and many new employees can be taken on a tour simultaneously. It is possible for employees to work in the hotel housekeeping department for years and never to have visited the showroom, dining rooms, ballrooms, or even the executive office areas. A tour of the complete facility melds employees into the total organization, and a complete informative tour should never be neglected. For ongoing operations, after acquisition, the new employee may be turned over to a department supervisor, who becomes the tour director. An appreciation of the total involvement of each employee is strengthened when a facilities tour is complete and thorough. If necessary, the property tour might be postponed until after the orientation meeting; however, the orientation activity of staffing is not complete until a property tour is conducted.

Employee orientation meetings that are scheduled too soon fail to answer many questions that will develop within the first two weeks of employment. The meeting should be held in a comfortable setting, with refreshments provided. It is usually conducted by the director of human resources and is attended by as many of the facility managers as possible. Most certainly, the general manager or hospital administration members of the executive committee, the security director, and the new employees' department heads should attend. Each of these managers should have an opportunity to welcome the new employees and give them a chance to associate names with faces. All managers and new employees should wear name tags. In orientation meetings, a brief history of the company and company goals should be presented. Although the new employee will be gaining confidence and security in the position as training ends and work is actually performed, informal orientation may continue for quite some time. The formal orientation, however, ends with the orientation meeting. Finally, it should be remembered that good orientation procedures lead to worker satisfaction and help quiet the anxieties and fears that a new employee may have. When a good orientation is neglected, the seeds of dissatisfaction are planted.

Responsibilities of Hotel managers

Hotel managers are being asked more and more often to assume responsibility for management of the sales staff. It is a job for which they have received little training and for which they have a number of challenges. Five years ago, when demand was high and the sales function was relegated to answering the phone and taking the order, it was relatively easy for managers to keep an eye on things in the sales department. Unemployment was at historic lows and in order to keep positions filled, we were reluctant to expect too much or discipline an under performing employee. There was a tendency to keep the chair warm rather than let a position go unfilled. Times have changed both in terms of demand of demand and the employment pool but often the attitudes of management have not. Sales people represent a distinct management challenge. The good ones are bright, aggressive, able to sell their managers as well as their clients but they are also very human. They like most other employees will take the path of least resistance, need to have expectations made clear and have objective standards of performance by which they are evaluated.

Hotel managers have a particular challenge in that they work long hours and very closely with their sales staffs. It is difficult to maintain an objective and professional distance that allows for the kind of management that gets results. There are a few simple steps you can take to make your monitoring of the sales effort more effective. They may also make the sales effort more effective. There has to be a line of familiarity that you don't cross. It negates your ability to lead and manage effectively. Have regular sales meetings with a fixed agenda. It should occur at least once a month, preferably once a week at a time when it does not interfere with Prime Selling Hours. This provides a structured environment in which you can ask the 'tough' questions without sounding picky and irrational. To a sales person, if you just casually ask a question about an account or ask for numbers, they are likely to feel that you are just in a bad mood and it will pass. Take a course in sales. If you come from another discipline in the industry, learn about basic sales. Read a book, take a course—take a course in sales not related to the industry. There are many fine resources for hotel sales available especially now when that function has become so challenging. Sales people who have worked on commission 'get it'.

Set realistic goals and involve them in the process. Goal setting should be an objective process. When you let them know what they need to produce and why, then involve them in figuring out how they are going to get there, they understand and ideally buy into the plan. Be supportive but expect results! Your head is on the line here too!. If your sales staff is making a ton of calls but producing few results, it could be a skills problem. Offer them some training. When a reasonable amount of time and training effort has passed, don't be afraid to make the tough decision. The fact of the matter is they are uncomfortable at their non-performance and may be happier and more satisfied in another position. A comfortable room, good food, and a helpful staff can make being away from home an enjoyable experience for both vacationing families and business travellers. While most lodging managers work in traditional hotels and motels, some work in other lodging establishments, such as camps, inns, boardinghouses, dude ranches, and recreational resorts. In full-service hotels, lodging managers help their guests have a pleasant stay by providing many of the comforts of home, including cable television, fitness equipment, and voice mail, as well as specialised services such as health spas. For business travellers, lodging managers often schedule available meeting rooms and electronic equipment, including slide projectors and fax machines. Lodging managers are responsible for keeping their establishments efficient and profitable. In a small establishment with a limited staff, the manager may oversee all aspects of operations. However, large hotels may employ hundreds of workers, and the general manager usually is aided by a number of assistant managers assigned to the various departments of the operation. In hotels of every size, managerial duties vary significantly by job title. For example, general managers have overall responsibility for the operation of the hotel. Within guidelines established by the owners of the hotel or executives of the hotel chain, the general manager sets room rates, allocates funds to departments, approves expenditures, and establishes expected standards for guest service, decor, housekeeping, food quality, and banquet operations. Managers who work for chains also may organize and staff a newly built hotel, refurbish an older hotel, or reorganize a hotel or motel that is not operating successfully. In order to fill entry-level service and clerical jobs in hotels, some managers attend career fairs.

Resident managers live in hotels and are on call 24 hours a day to resolve problems or emergencies. In general, though, they typically work an 8- to 10 hour day and oversee the day-to-day operations of the hotel. In many hotels, the general manager also is the resident manager. Executive housekeepers ensure that guest rooms, meeting and banquet rooms, and public areas are clean, orderly, and well maintained. They also train, schedule, and supervise the work of housekeepers, inspect rooms, and order cleaning supplies.

Front office managers coordinate reservations and room assignments, as well as train and direct the hotel's front desk staff. They ensure that guests are treated courteously, complaints and problems are resolved, and requests for special services are carried out. Front office managers may adjust charges posted on a customer's bill. Convention services managers coordinate the activities of various departments in larger hotels to accommodate meetings, conventions, and special events. They meet with representatives of groups or organizations to plan the number of rooms to reserve, the desired configuration of the meeting space, and the banquet services.

During the meeting or event, they resolve unexpected problems and monitor activities to ensure that hotel operations conform to the expectations of the group. Assistant managers help run the day-to-day operations of the hotel. In large hotels, they may be responsible for activities such as personnel, accounting, office administration, marketing and sales, purchasing, security, maintenance, and pool, spa, or recreational facilities. In smaller hotels, these duties may be combined into one position. Assistant managers may adjust charges on a hotel guest's bill when a manager is unavailable. Computers are used extensively by lodging managers and their assistants to keep track of guests' bills, reservations, room assignments, meetings, and special events. In addition, computers are used to order food, beverages, and supplies, as well as to prepare reports for hotel owners and top-level managers. Managers work with computer specialists to ensure that the hotel's computer system functions properly. Should the hotel's computer system fail, managers must continue to meet the needs of hotel guests and staff. Because hotels are open around the clock, night and weekend work is common. Many lodging managers work more than 40 hours per week. Managers who live in the hotel usually have regular work schedules, but they may be called to work at any time. Some employees of resort hotels are managers during the busy season and have other duties during the rest of the year. Lodging managers sometimes experience the pressures of coordinating a wide range of functions. Conventions and large groups of tourists may present unusual problems. Moreover, dealing with irate guests can be stressful. The job can be particularly hectic for front office managers during check-in and check-out time. Computer failures can further complicate an already busy time.

Lodging managers held about 69,000 jobs in 2002. Self-employed managers-primarily owners of small hotels and motels-held about 50 percent of these jobs. Companies that manage hotels and motels under contract employed some managers. Hotels increasingly emphasise specialised training. Postsecondary training in hotel or restaurant management is preferred for most hotel management positions, although a college liberal arts degree may be sufficient when coupled with related hotel experience. Internships or part-time or summer work are an asset to students seeking a career in hotel management. The experience gained and the contacts made with employers can greatly benefit students after graduation. Most bachelor's degree programmes include work-study opportunities. Community colleges, junior colleges, and some universities offer associate's, bachelor's, and graduate degree programmes in hotel or restaurant management. Combined with technical institutes, vocational and trade schools, and other academic institutions, over 800 educational facilities have programmes leading to formal recognition in hotel or restaurant management. Hotel management programmes include instruction in hotel administration, accounting, economics, marketing, housekeeping, food service management and catering, and hotel maintenance engineering. Computer training also is an integral part of hotel management training, due to the widespread use of computers in reservations, billing, and housekeeping management. Additionally, over 450 high schools in 45 States offer the Lodging Management Programme created by the Educational Institute of the American Hotel and Lodging Association. This is a two-year programme offered to high school juniors and seniors, which teaches management principles and leads to a professional certification called the "Certified Rooms Division Specialist". Many colleges and universities grant participants credit towards a post-secondary degree in hotel management.

Lodging managers must be able to get along with many different people, even in stressful situations. They must be able to solve problems and concentrate on details. Initiative, self-discipline, effective communication skills, and the ability to organize and direct the work of others also are essential for managers at all levels. In the past, many managers were promoted from the ranks of front desk clerks, housekeepers, waiters, chefs, and hotel sales workers. Although some employees still advance to hotel management positions without education beyond high school, postsecondary education is preferred.

Restaurant management training or experience also is a good background for entering hotel management, because the success of a hotel's food service and beverage operations often is important to the profitability of the entire establishment. Graduates of hotel or restaurant management programmes usually start as trainee assistant managers. Some large hotels sponsor specialised on-the-job management training programmes that allow trainees to rotate among various departments and gain a thorough knowledge of the hotel's operation. Other hotels may help finance formal training in hotel management for outstanding employees. Newly built hotels, particularly those without established on-the-job training programmes, often prefer to hire applicants who have hotel management experience.

Large hotel and motel chains may offer better opportunities for advancement than small, independently owned establishments, but relocation every several years often is necessary for advancement. The large chains have more extensive career ladder programmes and offer managers the opportunity to transfer to another hotel or motel in the chain or to the central office. Career advancement can be accelerated by the completion of certification programmes offered by various associations. These programmes usually require a combination of course work, examinations, and experience. For example, outstanding lodging managers may advance to higher level manager positions.

Employment of lodging managers is expected to grow more slowly than the average for all occupations through 2012. Additional job openings are expected to occur as experienced managers transfer to other occupations or leave the labour force, in part because of the long hours and stressful working conditions. Job opportunities are expected to be best for persons with college degrees in hotel or restaurant management. Increasing business travel and domestic and foreign tourism will drive employment growth of lodging managers.

Managerial jobs are not expected to grow as rapidly as the hotel industry overall, however. As the industry consolidates, many chains and franchises will acquire independently owned establishments and increase the numbers of economy-class rooms to accommodate bargain-conscious guests. Economy hotels offer clean, comfortable rooms and front desk services without costly extras such as restaurants and room service. Because there are not as many departments in these hotels, fewer managers will be needed. Similarly, the increasing number of extended-stay hotels will temper demand for managers because, in these establishments, management is not required to be available 24 hours a day. In addition, front desk clerks increasingly are assuming some responsibilities previously reserved for managers, further limiting the employment growth of managers and their assistants. Additional demand for managers is expected in suite hotels, because some guests-especially business customers-are willing to pay higher prices for rooms with kitchens and suites that provide the space needed to conduct meetings.

Importance of Effective Leadership

The hotel you just walked into has a certain crispness to it; a certain feeling. You get a sense of it all around you from the moment you arrive at the front desk. It isn't just that this place is spotlessly clean, though it is. It isn't just that everyone seems friendly and on their toes, though, that certainly is obvious. It isn't just that the hotel employees seem to genuinely care about meeting or exceeding your expectations, though that also is happening at every turn you make. No, it's something else; something intangible, yet unmistakably obvious. This is a hotel that exudes quality. But how did it get there? Why do you notice it here, and not somewhere else? The answer rests in the matter of Leadership. If something in a hotel environment leads you to the conclusion that you are in the midst of quality, it is because Leadership brought the organization into that state. For sure, quality doesn't happen on its own. Someone made it happen and brought others with him or her to ensure that quality would endure.

The mark of a good manager isn't how well things run when you're there. It's how well things run when you're not there. Managers must hire the right people; people who care and show a willingness to care for others—that's what hospitality means. Then, they must train their employees in the rudiments of the job and later, coach them to do their job well in a positive environment that inspires and motivates teamwork. Training and coaching are not the same things. Training teaches skills. Coaching teaches the application of those skills; and training must always precede coaching. Finally, the manager needs to get out of the way and let people do their job. Delegate tasks, authority and decision making, but don't abdicate them. Hold people accountable for their actions. Cultivate and nurture key players and you will develop winners along the way. The manager who works seven days a week to make sure things get done right has missed this important attribute of leadership. On the other hand, managers who are never around while the department is in a state of chaos have equally missed the point. People do what they do because of what they get after they do it. People behave within an organization a certain way because that is what is being culturally reinforced. Culture is nothing more than the collective attitudes of those who hold power. Managers who are not leaders and leadership that does not preside has abdicated power, but power will still be held by someone within the organization, and usually by tenured employees with lower standards than their customers.

Leadership's role is to use its authority as a means to influence behaviour. Reward is the only thing that initiates lasting changes in behaviour and in order for reward to succeed, it must be positive, immediate and certain. Giving reward is a Leadership behaviour that acknowledges someone for having done something correctly. Unfortunately, many managers see their role as correcting behaviour only when it is wrong. We've all worked for the manager that was always on our case when we made a mistake, was slow to give praise for having done something right and rarely said, "Good job." Good Leadership is always noticing when someone does something right and makes mention of it. Reward need be nothing more than a smile and a few kind words, but given routinely and as soon as a positive act is observed, it will set the culture moving in the right direction. Do it. Do it right. Do it right now. Leaders act. Leaders get it right the first time. Leaders take action the moment it is required and inspire others to do the same. If you've ever had a complaint, then explained the complaint to a frontline clerk only to be told that you'll have to see the manager, you might understand the importance of this Axiom. There probably is no more important place in a hotel where this Axiom is needed than in the Sales office.

A hotel where leadership has a certain operational intensity and sense of urgency about getting things done has embraced this philosophy, which is a hallmark of good Leadership. The attitude of any staff reflects the attitude of their leader. If a front desk crew is friendly and vivacious, their leader is, too. If a restaurant delivers outstanding service, you can bet that the leader exhibits the same attitude toward serving the customer. Leaders, by their very attitude, set the standard by which others will behave. Leadership sets an expectation, creates an environment where that expectation is routinely met and ensures that it will endure over time. This means managers have to be willing to deal with the nitty-gritty and the fundamentals of their department. Every service encounter that an employee will make and every expectation that Leadership has must be communicated and reinforced. You can grow, or you can be comfortable, but you cannot do both at the same time. Leadership isn't a state that is suddenly attained, at least not for most of us. And while it is true that great leaders are born, they still have to learn an awful lot about channelling their innate ability to become great leaders.

Leadership is a path of continual enlightenment that occurs over a lifetime. That path is often difficult. Hotel managers don't have an easy job, but any level of discomfort may well be precisely because that path has been taken. All leaders reach certain plateaus in the course of their development: that's called experience. But learning never stops and it's never very easy. Managers who rest in their comfort zone will eventually fail because the world all around them isn't static. The market isn't; the competition isn't; customers aren't and neither are employees. Leaders must continually challenge themselves to compensate for the changing environment and learn new ways to gain market share, beat the competition, find new customers and retain good employees. People don't always do what you expect. They'll do what you inspect. Checking behind your crew doesn't mean you don't trust them; it just means you accept your Leadership role. General Managers in particular should never stop checking rooms and you can almost always tell the hotels where they have.

At the heart of business is the need to be fiscally healthy and it is Leadership's responsibility to guide the organization toward that state. Junior managers in particular sometimes lose site of the fact that their decisions, on an hour-by-hour basis, are having financial impact on the hotel, both good and bad. Yes, put people before money and recognise that the organization deals with human issues every day; Leadership must always be caring and compassionate. But absent financial success, the business will fail, and then, all human conditions fall prey to unfortunate and often unsavoury outcomes: lay-offs, litigation, foreclosure or take-over.

Training of Employees

Employees, regardless of past experiences, always need some degree of training before starting a new job. Small institutions may try to avoid training by hiring people who are already trained in the general functions with which they will be involved. However,most institutions recognize the need for training that is specifically oriented toward the new experience, and will have a documented training program. Some employers of housekeeping personnel find it easier to train completely unskilled and untrained personnel. In such cases, bad or undesirable practices do not have to be trained out of an employee. Previous experience and education should, however, be analyzed and considered in the training of each new employee in order that efficiencies in training can be recognized. If an understanding of department standards and policies can be demonstrated by a new employee, that portion of training may be shortened or modified. However, skill and ability must be demonstrated before training can be altered. Finally, training is the best method to communicate the company's way of doing things, without which the new employee may do work contrary to company policy.

First training of a new employee actually starts with a continuation of department orientation. When a new employee is turned over to the housekeeping or environmental services department, orientation usually continues by familiarizing the employee with department rules and regulations. Many housekeeping departments have their own department employee handbooks. Training may be defined as those activities that are designed to help an employee begin performing tasks for which he or she is hired or to help the employee improve performance in a job already assigned. The purpose of training is to enable an employee to begin an assigned job or to improve upon techniques already in use. In hotel or hospital housekeeping operations, there are three basic areas in which training activity should take place: skills, attitudes, and knowledge.

Skills Training

A sample list of skills in which a basic housekeeping employee must be trained follows:

— *Bed making*: Specific techniques; company policy

— *Vacuuming*: Techniques; use and care of equipment

— *Dusting*: Techniques; use of products

— *Window and mirror cleaning*: Techniques and products

— *Setup awareness*: Room setups; what a properly serviced room should look like

— *Bathroom cleaning*: Tub and toilet sanitation; appearance; methods of cleaning and results desired

— *Daily routine*: An orderly procedure for the conduct of the day's work; daily communications

— *Caring for and using equipment*: Housekeeper cart; loading

— *Industrial safety*: Product use; guest safety; fire and other emergencies

The best reference for the skills that require training is the job description for which the person is being trained.

Attitude Guidance

Employees need guidance in their attitudes about the work that must be done. They need to be guided in their thinking about rooms that may present a unique problem in cleaning. Attitudes among section housekeepers need to be such that, occasionally, when rooms require extra effort to be brought back to standard, it is viewed as being a part of rendering service to the guest who paid to enjoy the room.The rooms are there to be enjoyed. Positive relationships with various agencies and people also need to be developed. The following is a list of areas in which attitude guidance is important:

— The guest/patient

— The department manager and immediate supervisor

— A guestroom that is in a state of great disarray

— The hotel and company

— The uniform

— Appearance

— Personal hygiene

The most important task of the trainer is to prepare new employees to meet standards. With this aim in mind, sequence of performance in cleaning a guestroom is most important in order that efficiency in accomplishing day-to-day tasks may be developed. In addition, the best method of accomplishing a task should be presented to the new trainee. Once the task has been learned, the next thing is to meet standards, which may not necessarily mean doing the job the way the person has been trained. There is a need to conduct ongoing training for all employees, regardless of how long they have been members of the department. There are two instances when additional training is needed:

— the purchase of new equipment, and

— change in or unusual employee behavior while on the job.

When new equipment is purchased, employees need to know how the new equipment differs from present equipment, what new skills or knowledge are required to operate the equipment, who will need this knowledge, and when. New equipment may also require new attitudes about work habits. Employee behavior while on the job that is seen as an indicator for additional training may be divided into two categories: events that the manager witnesses and events that the manager is told about by the employees. Events that the manager witnesses that indicate a need for training are frequent employee absence, considerable spoilage of products, carelessness, a high rate of accidents, and resisting direction by supervisors. Events that the manager might be told about that indicate a need for training are that something doesn't work right, something is dangerous to work with, something is making work harder. Although training is vital for any organization to function at top efficiency, it is expensive. The money and man-hours expended must therefore be worth the investment. There must be a balance between the dollars spent training employees and the benefits of productivity and high-efficiency performance.

A simple method of determining the need for training is to measure performance of workers: Find out what is going on at present on the job, and match this performance with what should be happening. The difference, if any, describes how much training is needed. If the employee could not do the job even if his or her life depended on the outcome, there is a deficiency of knowledge (DK). If the employee could have done the job if his or her life depended on the outcome, but did not, there is a deficiency of execution (DE). If either deficiency of knowledge or deficiency of execution exists, training must be conducted. The approach or the method of training may differ, however. Deficiencies of knowledge can be corrected by training the employee to do the job, then observing and correcting as necessary until the task is proficiently performed. Deficiency of execution is usually corrected by searching for the underlying cause of lack of performance, not by teaching the actual task. There are numerous methods or ways to conduct training. Each method has its own advantages and disadvantages, which must be weighed in the light of benefits to be gained. Some methods are more expensive than others but are also more effective in terms of time required for comprehension and proficiency that must be developed.

On-the-Job Training

Using on-the-job training (OJT), a technique in which "learning by doing" is the advantage, the instructor demonstrates the procedure and then watches the students perform it. With this technique, one instructor can handle several students. In housekeeping operations, the instructor is usually a GRA who is doing the instructing in the rooms that have been assigned for cleaning that day. The OJT method is not operationally productive until the student is proficient enough in the training tasks to absorb part of the operational load.

OJT requires progress toward daily production of ready rooms, simulation requires that the model room not be rented. In addition, the trainer is not productive in cleaning ready rooms. The advantages of simulation training are that it allows the training process to be stopped, discussed, and repeated if necessary. Simulation is an excellent method, provided the trainer's time is paid for out of training funds, and clean room production is not necessary during the workday.

Modern Trends in Training

Many hotels use training aids in a conference room, or post messages on an employee bulletin board. Aside from the usual training aids such as chalkboards, bulletin boards, charts, graphs, and diagrams, photographs can supply clear and accurate references for how rooms should be set up, maids' carts loaded, and routines accomplished. Most housekeeping operations have films on guest contact and courtesy that may also be used in training. Motion pictures speak directly to many people who may not understand proper procedures from reading about them.

Many training techniques may be combined to develop a well-rounded training plan. It is possible to have two students sitting side by side in a classroom, with one being trained and the other being developed. Recall that the definition of training is preparing a person to do a job for which he or she is hired or to improve upon performance of a current job. Development is preparing a person for advancement or to assume greater responsibility. The techniques are the same, but the end result is quite different. Whereas training begins after orientation of an employee who is hired to do a specific job, upon introduction of new equipment, or upon observation and communication with employees indicating a need for training, development begins with the identification of a specific employee who has shown potential for advancement.

Training for promotion or to improve potential is in fact development and must always include a much neglected type of training -supervisory training. Many forms of developmental training may be given on the property; other forms might include sending candidates to schools and seminars. Developmental training is associated primarily with supervisors and managerial development and may encompass many types of experiences. Development of individuals within the organization looks to future potential and promotion of employees. Specifically, those employees who demonstrate leadership potential should be developed through supervisory training for advancement to positions of greater responsibility. Unfortunately, many outstanding workers have their performance rewarded by promotion but are given no development training.

Development of new growth in the trainee becomes difficult when the training instructor or coordinator is not only developing a new manager but is also being held responsible for the production of some aspect of housekeeping operations. Whether you are conducting a training or a development program, suitable records of training progress should be maintained both by the training supervisor and the student. Periodic evaluations of the student's progress should be conducted, and successful completion of the program should be recognized. Public recognition of achievement will inspire the newly trained or developed employee to achieve standards of performance and to strive for advancement. Once an employee is trained or developed and his or her satisfactory performance has been recognized and recorded, the person should perform satisfactorily to standards. Future performance may be based on beginning performance after training. If an employee's performance begins to fall short of standards and expectations, there has to be a reason other than lack of skills.

The reason for unsatisfactory performance must then be sought out and addressed. This type of follow-up is not possible unless suitable records of training and development are maintained and used for comparison. Although evaluation and performance appraisal for employees will occur as work progresses, it is not uncommon to find the design of systems for appraisal as part of organization and staffing functions. This is true because first appraisal and evaluation occurs during training, which is an activity of staffing. Once trainees begin to have their performance appraised, the methods used will continue throughout employment.

As a part of training, new employees should be told how, when, and by whom their performances will be evaluated, and should be advised that questions regarding their performance will be regularly answered. Initial employment should be probationary in nature, allowing the new employee to improve efficiency to where the designated number of rooms cleaned per day can be achieved in a probationary period (about three months). Should a large number of employees be unable to achieve the standard within that time, the standard should be investigated. Should only one or two employees be unable to meet the standard of rooms cleaned per day, an evaluation of the employee in training should either reveal the reason why or indicate the employee as unsuitable for further retention. An employee who, after suitable training, cannot meet a reasonable performance standard should not be allowed to continue employment.

Evaluation of staff is an attempt to measure selected traits, characteristics, and productivity. Unfortunately, evaluations are generally objective in nature, and raters are seldom trained in the art of subjective evaluation. Initiative, self-control, and leadership ability do not lend themselves to measurement; therefore such characteristics are estimated. How well they are estimated depends to a great extent on the person doing the estimating. Certain policies on the use of evaluations should be established so that they are understood by both the person doing the evaluating and the person being evaluated. These policies must be established and disseminated by management. Evaluation should be used at the end of a probationary period, and the employee must understand at the beginning of the period that he or she will be observed and evaluated. Each item, as well as what impact the evaluation will have on future employment, should be explained to the employee. People undergoing periodic evaluations, such as at the end of one year's employment, should also know why evaluations are being conducted and what may result from the evaluation. In both situations, the evaluation should be used for counseling and guidance so that performance may be improved upon or corrected if necessary. Certainly, strong points should be pointed out.

Role of HRM in Customer Satisfaction

HRM involves all management decision and practices that directly affect or influence the people or human resource, who works for the organization. The main function of human resource management involves, HR panning, acquiring HR, building individuals and organizational performance, rewarding employees, and maintaining human resources. However, HRM has faced many changes over the past decades, making changes in both aspects and way of managing human resource of organizations. Agrawal pointed out that in a era of heightened competition alone has made it required that human resource management can no longer be content with simply executing a standard set of practices. There is a need constantly to develop and implement new and improve HR practices so as to remain completive in the market.

A new branch of HRM has emerged as a way of addressing this challenging issue, known as strategic human resource management (SHRM). The role of SHRM is to see that human resource issues are taken in to account when an organization develops its business strategy and that strategy then drives the development of human resource practices within the firm. It seems that all SHRM activities resembles around four major activities: (1) integration of HR within the strategic planning process, (2)partnership between HR and other members of the organization, (3) linkage of HR activities business activities and core cultural values of the organization and (4) restructuring the HR department.

It is interesting to note that it is under the function of integration that HR managers have to align HR practices of the organizations with customers' expectation known as customization of HR services. One of the objectives of integration with the customer group is to win customers for life which has direct implications for organizational success. HR manager has to formulate a set of strategies for his HR functions so as to meeting the customer expectations leading to their satisfaction. This is more relevant for service organizations like hotels and banks, since employees of these organizations have to make a physical contact with customers in serving for their requirements. Under this proposition, it is important to explore empirically how significant HR strategies are for making customers satisfied with the service.

The concept of customer satisfaction stands central in the most of marketing theories and practices. Since early 1970s the volume of customer satisfaction research has been impressive. Many researchers conceptualize customer satisfaction as an individual's feeling of pleasure or disappointment resulting form comparing a product's perceived performance in relation to his or her expectations. Generally, there are two general conceptualization of customer satisfaction, namely transaction specific satisfaction cumulative satisfaction. Transaction specific satisfaction is a customer's evaluation of his or her experience and relation to a particular service counter and cumulative satisfaction refers to the customer's overall evaluation of consumption experience to date. It is the commutative customer satisfaction the study used as the basis for assessing respondents' satisfaction.

Organizations today have found the important of keeping their customer satisfied with their products and services in fast-faced and increasingly completive business environment. This can be attributed to the fact that many researchers have pointed out the relationship of customer satisfaction with many organizational outcomes interested by the management. Among the possible outcomes of customer satisfaction are customer loyalty and profitability, better business performance, market share and customer retention and survival of the firm.

What make the customers of a firm satisfied with their product or service? Numerous studies have been carried out to identify the possible antecedents of customer satisfaction. Service quality has received relatively many attentions of researchers over the past years as one of the major determinant of customer satisfaction specially in service industry. This higher attention lies in the interest of researchers to explore the construct of customer satisfaction through a multi disciplinary perspective rather through single disciplinary perspective. The exploration of customer satisfaction with service quality brings three disciplines together, namely marketing, HRM and total quality management (TQM).

Bitner, Booms and Mohr define service quality as the customer overall impression of the relatively inferiority or superiority of the organization and its services. This definitions itself depicts the fact that customer satisfaction is highly correlated with customer satisfaction in service organizations. The level of inferiority or superiority of the service as perceived by the customer will determine the degree of satisfaction of the customer with that service. It is the characteristics or attributes associated with the service that are perceived by the customer in assessing the superiority or inferiority of the service.

The contribution of human resource practice to customer satisfaction has been amenable to many researches both in the field of Human resource management and marketing. Some researchers have pointed out organizational requisites for customer satisfaction. They claim that customer satisfaction can be achieved only when the firms design necessary structure, processes, cultivating customer-oriented values and developing customer-oriented workforce It is evident from the findings of these studies that the nature of the workforce or human resource of the organization is one of the determinants of customer satisfaction of the firms. But the question arouse in this regard is whether all types of employees in the organizations matter in customer satisfaction. Kelly argued that customer contact employees with customer oriented values and beliefs are of significant for the organizations customer focus and customer satisfactions. So it is clear that the behavior of the employees who has direct contact with the customer is of importance in this regards.

What are the aspects of human resource of the organization that are making their customer satisfied with the products or services of them? Researchers have identified number of factors relating to human resources of the organization associated with customer satisfaction. Rosemary listed out human resource factors for customer satisfaction such as ongoing investment in training, employee security, high relative pay and performance management system. Other than these human resource functions, attributes such a values and beliefs, employee behavior have been stressed.

The role of the human resource manager in improving and sustaining customer satisfaction is paramount important. The implementation of human resource strategies specially deigned for employee-customer linkage improves the service effectiveness resulting in customer satisfaction. The HR strategies for customer satisfaction are some HR functions identified as having special implication on customer satisfaction.

Among these HR strategies, compensation is standing as cornerstones. American quality foundation reported that more and more companies in U.S., Japan, Germany, and Canada have incorporated customer satisfaction criterion into their senior management compensation system. Few researchers have brought up the implication of compensation on customer satisfaction. The point to be concerned here is how the compensation system brings implication on customer satisfaction. Hauser et al. argued that customer oriented compensation focuses the effort of both employees and managers from short term sales to long term sales resulting high concerned for customer satisfaction.

Motivating employees is another area of HRM that records implication on customer satisfaction. Deming pointed out that it is the firm's responsibility to design an incentive system that result in consistency between the firm's and employees' objectives so that when acting in their own best interest, the employees take actions that also benefit the firm. The employees should be motivated in such a way that they focus not only on mere performance but also on customer satisfaction.

Training and development stands significant in the endeavor for satisfied customer base for an organization. Special attention is given here to change the attitudes and values of employees for high customer oriented behavior. Siguaw, Brown and Widing argued that an important aspect of implementing customer oriented strategies is to influence employees especially the salespersons to adopt chosen orientation in their selling efforts.

The customer oriented-attitudes and values prompt a sort of behavior in the employees which is valued by the customer to a greater extent resulting in customer satisfaction.

Employee empowerment is another dimension of HRM contributing to the improvement of customer satisfaction. Empowering employee can be defined as the process of enabling employees by giving them the power and the autonomy to exercise control over job-related situation and decisions.Bowen and Lawler pointed out several advantages that employee empowerment bring to servicing customer such as faster response to customer needs and problems, more-satisfied employees, enthusiastic and warm customer interaction, and innovative ideas. Further, empowered employees are also more likely to exhibit customer oriented behavior because they become more flexible and adoptive in the face of changing customer needs. Therefore, it is no doubt that the empowered employees may act or do their duties in such a way that it leads to higher customer satisfaction than the underpowered employees in organization.

Evaluation of employees is a core task in Human resource management. A particular type of employee evaluations termed as behavior-based employee evaluation bears much implication on customer satisfaction.Behavior-based evaluation is not only evaluate the performance of employee but also the behavior of those employees to judge whether they exhibit behaviors for long term durability. Much research has been carried out to assess the impact of behavior-based employee evaluations. They have come up with number of positive aspects related to employees such as employee competence, confidence, job satisfaction, and adoptability. Zeithmal, Berry and Paraguayan argued that behavior-based evaluation encourage employee performance that is consistence with customer expectation resulting in customer satisfaction.

Organizational socialization is another area where HR managers can contribute to the customer satisfaction efforts of organizations. Organizational socialization is defined as a process by which person acquires the social knowledge and organizational skills necessary to assume an organizational role. This will improve the knowledge and skills in employee resulting in developed social interaction between the members within the organizations and with outsiders. Hartine and Ferrell claimed that organizational socialization is a critical component in the dissemination of a customer oriented strategy to customer contact employees. it is clear that

HRM can assist in improving the customer satisfaction by effectively handling the socialization of employees specially the customer contact employees of the organization.

One of the outcomes of an effective HRM is to generate and sustain a committed workforce both towards the organization and the job. Hiltrop is consistent with the view that HR practices of an organization have a significant influence in making employees committed to exhibit the kind of attitudes and behavior that are needed to support and implement the competitive strategies of the organization. It is a well accepted proposition in management literature that it is the change of attitudes and behaviors of employees that leads to customer satisfaction of organizations specially in service organizations.

It is clear from the literature review that HRM can make a effective contribution to the enhancement of customer satisfaction of the customers of organizations. The areas and the ways that Human resource management can make a contribution to the customer satisfaction can be summarized as follows:

HR Area	*Highlights*
Empowerment of Employees	Empowered employees often feel more confident in their ability to contribute to the firm's success, a result that fosters creative thinking and problem solving. Bowen and Lawler pointed out several advantages that empowerment bring to the firm. Among these advantages are faster response to customer needs and problem, more satisfied employee, enthusiastic warm customer relations, innovative ways of ideas, and loyal customers.
Behavior-Based Evaluation	Behavior based evaluation is particularly suited to customer contact employees in that their performance in serving customer needs is directly related to customer oriented behavior. Employee behavior can become an important in service settings, because service customers often weight the service process heavily in their quality evaluation.
Shared Customer-Oriented Values	Shared values among a firm's employees can facilitate greatly the implementation of customer satisfying startegies and enhance firm's performance.

Work Group Socialization	By instilling confidence in employees and using effective role models, work group socialization can enhance the dissemination of customer-oriented strategy and value to customer contact employees.
Organizational Commitment	Commitment causes employees to believe more strongly in the goals and values of the organization. As a result, employees who are committed to the organization are more likely to buy into the value system and exert effort towards achieving organizational goals.
Performance-Based Reward System	A common theme from employees at the best service provider is that management provides feed back, recognition and rewards for excellent service delivery. it is also important for employees to view their compensation as fair, equity

References

Boomer, Lucius Messenger. *Hotel management; principles and practice.* New York: Harper, 1931.

Boni, G. de and Frederick Francis Sharles. *Hotel organization, management and accountancy.* London; New York: Sir I. Pitman, 1931.

Fisk, Warren Wells. *Evidence of needs of hotel managers in regard to training and education.* 1947.

Holmes, F. H. *Hotel training course.* Chicago: F.H. Holmes, 1937.

Woods, Robert H. *Quality Leadership and Management in the Hospitality Industry.* East Lansing: Educational Institute of the American Hotel & Motel Association, 1996.

4

Hotel Operation and Administration

The size and magnitude of a hotel management structure varies significantly depending on the size and function of the hotel. A small hotel normally consists of a small core management team consisting of the general manager and a few key department managers who directly handle day-to-day operations. On the contrary, a large full service hotel often operates more like a large corporation with an executive board headed by the general manager and consisting of key directors serving as heads of individual hotel departments. Each department normally consists of subordinate line-level managers and supervisors who handle day to day operations.

Hotel managers are generally exposed to long shifts that include late hours, weekends, and holidays due to the 24 hour operation of a hotel. The common workplace in hotels is a fast-paced environment, with high levels of interaction with guests, employees, investors, and other managers. Upper management consisting of senior managers, department heads, and General Managers may enjoy a more desirable work schedule consisting of a more traditional business day and having weekends and holidays off.

Depending on the size of the hotel, the hotel manager's day may include scheduling breaks, covering a window for check in or check out, handling cash, reconciling bank accounts, writing a review for an employee, disciplining an employee or handling dissatisfied guests. These duties may vary each day depending on the needs of the property. The manager's responsibility includes knowing about all current local events as well as the events being held on the hotel property. Managers will be required to attend regular department and company meetings. A hotel/casino property may require additional duties regarding special events being held on property for casino complimentary guests.

Developing a Hotel

The developer is the entrepreneur, the risk taker, who originates the idea for the hotel. Depending on the business structure selected, the developer often puts his or her personal wealth at risk when engaging in a hotel project. The developer, along with a small staff of people, networks with commercial real estate agents on the lookout for a suitable hotel site. Depending on the type of hotel to be developed, a site of at least two to four acres is required (for comparison, an acre is roughly the size of a football field).This property must be zoned by the city for a hotel, be visible from a freeway or major street arterial, and have city approval for such construction activities as curb cuts, lefthand turn lanes, and delivery truck access. Commercial realtors offer sites for the developer's consideration that include maps, aerial photos, and proof of hotel zoning. Sometimes the developer views potential sites by driving around the neighborhood within five miles of the site or touring multiple sites by helicopter, noting where the potential guests live and work and where potential competing hotels are located. The price per square foot of the land is considered. The higher the cost of land, the higher the rates the hotel will need to charge. Is the price too high for the average daily rate (ADR) in this particular market? Is it too low? Or is it acceptable? This is determined when the hotel financial pro forma budget document is created.

Feasibility Study

When the developer selects a site, a feasibility study is often commissioned to obtain an analysis of the site by an objective third party. Companies offer hotel feasibility studies for a fee and are experts in a particular market, or developers may use the consulting group of one of the major public accounting firms. The company retained to do the feasibility study can spend up to several months gathering detailed data to see if, in their opinion, it makes economic sense to build the hotel. Their conclusion offers an objective thirdparty opinion as to whether the project is feasible, hence the term *feasibility study.* Generally, the feasibility study considers, evaluates, and makes recommendations about the project based on the following variables:

The Site

- Proper zoning
- Size in square feet/acres
- Visibility from arterials/freeways
- Traffic counts/patterns
- Accessibility from streets, freeways, airports, train stations, etc.
- Proximity to where potential guests live, travel, or work
- Barriers that discourage competition coming into the market, if any
- How adjacent property and businesses are utilized
- Master area development plans
- Local permitting process and the degree of difficulty for that particular city
- Impact fees charged by the city

The Economy of the Area

- Major employers, government agencies
- Business trends for each employer/agency
- Hotel needs and the demand for each
- Leisure travel demand in the area
- Nearby tourist attractions
- Visitor counts
- Conventions, trade shows, and meetings history

The Hotel Market

- The competitors, both existing and planned
- Historical occupancy of hotels in the area
- Historical average rate
- Proprietary data on area travel

Identification of Which Hotel Market Segment to Serve

- Full service
- Limited service
- Extended stay
- Luxury

— Midprice
— Economy
— Budget

Selection of Appropriate Hotel Design

— High-rise
— Midrise
— Garden apartment style
— Hybrid design

Selection of Appropriate Hotel Brand

— Franchised (Marriott, Sheraton, Hyatt, etc.)
— Licensed (Best Western, Guest Suites, etc.)
— Independent
— Independent with strategic market affiliation (Luxury Hotels of America, Historic Hotels of America, etc.)

Ten-year Projection

— Occupancy projection by year
— ADR by year
— Estimated cash generated for debt
— Estimated cash generated for distribution to investors
— Estimated cash-on-cash return (after-tax income divided by equity invested)
— Overall projected yield
— Projected internal rate of return
— Net present value of the project over each of the next ten years

Once the feasibility study is completed, the developer is prepared to move forward with the project. Often, at this stage of the process, the developer purchases an option on the land to tie it up until the remaining development steps can be completed—and to prevent the competition from purchasing it.

Ownership Entity

An ownership entity (note that this is different than and separate from the development company) must be created to hold title to the land—and the hotel, once it's built. Considering the limitation of liability to the investors, tax consequences, estate implications for the investors, and potential requirements of the mortgage lender, a business structure is selected, normally in one of the following forms:

— Limited liability company (LLC)
— Limited partnership (LP)
— S corporation (formerly known as a Sub-S corporation)
— C corporation

Agreement

The newly formed entity now enters into a development contract with the development company to take the project to completion. The development company charges a fee, approximately 3 percent of the total project cost, for this service.The agreement generally covers such variables as:

— Selection of architect/engineers
— Selection and supervision of a general contractor
— Processing all building and occupancy permits
— Raising all the equity money from investors
— Securing a construction mortgage loan
— Selecting a franchise company
— Securing the franchise
— Selecting an interior designer that meets franchise company requirements
— Purchasing all opening furniture, fixtures, equipment
— Selecting a management company to operate the hotel
— Liability for cost overruns

Selecting Franchise

Depending on the type of hotel to be built (based on the feasibility study), the developer recommends a franchise company to the hotel owner. A major consideration is the best franchise brand for the market segment to be served. Each franchise company has different franchise fees, royalty fees, and marketing/ miscellaneous fees as part of its agreement structure with the operating company. Consideration must also be given to the brands already represented in the target market that may be available for franchise. The franchise company is approached and a franchise is requested, with the feasibility study offered as backup for the request.

The next step is for the franchise company to conduct an impact study of the market. This considers such matters as possible negative impact on existing hotels that carry the franchiser's flag. If the impact is judged to be insignificant, a franchise is usually granted to the ownership entity for a one-time fee of about $400 per room, depending on the franchise selected, with continuing royalty and marketing, usually based on a percentage of hotel revenue.

Selecting the Architect

Because the final product of this process is a building the operator has to run as a hotel, the architect's experience in designing hotels, his or her experience with the prototypical drawings of the franchise selected, the fee, and his or her on-time record must be considered. Architect fees can run up to 5 percent of the total project cost but are often negotiated down, if the project is big enough. The firm's experience and record on similar projects are critical. The architect does not have to operate the hotel when it is completed. The developer wants the architect to design a hotel that will be easy to operate and maintain.

Selecting General Contractor

Major consideration are the quality and reliability record of the general contractor and the firm's use of and relationships with the many subcontractors needed for a project as complex as a hotel. Again, experience in building the hotel type is important. It is hoped that the general contractor has learned from any mistakes made in building similar hotels. The general contractor and architect often bid the project as a team; this helps the developer determine the final cost. Often, up to a 10 percent contingency cost that allows for unforeseen circumstances is built into the project bidding process.

Financing

The following variables must be determined to qualify for financing:

— The cost of the land

— Design and construction cost of the building

— The cost of furniture, fixtures, equipment, and opening supplies
— Pre-opening marketing and labor costs
— A six-month operating capital cash reserve The sum of these constitutes the total cost of the project for purposes of securing financing.

With this information, the ten-year operating pro forma budget is updated to reflect actual costs. It's now time to go to the money markets for construction financing.The terms and conditions of a construction loan can vary widely depending on the individual lender. Important terms that can affect the cost of the loan include:

— Personal guarantees by developers and/or equity partners/investors
— Loan origination fees
— Interest rate
— Required loan-to-value ratio
— Terms of repayment
— A requirement that interest/taxes be held in reserve
— Required debt service coverage ratios
— Length of the construction loan; length and costs of extensions

These are only a few of the considerations that must be analysed when selecting a lender. The developer, on behalf of the owning entity, then approaches a number of lending institutions. The lending institutions analyse the deal and offer a proposed term sheet that answers all of the borrowers' questions. This allows the borrowers to select the lending institution with which they wish to work. The lender then commissions an appraisal of the project by an independent appraisal company such as Hospitality Valuation Services (HVS). Based on the appraisal, the lender issues a loan commitment for the project that usually offers up to 60 percent of the project cost.The balance must be raised as equity from investors.

With the bank committed to about 60 percent of the cost, the remaining 40 percent must be raised in equity commitments by investors. To pursue these, the developer prepares an offering solicitation document that meets current securities and exchange law. The nature of this document depends on the type of business entity that was formed. For limited partnerships or limited liability companies, a private placement offering circular and project description is prepared. For S or C corporations, stock offerings are prepared for sale consistent with applicable federal and state securities laws.

The developer now contacts money sources that have risk capital available to invest.

These can include:

— Individual investors
— Private asset managers
— Opportunity fund managers
— Venture capital fund managers

These potential investment sources are offered the opportunity to invest in the hotel. Based on their study and evaluation of the reports, documents, and studies detailed above, they decide whether or not to offer funding to the developer.

Once the loan is secured, the equity raised, and the building permit issued by the city, the land purchase option is exercised and the purchase is completed. Then the 12–16-month construction process begins. If the architect's plans work as intended, if the general contractor has no problems with subcontractors, unions, or permits, if all the furnishings, fixtures, and equipment arrive on time, if the weather cooperates, and if the employment market is such that human resources are sufficient to open a hotel, then congratulations!

Selecting Management Company

Often even before the construction activity commences, the owning entity selects an appropriate management company to manage the pre-opening, marketing and sales, selection and training of the opening staff, preparation of the operating budget, and day-to-day operations once the hotel is opened. Management companies charge 3–5 percent of revenue for this service. In recent years, management companies have charged 3–4 percent of revenue and 2–3 percent of gross operating profit so they can be measured and evaluated on both sales and profitability. The franchise company may offer to provide management services to franchisees.

Marriott International, Inc., for example, manages about 50 percent of all hotels that carry the Marriott flag under 20-year contracts. Independent management companies manage the remaining hotels under long-term management contracts of up to ten years' duration, often with several five-year renewal options.

This is a largely linear explanation of the complicated process that a developer goes through in order to create a hotel. It has been described in a step-by-step process, but in reality, many of the steps are carried out concurrently to save time (and money).

Nevertheless, the hotel development process takes about three years from original concep-tion to first guest. It is important to remember that during the initial stages of the process, the developer can have as much as $1 million or more at risk in the process before a final go/no-go decision is reached. Only after the project is approved and all financing is in place can the developer start to recover upfront costs and collect development fees. Hotel development with its component parts of hotel feasibility studies, hotel appraisal, hotel real estate finance, and hotel management are all among the career opportunities available to hotel and restaurant administration graduates.

Story of an Extended-stay Hotel Development Project

The City Development Commission in a Pacific Northwest community purchased a 1.55-acre parcel of riverfront land in the downtown area.The land was previously contaminated with industrial pollutants that made the parcel unsafe for habitation and construction. The City Development Commission used state, local, and federal grants to have the land decontaminated, created a master plan for the area, and then offered the parcel for sale and development.

The City Development Commission issued a request for proposal (RFP) that outlined the asking price of $2,076,240 ($30/sq. ft.) for the land and the design requirements set down by the Commission for a building that would fit the intended look and feel of the area.The RFP was sent to many major hotel companies and commercial real estate brokers, asking prospective buyers to submit a purchase price bid along with a statement of the buyer's development history and ability to develop a hotel of the type envisioned by the Commission. It listed a closing date by which all bids had to be submitted.

An area commercial real estate broker contacted a hotel development and management company with a long history of developing and managing extended-stay hotels in the Pacific Northwest, including a property located in a similar setting to that being offered for sale.The commercial realtor offered to represent the developer in negotiations with the City Development

Commission, which would be paying the real estate commission on the sale. An agreement was reached with the commercial real estate broker to represent the buyer to the seller, and the developer went to work in preparing a proposal.

The developer conducted a feasibility study to see all of the conditions in the marketplace that would be encouraging or discouraging to this development project.

Studies were conducted to estimate how many room-nights were being sold within a five-mile radius, how many extended-stay room-nights were available in the market, how many hotel rooms existed, and how many were being planned over the following five years. From this, the developer was able to estimate the number of extended-stay room-nights available needed to produce an 82 percent occupancy with an average daily room rate of $141 when the hotel achieved stabilisation three years after opening. That provided the basis for a ten-year revenue estimate.

The developer proposed a nine-floor, 258-suite extended-stay hotel with an indoor pool, spa, and exercise facility, a guest laundry, offices, meeting facilities, and a three-floor parking garage with parking for 193 automobiles, all at a total cost of $38 million, or $147,286 per suite.

The $38 million construction budget was broken down as follows:

Land	6.0%
Construction	66.0%
Office Equipment	1.4%
Furniture, Fixtures, Equipment	7.4%
Architecture/Engineering	2.8%
Permits/Fees/Environmental	2.8%
Appraisal/Legal/Tax/Insurance	1.3%
Pre-Opening Expenses	1.3%
Construction Loan Fee	1.1%
Developer Fee	2.8%
Construction Interest	2.8%
Working Capital	2.1%
Contingency	2.2%
Total	100%

The opening date for the hotel was projected at 27 months from the date of proposal acceptance.

The City Development Commission awarded the project to the developer, and work began.First, an ownership limited liability company (LLC) was formed as the ownership entity that would hold title to the hotel. The LLC, in turn, entered into a development and construction management agreement with the development company to manage the arrangements for financing and construction of the hotel.

The developer, as agent for the ownership LLC, also entered into a hotel management contract with a management company to manage the pre-opening marketing, preopening hiring and training, and the day-to- day operation of the hotel once it was opened.The arrangements called for the management company to be paid 3 percent of revenue and 2 percent of the net operating income for management services.

The ownership LLC then contacted a major hotel company and applied for a franchise to allow the development and operation of an extended-stay hotel. A 20-year franchise was granted with a fee of $400 per suite or, $102,800. This was to be followed by a 5 percent royalty and a 3 percent advertising fee once the hotel was open and operating. The developer, acting as agent for the owner, prepared a private placement memorandum document seeking investments from accredited investors.These investors were primarily defined as people with a net worth of $1 million, or those with an income in excess of $200,000 over the previous two years and expecting an income in excess of $200,000 in the current year.

The private placement memorandum offered $100,000 units of ownership to accredited investors, guaranteeing a 9 percent priority return on the investment and a combined 50 percent ownership in the hotel. A group of initial investors retained the other 50 percent in exchange for putting the project together.This effort was successful in raising 40 percent of the total cost of the hotel in anticipation that a lender would provide the remaining 60 percent in the form of a construction loan. In addition to the priority return, investors could expect to participate in any future capital gain realised should the hotel be sold.

The development company, continuing to function as agent for the owner, then sought a commercial bank to provide threeyear construction financing for the project. As $22,800,000, or 60 percent, of the $38 million development cost was to be borrowed, only major banks were considered as prospective lenders.The size of the construction loan was above the lending limits of most small regional banks. After a preconstruction appraisal by a third-party appraisal firm chosen by the lender confirmed the value at $38 million upon completion of construction, and for an origination fee of $400,000, a three-year construction loan was secured.The terms allowed the developer, as agent for the owner, to draw down the loan every 30 days after providing proof that funds had been properly disbursed in the construction process.The loan documents set an interest rate and also required that the ownership LLC seek a permanent mortgage prior to the three-year expiration date on the construction loan.

The development company then negotiated with and selected a general contractor with significant hotel construction experience who acted on behalf of the developer, as agent for the owner. The general contractor then selected design-build subcontractors and an interior designer to select colors, fabrics, furniture, fixtures, and equipment to meet the hotel franchise design requirements.

Building permits were applied for, and the building design was presented to the City Development Commission for its approval, along with other groups with a stake in the appearance of the finished building in relation to the area and neighborhood.With all of these approvals in place, construction commenced, and the hotel opened two years later.

Three years after the hotel opened, the ownership LLC had the obligation to secure permanent financing on the hotel to replace the construction loan. The September 11, 2001, terrorist attacks on the World Trade Center and the Pentagon slowed travel throughout the United States. As a result, the hotel did not achieve the projected occupancy or average daily rate during the three-year construction loan period. An appraisal that was primarily based on the hotel's trailing 12- month net operating income produced a value about $2 million below the original construction cost. The bank that had provided the construction loan notified the owners that they did not wish to provide permanent financing under these circumstances. The owners were forced to conduct a search for a new mortgage bank. They were able to find a mortgage, but only after buying down the loan by $2 million to bring the loan-to-value ratio back to 40 percent equity and a loan at 60 percent of the appraised.

This illustrates the risk that developers face when entering into a hotel project. However, as hotel values historically peak and decline on about a ten-year cycle, the owners look forward to the option of selling the hotel on the next peak, which will allow them to capture the original projected return through capital appreciation. Hotel development and ownership is a high-risk, highreward enterprise.

Changes in the Hotel Industry

Dramatic changes have affected the hotel industry over the past 30 years. These changes have had a disproportionately high bearing on the independent hotel owner, who, in the face of increasing pressure from large, wellfunded chains, struggles to maintain independence and to compete on the basis of distinctive hospitality and character.

Several organizations provide independent hotels and resorts with reservations and sales services. As competition has evolved and intensified, some of these organizations have modified their structure and enhanced their services to meet the changing needs of independent hotels and competitive market dynamics. Today, independent hotels may choose from among more than 20 such organizations delivering varying degrees of competitive advantage and ownership independence. In the new millennium, the face of the global hospitality market continues to change at a rate never before seen. Four factors contribute to this rapidly changing environment:

— *The broadening and diversification of the global consumer market.* Both the demographic and psychographic characteristics of the global consumer market are growing and changing radically.

— *The rapid advancement and availability of technology.* This includes internal hotel operating systems, revenue management, direct-to-consumer communications and booking technology (Internet), marketing technology (customer databases), and telecommunications and automated sales systems that enable central sales offices to become revenue producers.

— *The growth and importance of global brands.* Recognised brand names and brand attributes are important in reaching diverse customer segments and in creating customer loyalty.

— *Consolidation of multiple brands under a single global management.* The management and leveraging of multiple brands use similar technology platforms and shared sales and marketing infrastructures to consolidate and direct consumer demand.

Some established ways of doing business — long-term, high-fee management contracts and franchises, a focus on traditional distribution channels, and traditional hospitality industry marketing techniques—are no longer effective in the new consumer-focused market. More and more hospitality marketing budgets are being directed toward technologyenabled customer booking and communication; this shift away from traditional hospitality marketing techniques is expected to evolve over several years and involve millions of U.S. dollars in telecommunication, e-commerce, data warehousing, and one-to-one marketing investment. The independent hotel or resort and many small branded management companies may not be able to fund this requirement. However, this shift will not affect all independent hotels and resorts simultaneously.

The first wave of change will hit the global business and city hotel market. This is primarily because of brand competition and the fact that the business travel distribution network is more structured and driven by multinational corporations desiring lower and more predictable costs. The second wave will affect the leisure market, and the changes could follow quickly. Leisure travel content, including packaging on the Internet, will increase rapidly as the presently fragmented leisure travel distribution network becomes more unified and efficient through consolidation. The emergence of e-commerce modes in the hospitality industry is not eliminating the intermediary and empowering the individual property, as once thought; instead, it is creating new, more powerful intermediaries. Some of these evolve from the hospitality industry, while others are opportunistic e-commerce companies.

Management Contract

In the 1970s, hotel chains continued to evolve as the need for capital to invest in additional properties restricted growth opportunities. This pressure bolstered the proliferation of the *management contract,* whereby the chain offers the hotel owner the rights to use its brand name and established facility and service standards as well as trained operations management and reservation and marketing services—for a significant fee, usually a percentage of gross sales. The pressure to grow also fostered the development of the franchise concept and franchise system in North

America. The franchise differs from the management contract in that the owner is responsible for operations, including meeting the franchise standards. The growth of management and franchise contracts has been remarkable, and today, according to a recent study, 75 percent of the hotel rooms in North America are covered by some form of branded franchise or professional management agreement.

These new business structures continued to threaten the traditional independent owner by accelerating the growth of the chains' share of the lodging market. In response, the marketing/ referral organizations formed in the 1960s began to offer a wider range of services.

While these additional offerings leveraged linkages to the global distribution systems and led to strong relationships with travel agents, the consumer was largely ignored, and the organizations did little to generate consumer brand awareness. In the United States, strong consumer branded operators are attracting increasing amounts of capital to fund their growth at the expense of unbranded operators.

Brand Development

As the consumer market became more diverse and the hospitality product more segmented, branding became increasingly important. By the late 1980s, without a recognised brand affiliation or a close relationship with the lending community, owners/developers found it difficult to obtain permanent financing on a new hotel or resort. Lenders, believing that an established brand provided greater economies of scale and established infrastructure, opted for the lower-risk alternative.

In this brand-driven environment, the independent hotels' distinctive style and character became a competitive advantage, but only if they were able to meet recognised standards. As a result, the need for independent hotels to be associated with a clearly defined, trusted brand became more critical than ever. In the late 1990s, independent hotels, particularly those in Europe, began to face the daunting costs of upgrading their technological infrastructure and facilities to accommodate changing consumer needs. Such upgrades as new property management systems, highspeed Internet access, two-line phones, inroom faxes, and leisure and health facilities became critical to maintaining competitiveness. When coupled with ever-increasing costs of consumer marketing, these costs put unprecedented strains on independent hotels' finances. As a result, these hotels became increasingly focused on leveraging greater returns from their reservation affiliation.

Reservation Affiliations

The relationship of independent hotels and resorts to reservation affiliations has been long and generally successful. These relationships operated best in a market environment that was stable, somewhat homogeneous in terms of demographic market segmentation, and where travel influencers played a dominant role in transient business, group, and leisure travel. Reservation affiliations are most effective in regional hospitality markets that do not have multiple brand competition and when the goals and objectives of the reservation organization are in alignment with the goals of the independent hotel owners. A contributing element to the attractiveness of reservation affiliations has always been the networking and camaraderie opportunities for the professional management at independent hotels.

Reservation affiliations focus on traditional channels of distribution. Access to the Global Distribution Systems (GDS) is no longer a competitive advantage; the GDS is a universal pipeline. The new competitive playing field is proprietary distribution channels leveraged by consumer segmentation, e-commerce technology and partners, and innovative customer management programs.

In the new technology-driven and consumer- empowered global market, the strength and effectiveness of reservation affiliations are challenged by new market and operating imperatives. The cost to compete against chains will grow exponentially.As competition intensifies, it is probable that local and regional market share at independent hotels and resorts will be drawn off by local and regional licensees of strong global brands. Independent hotels, therefore, need to draw more national and international business to fill occupancy gaps.This requirement runs counter to the established business model and capabilities of reservation affiliations.

The average room-night contribution of reservations companies to affiliated inde-pendent hotels is less than 5 percent of available rooms.

At least four emerging factors are challenging the effectiveness of traditional reservation organizations:

1. The growing demographic and psychographic complexity of the global consumer market requires significant new expertise and resources in the area of segmentation and analysis.
2. The emergence of consumer direct-booking Internet technology requires significant new and ongoing investment.

3. The new marketplace requires innovative global brand management together with resources to establish and maintain a brand in the face of intense competition. To be competitive, a brand must attract new development and must therefore be strong enough to convince lenders to commit to permanent financing. Brand management also includes loyalty program management and the development of regional and global partners to strengthen and extend the effectiveness of the brand.
4. The corporate objectives and governance policies of traditional reservation organizations are influenced by the need to grow and meet shareholder profit requirements. These goals for growth can be at odds with the goals and expectations of independent hotel and resort members.

The traditional reservation affiliations must change not only their focus but also their structure if they want to succeed in this new competitive world.

The traditional reservation organization must be prepared to respond to competitive challenges by expanding resources and skills necessary to increase average room-night contribution to affiliated independent hotels to 15 percent—an average growth per member hotel of at least 200 percent over present performance levels. In response to this competitive environment and the need for more cooperative and focused business relationships, a new hospitality business structure is evolving for all scales of hotels: the branded distribution company.

Branded Distribution Organization

The ideal branded distribution organization is a conventional equity company with ownership shared (in some cases) by the individual hotel owners, who have direct input into the corporation through an elected board of directors. This ownership structure creates a true operating partnership and a sharing of energies toward the common goal of creating value through increased brand awareness and room sales. Corporate profits must be adequate to maintain technical and managerial leadership and to support the shareholders' investment.

Unlike a reservations and representation company, a branded distribution corporation owns and builds a branded distribution network asset that, in turn, provides services as set out in the diagram below.The sole focus is performance for the affiliated independent hotels and resorts.

Joining such an organization is appropriate for independently owned and managed hotels and resorts that want to keep owner control but require effective and low-cost distribution, global consumer brand awareness, and group purchasing benefits without the encumbrances and costs of a traditional hotel chain franchise or management contract. Above all, it promises the independent hotel awareness of, and access to, their target consumer and rapidly emerging technology through cooperative ownership.

This new business structure is attractive from an owner's or a developer's standpoint for a number of reasons, including:

— *Costs:* First, it requires less up-front cash; second, ongoing fees and reservation commissions are significantly lower than with either a pure franchise or management agreement. For example, a 9 or 10 percent franchise fee in many cases equals 50 percent of gross profits.

— *Contract terms*: The terms are typically shorter, easier to negotiate, and allow for substantial owner control over the operation, style, and character of the hotel. As a result, conflicts can be avoided, and the branded distribution contract can be completed and signed in as few as 45 days.

— *Marketing*: It frees hotel management from the daunting and increasingly expensive task of acquiring profitable new customers and allows them to focus their attention and operating skills on the delivery of an exceptional hospitality experience.

— *Common objectives*: Both the owner and the branded distribution company enter into the agreement with the same primary objective: revenue. The branded distribution company receives no revenue if it does not deliver to the hotel or resort.

This shared goal strengthens and energises the relationship between the two partners. From a branded distribution company's standpoint, this structure allows the brand to expand faster because capital is not used to subsidise additional construction or to support an older business model. Instead, funds are used to build and maintain an up-todate global distribution network and infrastructure composed of telecommunications, commerce functions, reservations software, data warehousing capability, and sales and marketing. The efficiency of the operation is assured by a focus that is almost entirely on the most important part of this business relationship—the generation of brand awareness and measurable room-night revenue for each affiliated hotel or resort. Unlike hard flags, which focus primarily on hotel operations and asset management such as the Marriott or the Westin, and reservation affiliations, which focus on professional camaraderie and traditional distribution channels such as the Best Western, the branded distribution company is primarily marketfocused; its full attention is on customer and travel influencer communication, relationship technology, and revenue streams.

In contrast, asset management, profitability, and operating efficiency are the major concerns of management companies, which tend to be public companies with stockholder expectations that must be met. It is often the case that strategic asset management concerns conflict with day-to-day tactical operating needs. This is evident in Marriott's recent move to separate its ownership and operating divisions, to the benefit of both.

The same conflict can arise between the independent owners of a hotel property, who are focused on real estate concerns, and the management company they hire. Such misunderstandings can sour what should be a mutually supportive relationship. The fact that management contract fees are charged and collected, even when the cash flow is negative, does not create owner confidence in the partner. A franchise relationship can cause a similar conflict and put a financial and operating burden on an owner.

In contrast, participation of independent owner/operators as shareholders in a branded distribution company enables them to move beyond these concerns and focus on their operation and the consumer—the source of their revenue and the basis of their success.

The owners of property within a branded distribution company must relinquish a minimal amount of control and decision making, mainly in the areas of branding and quality assurance. In certain cases, member properties may have to adopt and maintain specific quality standards. In addition, they may also be required to demonstrate their affiliation with the branded distribution company through using its logo on marketing materials as well as participating in e-commerce and inventory management initiatives.

However, these drawbacks can actually enhance a hotel's operations and market positioning while allowing the hotel to maintain independent ownership and management.

Independent hotels face significant risk in today's marketplace. Given the advances in technology and the profitability pressures put upon chain hotels by shareholders, competition for customers is intensifying. Keeping in step with competitive chain hotels presents a significant challenge to independent owners.To address this, they currently have several options outside of the branded distribution company, including representation firms, reservations services, flagged chains, and franchise management companies. However, given the economic, societal, and technological trends that are dramatically changing the hospitality industry, many of these oldeconomy options can offer only short-term solutions to long-term competitive pressures. A branded distribution company has an inherent advantage going into this new competitive arena. Its sole focus is on customer acquisition and management, achieved through the development of new technologies. This competitive advantage extends to the independent hotel aligned with a branded distribution company. By providing the independent owner with a global brand and the technology and expertise to acquire profitable new customers, the branded distribution company enables the hotel management to focus its attention on the delivery of exceptional service and profits to the owners. This separation of skills, expertise, resources, and operating cultures in a cooperative business relationship provides a model and formula for success.

Hotel Operational Practices

If you ever have the chance to be involved with opening a hotel, jump at the opportunity. Opening a hotel is one of the most rewarding jobs in the hospitality industry despite its frustrating and exhausting aspects. Walk into any hotel, anywhere, and look around. Everything you see, hear, and feel, every detail, involved many people and countless decisions.

The operations project manager (OPM) is the third person hired, after the general manager and the director of marketing. The role of an OPM is to pull together the visions of the architect, interior designer, owner, operator, and others. When these visions are successfully melded, the hotel guest satisfied, the owner makes money, and the architect and interior designer can add the project to their list of successful accomplishments. The OPM oversees the following aspects of a project:

— Reviewing blueprints and specifications for the entire building
— Assisting with the creation of a model room
— Developing the pre-opening staff plan

- Developing and managing the pre-opening budget
- Developing the operational supplies and equipment budget (OS&E)
- Overseeing the purchasing, warehousing, delivery, and installation of the OS&E
- Developing the interior graphics package
- Coordinating the installation of thirdparty vendors

The OPM's responsibilities start with the architectural blueprints.The focus is to ensure a good flow for guests, staff, and goods. The bellperson bag storage room should be located between the porte cochere (entry) and the elevators and contain 1 square foot of space for each guest room. If valet parking is offered, ensure that a convenient cashier's station is located near the porte cochere. Arrange for a key rack to hold the keys for each valet parking stall.

Given a 10,000-square-foot ballroom, the catering department can sell functions for 800 for dinner.This requires 80 6-foot round tables, 800 chairs, a dais for the head table, a dance floor, and staging for the band. If sold for a 700-guest all-day meeting, the classroom setup requires 1,400 linear feet of narrow tables and 700 chairs. A short theater meeting setup for 1,000 requires 1,000 chairs, a podium, staging, and audio visual equipment. The same space accommodates a cocktail reception for 1,400 guests; this requires cocktail tables, portable bars, buffet stations, and so on. This all boils down to ensuring ample storage space for equipment not being used—at least 1,500 square feet.

Moving goods from the back of the house to the front requires careful planning to ensure that precious labor dollars are used efficiently. Are the rollaway beds, cribs, and high chairs stored near an elevator for quick delivery? The housekeeper closets should be centrally located on guest room floors to cut down on access time. A 6-foot, 2-cubic-yard garbage cart will not work if the elevator is only 5 feet deep.

If ice machines are offered for guest selfservice, they must produce an ample supply (10 pounds per room per 24-hour period) for the number of guest rooms on that floor or floors. The ice machine room requires the proper utilities, including electricity, plumbing, lighting, and HVAC. Don't forget the sign on the outside of the room, which must meet ADA standards!

Build a typical king and double/double guest room close to the site so you can review every single item in them. Are ample electrical and telecom outlets placed exactly where the TV, lamps, clock radio,mini-bar, coffeemaker, hair dryer, Internet access, and telephones are located so the cords are hidden? Are spare outlets offered for guest use (computer, iron, etc.)? Is the closet rod hung so the ironing board organizer and iron board fit in the closet? Is the thermostat location convenient for guest access?

Are the case goods (dresser, nightstands, headboards, chairs, etc.), designed for commercial heavy-duty use? Will they hold up to abusive use? Do they have sharp corners that will snag guest clothing? Does the bedskirt hang ½ inch off the floor? Do the bedside lamps give off enough lumens so guests can read in bed? Does the room meet or exceed every operator brand standard? These model rooms serve as sales tools for the sales and marketing staff selling group rooms up to three years before opening.

Pre-opening Staffing

The pre-opening staffing begins with an organizational chart with all positions. Once the titles and staff counts by position are finalised, then spreadsheets are created to include the position titles, start dates, pay rates, bonus, transfer allowances, and number of full-time equivalents (FTEs) for all positions.

The pre-opening staff plan is a comprehensive document that states who is hired, when they start, how much they are paid, and whether or not they are allocated a relocation allowance and benefit costs. Each of these pieces is used to build the pre-opening staff plan budget. If hiring has already begun and the opening date changes, the budget must be amended. Hiring a position that does not conform to the plan, such as bringing on a renowned chef one month earlier than planned, also requires the budget be modified.

Pre-opening Budget

The OPM develops and manages the preopening budget.This budget typically consists of three major categories; labor cost (40 percent), sales and marketing efforts (40 percent), and miscellaneous (20 percent).

The labor cost is taken directly from the pre-opening staff plan. Sales and marketing activities comprise advertising, collateral, public relations, and travel to see clients. Rounding out the budget are all of the miscellaneous items. These include office space rental before moving into the hotel, utilities (power, water, Internet, and telephone), human resources recruitment (ads, headhunters, drug testing, etc.), training materials, association dues, and licenses and permits (business, liquor, sales tax collection, etc.). If the hotel opening date is delayed for any reason, the pre-opening budget is affected. Additional costs include labor, office rent, utilities, and marketing efforts. If the opening date changes within three weeks of the original plan, major costs are encountered, as most of the staff is already hired.

Operational Supplies and Equipment

The largest and most complex aspect of the OPM's responsibility is specifying, quantifying, and budgeting for the operational supplies and equipment (OS&E) list.This budget typically pencils out to $8,000 to $10,000 per guest room for a typical four-star property. The list of goods typically exceeds 2,500 line items. Add a little more for a full-service resort; deduct a little for an in-city business hotel.

The OS&E comprises all of the items that are not nailed down, with the exception of the furniture, fixtures, and equipment (FF&E). The FF&E is typically specified and ordered by the interior designer.

Typical guest room items include bedding (frames, box springs, mattresses, mattress pads, sheets, pillows, pillowcases, towels, etc.), clock radios, hangers, laundry bags, laundry tickets, iron, ironing board, ironing board organizer, luggage rack, guest amenities (soap, shampoo, lotion, etc.), hair dryer, shower curtains, and shower curtain hooks.

Housekeeping equipment includes vacuums (guest room and wide-area units), carpet shampooers, carpet extractors, housekeeper carts, laundry bins, garbage trucks, valet delivery carts, and shelving, to name a few of many items. Housekeeping must also keep an inventory of guest request items including humidifiers, dehumidifiers, cribs, high chairs, rollaway beds, bedboards, spare pillows, towels, amenities, refrigerators, laundry soap, and so on.

Food and beverage front-of-the-house items include flatware (knives, forks, and spoons), hollowware (serving trays, serving utensils, chafing dishes, sugar bowls and sauce boats, punch bowls), glassware, table linen, napkins, skirting, salt and pepper shakers, china, plate covers, espresso machines, menu covers and the list goes on and on.

Banquet items include all of the above plus tables, chairs, staging, staging steps and railings, dance floors, carts, carving boards, ice carving trays, flags, podiums, portable bars, ice bins, pianos, and tray jack stands.

The largest purchase order—typically over 100 pages long—is for a full-service kitchen and includes everything a chef needs to produce the menus being sold at the hotel.

Every utensil, pot, pan, dish, and glass rack, warewashing chemicals, mops and buckets, specialty items (roller-docker, anyone?) must be reviewed by the chef, purchased, and delivered the day before the chef starts burning in the kitchen.

On the hotel administration side, the OPM specifies the office desks, chairs, cork and dry-erase boards, conference tables, filing cabinets, safes, bullet-proof window for the general cashier's office, fax machines, copiers, currency and coin trays, and a set of flags for the exterior flagpoles.

Before quantifying uniform needs, many questions are asked. Do we need summer and winter uniforms? Will the uniforms be laundered by the hotel or the hotel associates? How many extra servers are needed for a capacity dinner function in the ballrooms? Is the intent to have a large percentage of parttime staff? Which uniforms need custom embroidery (restaurants, culinary, engineering, etc.)? What percentage of spare uniforms are needed in reserve?

Once these questions are answered, then the selection process begins. Operations and the interior designer review the look and feel the options available. Each position (housekeeper, bellperson, etc.) or similar position (front desk clerk/concierge) has different requirements. Housekeepers and bellpersons require durable uniforms that breathe and can handle lots of bending and stretching.The uniforms of the culinary and engineering staffs are often stained and must hold up to numerous launderings.

The uniform order is placed 90 to 120 days before the first uniformed staff is hired. To quantify the sizes required, a typical bell chart sizing curve is used for the particular country or region of the hotel. The uniforms are delivered and sorted prior to the individual fitting process. On the line staff's second day on the job, each individual is measured for uniforms. An army of seamstresses then takes the pants, jackets, and dresses and alters each piece for each associate. The fitted uniforms are issued a few days before opening day.

In an ideal process, the 500 purchase orders are issued beginning six months prior to opening. Each order is tracked to ensure it is delivered to the proper location on the desired date. Most goods are delivered to a local warehouse and pulled for delivery to the site as the general contractor completes construc-tion and turns over areas. Some goods are shipped directly to the site to eliminate double handling. These large orders include bed sets (21 40-foot shipping containers for the Kona project), televisions (3 containers), banquet chairs (2 containers), banquet tables (3 containers), and guest room safes (1 container).

The linen order for guest rooms and F&B are shipped to an off-site laundry facility for initial washing.Once the goods are on site, they are typically staged in the largest ballroom for unpacking and distribution. The unpacking process requires a plethora of workers. For example, each clock radio must be unpacked, the electrical twist tie removed, the 9-volt battery installed, and the time set. Then the unit is placed in a guest room on the nightstand. For the 525-room Kona project, this task required two people for three eight-hour days.

Once they completed this task, they spent the next five working days installing the 7,000 shower curtain hooks, 525 shower curtains, and 525 shower liners. Then they unboxed 30,000 glasses and placed them in glass racks for washing.These kinds of tasks must be carried out for each of the 2,500 line items.Once receiving and distribution begins on site, another element comes to the forefront: garbage. During the five-week Kona installation process, over 3 tons of packing material were generated *every day!* Making friends with the local waste-hauling service is a priority.

Interior Graphics Package

The project manager reviews the interior graphics package for errors and omissions. This package includes every sign needed to direct guests and staff in front and back of the house areas. The recent Kona project included 1,600 signs, 98 percent of which were one of a kind.The text must be correct, the directional arrows must point the correct way, and most are required to include raised Braille text, per the ADA. The OPM works with the marketing department to develop the identity for the unique areas within a property.These include the restaurants, bars, pools, spa, and retail areas. These logos are incorporated into the signage package, collateral (cocktail napkins, menus, check presenters, etc.), and uniforms.

Third-party Vendors

Many third-party vendors must have access to the property prior to opening.

The project manager schedules and directs all of these vendors, including the soft-drink vendor (who installs soda guns for the bars and vending machines for the guest floors), the coffee company (which must install and test equipment), the pay-per-view TV vendor (who must connect every television in the building and test the signal strength), the warewashing chemical vendor (who must install and calibrate the dishwashing machines), and the office furniture installer (who must assemble all office equipment). Among the other vendors are those dealing in copier services, postage machines, telephones, fitness center equipment, security systems, and first aid supplies.These vendors are constantly informed when they can install their equipment based on the general contractor's completion dates. When the construction schedule changes, vendors must be updated so they show up when the area they need access to is ready.

Human Resources Management

The OPM assists the human resources personnel during the last two months of preopening so that they have all of the tools they need to recruit and hire the staff. On average, the HR department interviews at least five applicants for every position. This works out to over 1,000 applicants for a typical 300-room four-star hotel. This process is referred to as the *mass hire.* The mass hire is typically conducted over a two- or three-day period six weeks before opening. To interview this many job seekers, HR requires office space, reception space for up to 200 at one time, rest rooms, and break rooms for the interviewers. The OPM coordinates all of these details so that the operations team can focus on the recruitment.

Once the offer letters are accepted, all line associates start work about three weeks out. The first few days on the job are dedicated to group training, operational philosophies, code of conduct, and other general policies. On day three, divisional training takes place. In the second week of training, the staff is broken out into departmental or job-specific duties.Departmental training includes teaching staff to make beds, clean a room, cook every menu item, the most efficient route to each guest room, and what to tell the guest en route to the room.

Online Pricing

The importance of electronic hotel-distribution routes has grown substantially in recent years. According to statistics quoted in the Horwath

Worldwide Hotel Industry Studies, direct reservations fell from approximately 39 percent in 1995 to 33 percent in 1999, with the shift in sales going almost exclusively to electronic channels.

While hotels continue to make extensive use of travel-agent-oriented global distribution systems (GDSs), consumer adoption of the Internet as a reliable and secure commerce medium has prompted a change in the way in which hotel rooms are being distributed. The Internet has dramatically changed the way people communicate, research information, and buy goods and services. Travel products in particular have proven to be suitable for sale on line. The typical Internet user—an affluent, frequent traveler who spends more than the average on leisure and entertainment—is an attractive market for travel suppliers.

Furthermore, from a consumer's perspective purchasing travel products on line has, in many instances, become faster, easier, and more convenient than contacting a travel agent or telephoning a supplier directly. As a result, on-line travel-related revenues are forecast to grow sharply. For example, according to a recent report by Jupiter Media Metrix, on-line travel sales will more than triple in the next five years—from US$18 billion in 2002 to US$64 billion in 2007.

Booking volumes are also forecast to climb. The Travel Industry Association of America (TIAA) estimated that by the end of 2002 between 6 percent and 10 percent of all travel reservations would originate on the web. If Jupiter's 2007 prediction comes true, travel will be the biggest selling on-line product, with a volume nearly double that of the current leading product, PC hardware.

Price is key to selling successfully on line. Studies by Internet analysts Gomez and PhoCusWright, and also a study by TIAA, all identified price as being one of the key motivating factors that encourages consumers to purchase travel on line. For example, the PhoCusWright study found that competitive pricing is the best way to attract customers. When travelers who haven't bought on line were asked what would encourage them to do so, 64 percent said that saving money would make them more interested. No other benefit—whether saving time, getting bonus loyalty-club points, more control, or obtaining better information came close to this level of response.

Yesawich, Pepperdine, and Brown found in a 2000 study that almost six out of ten leisure travelers now actively seek the "lowest possible price" for travel services. Similarly, a 2001 Forrester Research study found that

66 percent of all buyers had used an on-line discount in the previous 12 months to buy travel on line, and a study by the Joint Hospitality Industry Congress found a real expectation among consumers that Internet prices would be lower than those available in the "bricks and mortar" world.

Such a perception has developed for several reasons. First, many of the best-known Internet retailers initially competed with traditional outlets based, to a large extent, on price. Second, savvy consumers are aware that webbased distribution costs are lower than those of other channels. As Jack Geddes, Radisson Hotels Worldwide's managing director, sales and marketing Asia, has pointed out: "Consumers now understand that suppliers are cutting costs through this channel and expect savings to be passed on to them, as well as being rewarded for making the booking themselves". Such expectations are being reinforced by the budget-airline sector, which offers substantial discounts for online bookings.

Companies such as EasyJet, RyanAir, and Buzz estimate that by avoiding telesales and travel agents, they can achieve savings of up to 30 percent—which they pass on to customers in the form of lower fares. Many hotels (and airlines) use the web to sell last-minute deals—packages at relatively low prices but with short lead times. While such promotions can help dispose of unsold inventory, they have also resulted in the public's associating rooms sold over the Internet with lower prices.

These factors have combined to make consumers associate on-line booking with good value, which in the consumer's mind translates into low prices. However, in the case of hotel brands' own web sites, industry practice frequently seems to be the opposite of theory. In a 1999 survey, for instance, it was found that rates obtained from the web site were usually substantially higher than those obtained by contacting the central reservations office. That study was limited, however, in that it focused only on direct sales over hotel chains' own branded web sites. Electronic distribution is rapidly evolving for hotels, and a large number of other on-line consumerfocused channels are now available, with most chains using multiple routes to reach the consumer.

The availability of numerous points of sale poses some interesting questions. Foremost among these is: Is there consistency between the room availability and prices being offered over each of the channels? Unlike in the physical world, where a potential customer would have to telephone or visit several suppliers, comparison shopping on the web can generally be accomplished relatively quickly. Research has shown that consumers shopping for travel on line almost always check more than one site before purchasing.

Both the range of channels through which hotels can be booked and the complexity of such channels have grown. The majority of hotel brands now use simultaneous, multiple electronic channels of distribution, making their rooms available to a relatively wide audience.

While the use of CRS-based reservations has fallen slightly, there has been a growth in the availability of hotel companies' own web sites, and make their rooms available for sale in this manner. The differences between this study's findings and earlier published research indicate a major expansion in hotel chains' use of the web as a direct-sales medium, perhaps accompanied by a realisation of the web's benefits in comparison with other, more traditional, electronic channels of distribution. Most companies offer multiple rates to customers over each channel. It is interesting to note, however, the large number of companies that now offer consistent pricing across all channels.

It is clear that for those with a taste for upscale products, the hotel brand's own web site is not the place to shop, as better value can be obtained in most cases through other channels. More interesting, however, is the fact that, in general, prices have become more or less equal across many of the channels investigated, and by implication, across many other electronic distribution channels as well. It is well established that time is a valuable commodity in today's society. Since the number and variety of ways that a consumer can book a hotel room has become undeniably manifold, the cost associated with searching through even a small number of the many consumer-focused channels currently available in the marketplace in an attempt to find a low price has increased. Given that this study has found that many of the rates being offered over alternative channels are more or less the same for many hotels, customers should reconsider whether all that time and energy searching for the lowest rate is actually worthwhile.

The implications for the hotelier are more pressing. My findings suggest that many hotel chains are not actively managing the room rates being offered in their portfolio of electronic distribution channels. Most companies offer multiple rates on each channel, which, as discussed earlier, can be beneficial as it gives a choice to the customer. Displaying too many rates, though, can be counterproductive, if the customer becomes overwhelmed. Presenting a small number of tightly defined rates would be the most appropriate solution. However, most companies currently display about five rates in response to a customer inquiry, with others showing significantly more, usually with little or no apparent product differentiation.

In addition, there appears to be inconsistency in terms of the rates being offered over electronic channels. In many cases, no clear or logical pricing strategy is apparent. The lowest prices are offered on channels with the highest transaction costs, and vice versa. A small number of companies offer consistent pricing irrespective of the channel being used to make the booking. Informal follow up with those companies revealed that they follow this strategy as they believe in the principle of one "correct" price for each customer. In this way, they do not have to address the issue of customer dissatisfaction as a result of a person's being quoted a lower price for a room on a different channel after having already made a booking. However, such an approach ignores the issue of the cost of processing a booking over a particular channel. Such costs vary greatly depending to a large extent on the number of intermediaries between the supplier and the customer. The greater the number of intermediaries, the greater the transaction cost and processing fees—and therefore the greater the distribution cost.

This would seem to argue for having high rates on the channels that have high-cost structures and low prices on those with lowcost structures. Coupled with this matter is the fact that customers have become more knowledgeable about and comfortable with e-commerce issues in general, are more aware that distribution costs are lower in the virtual world than the bricks-and-mortar one, and thus increasingly expect to find the cheapest prices over electronic, and particularly direct electronic, routes. Put simply, when they go to a hotel company's web site, they expect to find the best value there.This study has shown that in many cases this is simply not the case, given that luxury hotels in particular tend to offer their highest rates over direct channels — and (ironically) their cheapest rates over the most expensive on-line intermediaries. Informal follow up to the study revealed that this may be due to the proactive approach of the on-line companies in contacting hotel companies on practically a daily basis and encouraging them to reduce their rates in return for better positioning on their search listings. In contrast, the rates on hotel companies' web sites go largely unmanaged, in many cases being set far in advance and not adjusted to reflect changing supply and demand.

Irrespective of its root cause, the behavior of hotel companies is driving Internet shoppers into the arms of the waiting on-line intermediaries, where in addition to consistently low prices, they also find wide product choice. Because of this, it's likely that many hotels are losing potential bookings to competitors as a result of consumers' migration toward the on-line travel sites that offer relatively low rates from many different hotel chains. Instead of being presented with a list of a chain's properties on a company's web site, prospective guests see a much wider variety of options from the on-line intermediary and may be tempted to book a competitor's room (especially if price becomes an issue).

Once consumers conclude that they will usually find better prices on a third-party channel, they will make Expedia or Travelocity, for example, their first port of call for future bookings—threatening brand loyalty, driving up transaction fees, increasing reservation leakage, and strengthening the third parties' power to demand "special rates" or commission overrides for a company to gain premium positioning (or even inclusion) in their search listings. Hotel companies need to take urgent action if they are not to lose control over the sale of their own product. At the very least, this means offering consistent prices over all channels, but more probably means providing customers the lowest rate over their own web site. This would decrease guests' motivation to book on alternative electronic channels, would help build web-site traffic, and should help to decrease distribution costs.

Organizing the Hotel

The success of hotel organizations will be driven in large part by the ability to foresee—and capitalize – on change. Beyond this truism, however, there is an urgent need to identify what will be required in the competitive environment of the future with its intense focus on serving customer needs. The hospitality industry—as is the case with business generally—is subject to deep currents of change set in motion as economic and social systems shaped in the industrial era evolve to a knowledge-based era driven by technology advances. In this period of global transition, it behooves hotel organizations to examine the key factors that will not only define success, but the ability to survive in coming years. Its mission was to identify the characteristics needed to lead successful businesses in the next century. These executives offer a number of compelling messages regarding the key success factors of the future. Customers will have the strongest influence on the corporation in the year 2000. Indeed, these executives believe that the customer will be "king" in the new century. Exceptional leadership was by far the attribute most frequently cited by CEOs and senior executives; the consensus appears to be that successful companies in the year 2000 will be led by corporate visionaries.

A strategic planning focus is not only essential, but must embody a concept of planning for the future that anticipates change, rather than being based exclusively on historical models. In structuring organizations for the future, companies must build management capabilities to deal with one of the most critical challenges—diversity in the marketplace. Employing information technology to drive business success in this information-driven era is not only the path of least resistance, but vital to virtually every aspect of operations. Recognizing that the hotel industry has a somewhat split personality reflecting the inherent conflicts between its real estate and operational aspects, it is important to understand the industry's real estate origins and how they are shaping the challenges ahead.

The origins of the industry's real estate persona are embodied in the classic theory of location - "if we build it, they will come." As a result of this "building" complex, the industry has tended to have a real estate and asset orientation, rather than a customer focus. From the hotel company perspective—especially that of the brand-oriented "chain"—the varied interests of a diffused property ownership group can be quite different than the singular interest of the chain that operates and markets the properties. Even when the ownership of geographically dispersed hotel properties is controlled by a single hotel organization, the financial structuring tends to be property-specific. Corporate financial strategies are frequently subjugated to the needs of the last property deal brought into the company's fold. Each property in a so-called "chain," is frequently the subject of a unique and distinctive ownership and financial structure. This phenomenon—quite common in the real estate sector, but unusual for business enterprises generally—makes for elusive economies of scale in the structuring and financing of property-driven expansion. Collectively, these factors have produced low comparative returns in real estate, although criticism leveled at commercial real estate returns is somewhat less germane to the hotel industry, where management and franchise fees can produce high returns for those companies where property ownership is held by third parties.

While hotel chains have adopted traditional corporate frameworks, there are a number of predominantly real estate-driven, family-owned businesses in the hotel sector that continue to operate as relatively unstructured organizations. In meeting the future, these businesses will need plans, people and processes in order to establish viable corporate forms that can compete in tomorrow's marketplace and capitalize upon its opportunities. In today's changed environment, the hotel organization must deal with a number of new realities. Investors in our industry are no longer satisfied with long-term capital appreciation and psychic income that heretofore were often the justification for otherwise seemingly uneconomic investments in hotel property or, indeed, hotel chains. The first reality is that there is a very specific and identifiable relationship between bottom line performance and value. Improvements in business operations raises values. It is not surprising, therefore, that the new owners attracted to this industry in recent years have new sets of demands. This transformation from an old-guard group of investors and owners to income and return-driven newcomers has meant that the once "quiet enjoyment" of operators in their management of hotels for third parties is being disturbed, interrupted and overturned. These challenges all take place in an environment where capital has become extremely selective in markets that have little stability. A global shortage of capital will not remain a short-term problem, and future hotel organizations must have a stronger alignment to capital providers—a critical "customer" group. Hotel companies will need to compete by offering better returns and performance than in the past.

Hotel chains have found their development timetables quashed in recent years, making it difficult to achieve goals of critical mass often required to improve performance. These factors are driving consolidation in the brand "sweepstakes." Capital markets, therefore, continue to favour well-established companies, a reality that must drive entrepreneurial organizations to meet the future now by planning for an evolving corporate context in which to operate. Hotel developers, owners and management companies will all need to develop new strategies, skills and processes that look forward to the competitive demands of the future. These ultimately must address issues related to vision and planning, as well as organizational skill sets and processes to attract and retain customers. To stake a claim in the future, current business practices should be examined in light of what can be expected to be the key success factors in the year 2000.

As the information age produces greater worldwide integration of business activities, a global knowledge base will become invaluable. Success in local and regional hotel markets will be shaped decisively by a global business environment that defines capital movement, customer expectations and applications of new technologies. If the customer is king in the 21st century, hotel organizations will be best served by focusing less on their hotel assets as measures of success, and more on their customers. This involves a fundamental shift in viewing the real estate asset as the wealth creator—to the customer as the key to building shareholder wealth. A customer focus must imbue business decisions at all levels of developing and operating a hotel organization. Pursuing such a course will inevitably impact shareholder wealth. To accomplish this, however, customers need to participate in the product development process.

Fully realizing a customer focus in the industry poses a significant challenge. The hotel industry must confront problems due to conflicts between operational needs and real estate goals. Quite simply, an operator must remain customer-focused, but the short-term strategies to meet these needs may be inconsistent with the long-term objectives of property owners. Balancing those goals will be essential. A customer focus implies a significant shift in what drives hotel development—placing primary emphasis on the customer with the locations to follow. Nevertheless, a hotel organization with its large investment in fixed assets—the real estate—can never be as nimble as a consumer products company in adjusting products and services to match rapid shifts in the marketplace.

Hotel services are based primarily on people, not computers or other equipment. Quality that surprises takes the concept of zero defects a step further. Yesterday's surprising product or service is today's status quo. Twenty years ago, a business executive did not expect a consistent and predictable level of service wherever he or she traveled in the world. Today that is a standard—not the exception—as is the expectation for sophisticated technology in hotel rooms to support business needs. With customer discrimination so acute, it is not surprising that brand loyalty is a diminishing "commodity" in the hotel industry. Find the ingredients for visionary leadership. Today's hotel organizations need to recognize the need for visionary leadership. The ability to forecast the future—to anticipate change rather than react to it—will be one of the single greatest determinants of market dominance in the years ahead. The old "command and control" model of leadership is giving way to a focus on leadership in ideas, information, inspiration, vision and teamwork. "For the most part, failing organizations tend to be over-managed and under-led. The leader sets the tone for the moral character, the vision, the corporate culture and the fiber of the institution."

While visionary leadership is essential, it must be linked to business operations and foster a risk bias, rather than a procedural bias. This will allow the organization to stretch and, in turn, change. And it must be shared by empowered professionals and staff throughout the organization, including those who meet the customer. Overcoming the resistance to change can be a daunting task, particularly in large hotel organizations in which diversions from the status quo may threaten established management lines. It suggests that a culture based on conformance may need to be replaced by an emphasis on flexibility, learning and cooperation.

Management competencies will need to be aligned in order to achieve the desired result. For many organizations, this may mean a shift from traditional hierarchies typical of companies in an industrial era to a flatter organization with a more transparent interface between leadership, organizational functions and employees. Create a defensible position through corporate strategy. For many of the industry's leaders, vision is driven by the strategic planning process, a function which has become critical for success. Strategic planning, however, has at times been a step-child in the hotel industry, and it is often the first to be cut when organizations are downsized. It is clearly in transition. There also has been a tendency to decentralize and simplify this function—both actions of potential benefit. Strategic planning must be led by the top people in the organization—the CEO and COO.

Beyond the ability to envision the future, core management capabilities will make the difference—they are essential. A clear vision without the management skills to support it cannot be a recipe for success. First and foremost, hotel management must have strategic development skills and the ability to integrate complex factors affecting success. Market volatility has become the norm, in part caused by the rapidly changing tastes of customers. Customers are increasingly approaching the hotel industry with widely different social, economic and political backgrounds, to say nothing of employees. Being able to deal with these diversities in a positive and constructive fashion that capitalizes on the differences, rather than working to find ways to mitigate them, is the clear path for successful management in the future.

The organization will also need to be imbued with a sense of entrepreneurship that reacts proactively to the market's diversity. Traditional organizations that follow well-documented rules must give way to leaders who can balance a sense of discipline with that of flexibility. Talent and resources must be marshaled and leveraged. In an industry with high fixed costs and labour intensity, the concept of leverage in the hotel business is an all-important one. Improving labour productivity through technology must be a goal for today's forward-looking hotel organization. Management must also be able to narrow the gap between the employer and the employee, forcing a flatter organization in the process. This will put management closer to the customer and speed the two-way communication process up and down the organization.

Pitfalls in Hotel Development

Cost overruns and construction delays can easily turn a profitable project into a development nightmare, of ten losing millions of dollars in the process. The careful selection and engagement of a professional Project and Development Services manager who represents the owner's best interests will be the most valuable project cost allocation made in a hotel development. In this section some of the pitfalls encountered in hotel development are describes.

Building a Dream Rather than a Financial Winner

Historically, many hotels were developed as trophy assets, often with little regard to the underlying economics of the development. While these types of developments were common in the late 1980s, they have by in large become the exception today. The first question that needs to be asked is why build a new hotel. The answers will range from financial to fantasy. The first step in any development process is to "prove" the vision; the most successful hotel developers set aside a judicious amount of time in the development cycle to validate their ideas.

The first and indispensable step of a project delivery process is the confirmation of the owner's goals and objectives. Even if they have already been established, a thorough review of the goals and objectives is appropriate when a development team is retained. Constraints should be investigated to assure all budget and schedule risks are exposed. Objectives for image and costs must be tested in the market to assure expectations can be met. The owner's decision-making process, financing requirements and similar concerns will be explored to unearth unforeseen risks.

Project planning, including the selection of all consultants, needs to be reviewed and coordinated from the beginning. The financial objectives of the development need to be established and clearly communicated, including the holding strategy, return on investment, equity available and the likelihood of raising construction and long-term financing.

As a development team will be responsible for the implementation of the owner's decisions made early in the process, it is beneficial to introduce the development manager early in the development cycle to avoid divergent agendas of architects, contractors, operators and owners.

Having the Wrong Entity Driving The Process

Very early in the development process, the owner must form their team. This team includes the owner, developer, architect, engineer, interior designer as well as other consultants unique to the project such as contractors, attorneys, financial advisers, appraisers and operators. Usually, there are three drivers jockeying for the lead position: the owner, the developer and the operator. All believe they have legitimate reasons for why they should spearhead the project.

Developers assume they should take the lead because they know how to convert the vision into a building. Operators think they should run the show because the hotel must be built according to specifications of their brand. Owners presume they should be in charge because their capital is financing the project. Although the team is assembled based on the owner's concept, the developer and the operator each has a tendency to craft the agreement in a way that allows minimum interference from the owner.

The fact of the matter is that the owner should drive the process at all times and should be the ultimate decision-maker. After all, the owner is the risk taker and without his or her financial support, the project might remain on the drawing board. This does not mean that the owner should be involved in every detail of the project. Rather, it is assumed that the owner would have selected a competent project team and negotiated with the best suitable operator for the property.

To ensure the owner's best interests, it is wise to assemble a development team with experience in completing complex hotel projects that can objectively oversee the development activity of a third party. To ensure a timely and successful delivery of a project, a qualified development adviser should initiate the following related processes that are critical to any development.

Pre-construction
- Project Planning
- Capital/Financial Plan Development
- Design Team Selection/Design Management Plan
- Pre-Construction Services and/or General Contractor Selection
- Governmental & Regulatory Requirements
- Hotel Operations Planning & Asset Management Approach
- Schedule & Budget Management Systems
- Bid and Negotiation Services
- FF&E Design, Procurement & Installation Planning

Construction
- Contract Administration, Management Control & Reporting
- Project Coordination & Conflict Resolution
- Budget & Schedule Control
- Change Order Administration
- Quality & Safety Control
- Invoice Approval/DrawPreparation/Cash Flow Management/Reporting
- FF&E Procurement & Phased Installation
- Preparation for Occupancy and Hotel Management Start-up
- Project Close-Out & Operations Turnover

Form at the Expense of Function

Unlike other types of real estate, the development of a hotel is the creation of a new business entity. Design decisions made early in the development process stay with the property for its lifetime and can become an operations benefit or nightmare. Decisions about technology, room size, meeting facilities, flexibility with current brand standards, and the mix of food and beverage must be the driving force in "future-proofing" a design so that the property remains competitive well into its future.

In order to achieve maximum value as well as budget control, a development team needs to ensure that a comprehensive construction estimate and updated project budget is prepared at the end of each design phase (conceptual, schematic, design development and construction documents). This process results in constant checks of the evolving design versus the project budget, which allows issues to be addressed while there is still time to adjust the design or the budget.

Throughout a project, a systematic value engineering approach needs to be adopted to maximize the cost/benefit impact of every dollar invested in the project. The goal of value engineering is to analyze every opportunity, recommendation or new technology/material during the design and construction phase that has the potential to "enhance" the project while maintaining budget and schedule control. Value enhancement can occur (1) when a project can be constructed more economically and efficiently from a cost and schedule standpoint; (2) when new products or more durable material is developed that will decrease operations and maintenance costs, and (3) when operators provide input on functionality, work flow and overall building performance. The discipline of value engineering requires the evaluation of everything against a pre-determined set of criteria, which are established in the initial development phase with the owner.

Local and Regional Civic Participation

A hotel should ultimately be developed because it is financially sound and provides the type and quality of services that the market desires. By developing a hotel, the owner is contributing a tangible asset to a local community by providing additional tax revenue and gainful employment. In exchange for these benefits to the community, an owner/developer should take advantage of its privileged position and get support from the local government. Although not always available, this support can take various forms, from building the access infrastructure to tax incentive financing. The key is to ensure that all forms of available incentives are investigated and incorporated into the financial plan, if they are favorable to the owner's overall goals and objectives.

During early due diligence on the project and the site, the owner/ developer needs to be familiar with potential public incentives in the municipality where the project will be built. With the right approach, a developer can often obtain financial support from the local and federal government for the project. Following are a few of the options an owner/ developer should consider:

— Municipal tax free bonds
— Access infrastructure improvements

— Tax incentive financial (TIF) districts
— Federal historical tax credits
— Environmental clean-ups
— Beach restorations

Limited Contractor Accountability

Hotel projects are notorious for last minute installations of case goods and scrambles to complete interior finishes. The final push toward the opening deadline of ten forces contractors to cut corners to avoid financial penalties or liquidated damages for missed deadlines. Without defined project controls, the keys to the hotel are often handed to the hotel manager, only to find substandard materials and workmanship that create operating problems well after the contractors have moved onto their next project.

A comprehensive quality control programme is the backbone to any hotel development and should focus on three primary goals:

(1) knowledgeable design phase input,

(2) clear communication of expectations to contractors, and

(3) regular on-site inspections to review the construction and conformance to the quality standards contained in the design specification and, if necessary, formulate an aggressive programme to correct non-complying work.

As the project progresses, continual reviews of each phase of the project will minimize the final punch list and turnover process so project closeout can be expedited and hotel operations can proceed with minimal interference.

During the final phases of the project, it is imperative to coordinate the efforts of the general contractor and the local authorities to gain all necessary licenses and permits required to open the hotel in conjunction with the hotel operations plan.

The entire project team must be aligned to the goal of opening the hotel on time, with minimal remaining punch list items at the time of turnover to operations. Preliminary and final punch list procedures must be established early in the project to allow sufficient time for completion prior to turnover.

Prior to the expiration of all project warranties, inspections must be conducted to determine the existence of any warranted defects and arrange with the respective manufacturers and subcontractors to correct the defects prior to the expiration of the warranty.

Functional Obsolescence

Now more than ever, hotel guests are being exposed to ever increasing service levels, design innovations and new technology. Hotel guests are traveling more frequently and are being exposed on a regular basis to the latest in hotel trends and gadgetry. The process of one-upsmanship is nothing new, but to build a hotel today without consideration of future trends may create an asset that soon loses value through functional obsolescence. The mega trends in the lodging industry continue to evolve. We are seeing a continued shift toward quality not quantity, such as the proliferation of boutique hotels offering a unique experience over the cookie cutter approach to corporate lodging. With this evolving landscape, it becomes important to the long-term profitability of a project that every effort is made to incorporate product flexibility in the initial design.

The time frame on large projects from conception to completion can take anywhere from two to four years. This time frame is a lifetime in terms of technology and means that the available technology, materials and techniques at the start of a project can be vastly different from those available at completion.

To ensure that the "latest thinking" is brought to bear on a given project, it is important to draw from global experience on asset management, project management and financing. It is critical to balance the financial objectives of the project with the overall financial objectives of the asset during operations. Additionally, as stated previously, the discipline of value engineering will ensure that new technology, materials, products and design changes will be constantly evaluated against the overall design parameters and incorporated into the project should an overall benefit be substantiated.

Back-Door Procurement

The procurement process needs to be expertly managed and tightly controlled until the last towel is placed in the guestrooms. The hotel FF&E procurement process is full of stories of kickbacks, inferior products being delivered late or the wrong product arriving at the last minute. The procurement process is a haven for cost padding and political and self-serving decisions that affect the hotel operations for the useful life of the products.

Cost control and quality can be maintained by implementing a coordinated FF&E procurement process including:

— Establishing the RFP process for procurement & installation providers and controlling the process all the way through.
— Challenging the interior designer, the procurement company and the vendors to evaluate and recommend best-in-class solutions to FF&E.
— Reviewing product data and samples proposed with the owner and the hotel operator to make sure they are in compliance with the client 's requirements.
— Developing a plan and coordinating the installation of FF&E in conjunction with the contractor's construction turnover schedule and the operator's training schedules on all elements of the project, including furniture delivery strategies and inventory security.

Costs Spiraling out of Control

Without a clearly conceived strategy for implementing the project, together with experience, coordination and communication, a project can literally spin out of control. The financial implications that result from development pitfalls can be devastating. Following are some of the potential hazards:

— Labor disputes
— Legal disputes
— Less than ironclad agreements with general contractors and trades, allowing for uncapped price fluctuation
— Accumulation of delays, causing loss of business and increased construction costs
— Accumulation of change orders due to a flawed or incomplete design prior to construction
— Construction conflicts adding to delays
— Lack of contractor/trade warranties
— Non-bonded contractors and trades on the job
— Uncooperative neighbors
— Potential loss of business and goodwill

The business of building a hotel from the ground up is complex and multifaceted. Of ten owners and developers do not account for cost overruns, which can have dramatic implications on the project.

Experience is key to the hotel development process and qualified advisers can mitigate most of these issues with minimum involvement by the owner. The primary objective of advisers is to ensure that the owner's best interest is met during all stages of development. To accomplish such a project, the development team must focus on the following:

1. Establishing benchmarks and performance targets:
   — Assembling a design and construction team of best-in-class providers;
   — Maximizing the buying power of each dollar spent on the project by testing, evaluating and expanding local contractor and subcontractor relationship negotiations to take advantage of current market conditions and discounts; and
   — Challenging design solutions to ensure optimum value for construction dollars and efficient and economical future flexibility.
2. Bringing market leverage and pressure to all cost categories.
3. Mitigating risk and liability.
4. Retaining a high level of control:
   — The control of a project's schedule is essential to minimize cost overruns. Process control, scheduling and project management cost reporting systems put real cost containment into the hands of the project team and owner management.
   — Expert management provides important initial feasibility information and manages the design and construction process to the interests of the owner. This will produce an end result that is consistent with the overall project goals and business plan.

Overlooking Small Details

Finally the hotel is built and almost ready to open for business. Often this is when the owner must feverishly scramble to secure all licenses and permits necessary to open the hotel. Time is money, and any delay in the hotel opening can be costly. Construction delays are one aspect of the equation. The other side of the equation is the lack of understanding and knowledge of the process for obtaining the necessary permits, licenses and certificates to open a hotel. The following list represents some of the required licenses and permits prior to opening:

— City Occupational Licenses
— County Occupational Licenses

- Certificate of Registration—Collection of Sales & Use Tax
- Business License (Rooms, Miscellaneous)
- Food & Beverage (Bars/Restaurants)
- Food & Beverage (Kitchens/Food prep areas)
- Beverage Licenses
- Special Tax Stamp
- Swimming Pool Permits
- Elevator/Escalator Certificates of Operation
- Certificate of Balcony Inspection
- Boiler Certifications
- Certification of Fire Protection System
- Fuel Storage Tank Licenses
- Dry Cleaning System Permits

There is no excuse for not having all the licenses, certificates and permits in place upon completion of the development. These documents may require planning months in advance and should be an integral part of the development's critical path planning. To ensure a smooth process of attaining the necessary licenses and permits, it is important to remain in constant contact with the local government agency throughout the various development phases of the project. Issues are addressed during regular visits with the local inspectors and, therefore, do not accumulate over time to the point that they become unmanageable. Lack of communication translates into licensing delays.

Missing the Deadline

Project delays resulting in the postponed opening of a hotel can have many adverse consequences. In order to ease the financial pressure of the typical hotel start up, the sales and marketing team will begin to book association and group business 12 to 18 months prior to opening. The importance of establishing an opening date and completing the hotel on schedule is critical to avoid the cost of relocating group bookings and the associated negative publicity. The same can be said for the various publications and directories catering to the corporate and leisure travelers. If group business cannot be layered in and publications and promotional material do not accurately reflect a hotel's opening, the hotel opening is likely to produce poor financial results.

Critical path planning and adherence to development schedules are imperative to a hotel project's financial success. Managing the development schedule and assuring compliance requires that all interaction between the owner/developer, the hotel operator and the design and construction team are managed.

Management of the development schedule requires an intimate understanding of the owner's decision-making processes, the creation of interim milestone dates with the necessary tracking process, and the necessary expertise to provide real time solutions to remedy construction delays.

To ensure that a hotel opens on time, many construction contracts will include performance clauses such as bonus incentives for early completion or liquidated damages as a penalty for late completion. Other steps that can be implemented to ensure timely openings include staged occupancy of critical components of the hotel. Typically kitchens, training facilities, computer rooms, and laundry and operating supply areas are brought online three to four months before opening, while guest rooms, front office and reception are turned over four to six weeks ahead of opening.

The strict management of the development schedule, including establishing and tracking critical milestones, managing an "Action Item List" throughout design and construction and identifying and tracking long-lead items will result in a smooth ending of a long and demanding development process.

Partnership and Outsourcing

Outsourcing happens when a company determines specific tasks are better and more efficiently performed by a provider outside the company that specializes in that particular field. For most companies, cost savings is the main reason for outsourcing. Outsourcing is usually a profitable option when outside providers are more efficient or better able to achieve economies, are capable of reducing over-head or debt, or are able to save on the cost of benefits and administration.

While cost savings is the main reason for outsourcing, it is clearly not the only reason. Outsourcing enables a company to benefit from the knowledge base of the outsource company, which can often provide expertise on complex business issues and processes that are not among the firm's own core competencies. By using outside professionals, management can focus on issues related to growth of the core business.

In the administrative/ finance areas, the functions most frequently outsourced are payroll, tax compliance, internal auditing, accounting and human resources/hiring. Internal operations primarily in the areas of manufacturing, processing and assembly are outsourced by almost half of the fast growth firms surveyed. Outside maintenance and equipment services are used by 19 percent, and information technology outsourcing is used by 17 percent; up eight full points from three years ago. Sales and marketing are a rapidly growing outsourcing category as well; up nine points in three years. Web site management, a new outsourcing category; is used by 11 percent of fast growth companies.

Partnering promotes a win-win situation for both companies. Instead of paying an out-side vendor to merely perform a task for a fee, partnering puts two companies with differing strengths together to create something much bigger Something along the lines of "the whole being greater than the sum of its parts". Each company brings a level of expertise, or distinction, that benefits the other. Both companies grow and create a better product or service jointly than they could have done individually.

References

March, C. A. *Building operation and maintenance.* New York: McGraw-Hill, 1950.

Rogers, R. Vashon. *The law of hotel life; or, The wrongs and rights of host and guest.* San Francisco.

Van Hoof, Hubert B. *A Host of Opportunities: An Introduction to Hospitality Management.* Chicago: Irwin, 1996.

Virts, William B. *Purchasing for Hospitality Operations.* East Lansing: Educational Institute of the American Hotel and Motel Association, 1996.

Walker, John R. *Introduction to Hospitality.* Upper Saddle River: Prentice Hall, 1996.

5

Customer Relationship Management

Customer Relationship Management (CRM) is currently one of the hottest topics in the fields of business strategy, information technology, and marketing management. Put simply, CRM is a management philosophy that calls for the reconfiguration of the firm's activities around the customer.

CRM can be the single strongest weapon you have as a manager to ensure that customers become and remain loyal. Great employees are, and always will be, the backbone of any business. But employee performance can be enhanced or hampered by the strategy you set and by the tools that you give employees to get the job done. Done right, CRM is both a strategy and a tool, a weapon, if you will. In your hands, and in the hands of your employees, CRM comes to life, keeping you and your team on course and able to anticipate the changing landscape of the marketplace. With CRM, loyal customers aren't a happy accident created when an exceptional customer service representative, salesperson or product developer intuits and responds to a customer need. Instead, you have at your fingertips the ultimate advantage-customer intelligence: data turned into information and information turned into acustomer-satisfying action.Implementing CRM is a nonnegotiable in today's business environment. Whether your customers are internal or external, consumers or businesses, whether they connect with you electronically or face to face, from across the globe or across town, CRM is your ticket to success.

Customer Relationship Management is a comprehensive approach for creating, maintaining and expanding customer relationships. Let's take a closer look at what this definition implies.

First, consider the word "comprehensive." CRM does not belong just to sales and marketing. It is not the sole responsibility of the customer service group. Nor is it the brainchild of the information technology team. While any one of these areas may be the internal champion for CRM in your organization, in point of fact, CRM must be a way of doing business that touches all areas. When CRM is delegated to one area of an organization, such as IT, customer relationships will suffer. Likewise, when an area is left out of CRM planning, the organization puts at risk the very customer relationships it seeks to maintain.

The second key word in our definition is "approach." An approach, according to Webster, is "a way of treating or dealing with something." CRM is a way of thinking about and dealing with customer relationships. We might also use the word strategy here because, done well, CRM involves a clear plan. In fact, we believe that your CRM strategy can actually serve as a benchmark for every other strategy in your organization. Any organizational strategy that doesn't serve to create, maintain, or expand relationships with your target customers doesn't serve the organization. Strategy sets the direction for your organization. And any strategy that gets in the way of customer relationships is going to send the organization in a wrong direction. You can also consider this from a department or area level. Just as the larger organization has strategies-plans-for shareholder management, logistics, marketing, and the like, your department or area has its own set of strategies for employee retention, productivity, scheduling, and the like. Each of these strategies must support managing customer relationships.

CRM is about the entire customer cycle. When you implement your CRM strategy, you will capture and analyze data about your targeted customers and their targeted buying habits. From this wealth of information, you can understand and predict customer behavior. Marketing efforts, armed with this customer intelligence, are more successful at both finding brand new customers and cultivating a deeper share of wallet from current customers. Customer contacts, informed by detailed information about customer preferences, are more satisfying. Are you a manager whose area doesn't deal with external customers? This part of the definition still applies.

First, you and your team support and add value to the individuals in your organization who do come into direct contact with customers. Again and again, the research has proven that external customer satis- faction is directly proportional to employee satisfaction. That means that the quality of support given to internal customers predicts the quality of support that is given to external customers.

Second, consider your internal customers as advocates for your department or area. For you and your team, CRM is about growing advocates and finding new ways to add value.

Finally, what do we mean by "customer relationships" in today's economy, where we do business with individuals and organizations whom we may never meet, may never want to meet, much less know in a person-to-person sense? CRM is about creating the feel of high touch in a high tech environment. Consider the success of Amazon.com. Both of us are frequent customers and neither of us has ever spoken to a human being during one of our service interactions. The CRM tools that support customer relationship strategy allow to:

— Add value to customer transactions by identifying related items with their "customers who bought this book also bought" feature, in much the same way that a retail clerk might suggest related items to complete a sale.
— Reinforce a sense of relationship by recognizing repeat shoppers and targeting them with thank you's ranging from thermal coffee cups to one-cent stamps to ease the transition to new postal rates.

In short, customers want to do business with organizations that understand what they want and need. Wherever you are in your organization, CRM is about managing relationships more effectively so you can drive down costs while at the same time increasing the viability of your product and service offerings.

CRM differs from traditional marketing initiatives in that, while the latter take predominately a short-term, transaction approach, CRM focuses on maximising revenue from each customer over the lifetime of the relationship by getting to know each one intimately. CRM is also, by definition, a crossfunctional philosophy that calls for substantial business integration. Thus, to implement CRM successfully, a very different mindset is needed: The firm no longer markets to customers, but it fosters a relationship with them through programs that span marketing, operations, information systems, accounting, and other organizational functions.

One of the questions most often asked about CRM is, "why bother?" Changing an organization's philosophy and methods of operation is troublesome; developing and maintaining in-depth customer databases is expensive and the benefits of the approach are not guaranteed. Day, Dean, and Reynolds neatly summarise the benefits of using CRM.

First, by developing a closer relationship with customers, the firm may gain a competitive advantage and, through increased switching costs, may be able to defend it. Over time individual customers typically educate a company about their individual needs, wants, and preferences—a costly process that they are reluctant to repeat with a rival. Thus, getting to know customers intimately creates a barrier to imitation of the leader's strategy.

Second, effective CRM can lead to increased customer satisfaction. Properly implemented, the customer-company dialogue facilitates the tailoring of products and services closely to individual needs, and the development of new products and services to meet changing needs or even anticipate future needs.

Third, using CRM techniques contributes to decreasing overall marketing expenditure. Acquiring new customers is estimated to be more expensive than keeping existing ones. Figures of between five and seven times as much have been quoted. And, last, developing a closer relationship with customers is thought to increase customer loyalty, and loyal customers are thought to stay with the firm longer, buy more from it, and buy more often. An oft-quoted statistic is that companies can improve profitability by between 25 and 85 percent by reducing customer defections by 5 percent. While the value of loyalty is currently being debated, for some time now lodging firms have been fostering loyalty through frequenttraveler programs and CRM may be seen as the logical next step.

CRM leads to higher profitability due to increased sales, declining customer acquisition costs, and increasing profitability of customers willing to pay a premium for "better" service. Substantial investments in CRM are not right for everyone. In a small or niche business, for example, it is relatively easy to keep in touch with customers' preferences.But because of the significant increase in the amount of information that must be managed as the firm's scale and scope increase, successful CRM requires significant investments in technology, process redesign, and people. An airline or a major international hotel chain must manage substantially larger amounts of data than does a small inn to achieve a similar relationship with its customers. However, information technology (IT)—used appropriately can help mitigate the problem.

Between 1990 and today, the world has seen enormous transformations in the extent to which organizations can deploy computer power. IT allows customer data to be collected, consolidated, manipulated, and analysed on an unprecedented scale, and IT has been identified by many authors as one of the key success factors for CRM implementation. IT allows increased reach into new markets without high incremental entry costs, and facilitates specifically tailored customer marketing and increased responsiveness.

The role of IT in CRM efforts is so important that some writers, and many practicing managers and vendors, associate CRM with the technology that is used to support the approach.Many use the term in the highly specific sense of database marketing, where a range of demographic, lifestyle, and purchasing activities are recorded and tracked, and subsequently used as the basis of targeting differentiated products to selected customer groups. In turn, their response to each marketing contact is tracked and used to further refine the approach. However, CRM is a broader concept than just technology. For example, CRM has been defined as "an enterprise- wide commitment to identify your named, individual customers and create a relationship between your company and these customers so long as that relationship is mutually beneficial".

This definition highlights several key CRM concepts —that the company will actively seek out the right customers (and, by implication, will not target those that will not do business with them), will develop a long-term, mutually beneficial relationship with each customer by starting and maintaining a two-way dialogue, will strive to satisfy customers' needs and solve customer problems, and will support customers throughout the life cycle of their interactions with the firm.

This approach to CRM demands more than computer systems and information technology. The customer must become the focal point of the organization. All members of the organization must understand and support the shared values required for CRM, its philosophy must encompass not just marketing but the entire organization, and it must be used to manage all aspects of the customer relationship in a coordinated way.

Although limited research about the effectiveness of CRM has been published to date, most observers agree that successful CRM is predicated on the ability to effectively capture exhaustive data about existing and potential customers, profile them accurately, identify their individual needs and idiosyncratic expectations, and generate actionable customer knowledge that can be dis-tributed for ad-hoc use at each point of contact. The objective is to achieve a comprehensive view of customers, and be able to consistently anticipate and react to their needs with targeted and effective activities at every customer touch point.

CRM requires the firm to keep track of the information produced through each interaction so that it can "learn" on a continuous basis, get to know each guest better, and enrich its database of individual customer knowledge. Godin has likened CRM to "dating a customer," in that it is a long-term process that requires an investment of time, information, and resources by both parties. The result is an active, participatory, and interactive relationship between customer and supplier.

Lastly, CRM is about customisation, or the ability to consistently treat different customers differently. Relationships differ as they develop. We do not treat old friends in the same way as new friends or good friends in the same way as casual acquaintances. Such consistent personalised interaction requires integration and synchronisation of many organizational functions, from marketing to accounting to operations and information systems. Failure to understand the scope, essence, and magnitude of CRM is likely to result in problems, rather than its promised benefits.

CRM in Lodging-industry

The past several years have witnessed an explosion in CRM tools, especially software applications. Your CRM strategy should drive your organizational structure, which should in turn drive choices around technology implementation. Yet, individuals and organizations become enamored of the technology applications and forget that that they must start with a CRM strategy. The language confusion doesn't help. Countless articles and reviews of CRM tools and technologies never mention strategy. They imply, or even come right out and say, that the only thing you need to do to have effective CRM is buy the right application. Yes, the right application is critical. But it is your CRM strategy that informs which application will be right for you. The power of CRM comes from the clarity of your approach. Think for a moment about your personal planner and organizer.

Lodging-industry participants face an increasingly competitive market. In addition, the basis of competition is changing. Location, a key driver of business, is fixed in the short and medium term, and attracting and retaining customers based on facilities and amenities is becoming increasingly difficult as they have become increasingly standardised across competing brands. Price competition is unattractive, even more so as consumers are able to easily find and compare prices over the Internet. As a consequence consumers are increasingly displaying less brand loyalty, and CRM is becoming increasingly attractive as a way for hotel companies to differentiate themselves from their competitors.

The lodging sector is ideally suited to applying the principles of CRM. In few other industries is there such potential to build up a comprehensive and accurate picture of the client. In few other industries do customers provide the significant amount of information hotel guests divulge when making a reservation and during their hotel stay. Every interaction between the guest and the customer is an opportunity to refine knowledge about her or him and to further build a relationship. By methodically collecting, consolidating, and analysing both guest preferences and transactional data, hotel chains have the potential to develop a deep understanding of each customer's needs and preferences, provide substantially improved service levels, individually tailor the customer experience, and generally offer more personalised service.

Providing outstanding personal service is certainly not a new concept in the hotel sector. Companies such as Rits-Carlton and the Savoy group historically maintained extensive manual guest-history systems recording guest preferences in an effort to better serve their best customers. However, when oper- ated manually, such systems are expensive to maintain, are frequently inaccurate, and can only be used to track a limited number of clients at individual properties.

Developments in information and communications technologies have enabled automation and efficiencies in these processes, reducing costs, increasing accuracy, and allowing comprehensive knowledge about each customer to be shared on a global basis. As a result, many companies are turning to technology to improve customer service by implementing large-scale CRM programs.

Analysis of the lodging sector shows that, driven in most cases by pressure from the marketing function, many of the dominant hotel chains are in the process of deploying (or have already deployed) the technological infrastructure to support CRM. A recent study by Arthur Andersen and New York University found that over one-third of U.S. hotel chains had a data warehouse in 2000, with another 50 percent planning to install one in the near future. Many chains have introduced information systems to improve the targeting of marketing and sales efforts. Such systems can help the firm to assess the value of each customer as well as their propensity to respond to various offers, and to market to them individually.

While important, such initiatives do not imply that the company has adopted CRM. In most cases, such developments focus solely on marketing objectives and lack the integration among functional areas that characterises a CRM initiative. Only where the company reconfigures its operations to deliver a comprehensive view of the customer and to support consistent, highly personalised service at every customer touch point could it truly be regarded as CRM. Few companies in the lodging sector appear to have progressed to such an advanced stage. Given the geographic dispersion of hotel properties and the role of brands in marketing and distribution, large-scale CRM initiatives seem most justifiable at the brand level.

Implementing CRM at this level would help to increase consistency and personal service throughout the chain and at each customer touch point. However, to achieve this, consistent and comprehensive information must be captured from all properties within the brand and then consolidated, analysed, interpreted, and subsequently disseminated to each property in time to influence the next customer interaction.

Two barriers currently prevent that from happening—a lack of standardisation and ITsystem integration within each franchise, and the fact that at any one time there may be up to three parties holding a stake in the operations of a particular property.The two issues are largely interconnected as the industry's generally reactive attitude toward IT has been exacerbated by its structural characteristics. .

Right Order for Effective CRM

This section describes the right order for effective CRM, and points out some classic mistakes that lead to failed CRM implementations. The most typical approach to CRM has companies developing point solutions, something that solves one particular problem, out of acute necessity. However, whether you use a consulting firm to help you implement the point solution or you go it alone, you should be sure that the key questions around direction, integration, processes and people are being asked. Generally speaking, the questions are a lot more easily asked than answered, which leads most companies back to the need for an overarching strategy and the realization that CRM really is a way of running the business, not just the program du jour. Additionally, CRM is a way to increase revenues and/or reduce costs. Not understanding the fact that this is a bottom line strategy could lead you to make the wrong decisions in establishing your strategy.

Everyone wants to be a CRM Hero — the desired outcome. No one wants to be a CRM Zero — the career-limiting option. Allow us to offer five words of advice: don't start by picking software. In addition, it would be prudent to watch for these classic mistakes:

1. *Thinking that CRM is, at its heart, technology-based.* The best example of this is the client who told us, "We need to get a CRM." That makes no sense, for it is not the technology that makes you a hero, it is the recognition and belief by your organization that CRM is a way to operate the company. To accomplish this, the CRM Hero must demonstrate the leadership necessary to develop a CRM strategy and get the rest of the company to come along for the ride. At the risk of stating the obvious, too many companies we've seen have adroitly demonstrated that they have no clue where their CRM program is going – but, wow, look at all that data! Never mind that they will soon be another case study in failed expectations. However, with a well-conceived strategy that highlights all aspects of the customer relationship, they would be able to clearly articulate the specific changes, tools and techniques that must be employed over time within their organization to deliver measurable results.
2. *So I've made a strategy, let's go get the software.* Not so fast. With clear articulation comes the second step: communicating the strategy to the rest of the company and your guests. Not much new technology is needed for this step, either. However, you are guaranteed to fall short of your CRM goals without effective communication throughout the company. Meanwhile, the CRM Hero grows ever more frustrated that people don't "get it." Yet, people are the most vital, and the most frequently overlooked, part of the equation. As service providers, we all know that our frontline people have the power to make or break the relationships we enjoy with our guests, but it is stunning to note that occasionally this basic truth gets forgotten. If our people don't understand the importance we are suddenly placing on effective relations with our guests, those relations will be anything but effective.

4. *OK, we've got everybody jazzed about this CRM thing; let's get some technology in here to help them.* Sounds great, but help them do what? The same things they did before you got them the technology? While those things worked really well for you under your old way of managing the business, remember that this is a new way of thinking you're trying to impart. With new thinking must come new ways of working, which means you will need to lead the way in helping your company look at things the same way your guests look at things. These guest-centric business processes are simple in concept, but much more difficult to get your people to design. Some companies have taken the radical step of inviting customers into their process design meetings to be sure they're taking a customer-centric approach.

4. We know what we're trying to do, everybody's on board and our processes are aligned with the desired guest experience – now all I need is a new POS system, a data warehouse, a campaign management tool, new call center software for my reservations agents, a good PMS built on the latest platform and a new yield management tool. It's finally time for technology, but if you follow this approach your systems integrators will be happy, though your IT shop won't be when they have to keep all of these balls in the air. Integration is the key – single points of data collection, techniques for data cleansing and easy ways of getting the right information to the right people in a way that allows for seamless, consistent, personalized service.

Keys to Successful Implementations

1. *The Keep It Simple, Stupid (K.I.S.S.) Principle.* There are a few home truths about successful CRM implementations. The K.I.S.S. principle is highly applicable. Over-complicating the process does one thing – it succeeds in extending the duration, potentially causing budgetary overruns. In the words of Dr. Chekitan Dev, associate professor of strategic marketing at Cornell University's School of Hotel Administration, "Do not draw up a long-winded program. It is important to have quick hits that show short-term benefits – this will help to get people on board, since they want to see results. Maintain the built-in potential to upgrade... a simple process that grows organically will be the most successful, and yield the best results." If you must plan a gargantuan CRM program, "break it down into shorter-

term, focused projects with clearly defined business benefits and success metrics". This brings us to the second key to success.

2. *Actionable Measurements and Performance Metrics.* It is important to ensure that adequate emphasis is placed on establishing timely and actionable measurements. It is crucial to be able to identify the bottom line impact on an ongoing basis of the program that has been established.
3. *Stakeholder Ownership.* If you want to ensure a successful implementation, it is important to ensure that all stakeholders are on board. It is not merely sufficient if key players buy into the process. They must take ownership of, and be actively engaged in the process. For a successful project it is important to have internal champions.
4. *GIGO.* Better known as "Garbage In – Garbage Out," this is the test of stakeholder ownership. Realize that none of the exciting new capabilities are worth anything without good data. In our experience, legacy systems generally have errors in roughly half of their customer records. These could be as simple as an address that reads "road" instead of "street," or as complicated as multiple customer records for the same customer, each with slight differences. Yet you have countless opportunities to capture good data in the course of a guest experience. Part of your business process work has to be to ensure effective capture and cleansing of customer data. Effective capture implies not sticking all of the good stuff in the comments field, where it likely resides today, completely unread in the hustle and bustle of the typical front desk.
5. *Consider the Value of the Customer.* Successful CRM is not about providing the best service on the block; rather, the key to effective relations with your customers is in providing appropriate service. We all know that customers are not equal. That's why loyalty programs were invented. Yet far too frequently we see clients that developed sophisticated segmentation capabilities and tiered loyalty programs who have no means of differentiating the service they provide to these segments of guests. One resort client was excited about his newfound ability to execute real-time marketing campaigns to fill short-term availabilities at the hugely popular property. Yet he had not considered the value associated with different customer segments and was disappointed when the realization from these last-minute guests was not up to the usual standards of the resort. Simply put, this client was

ignoring all of its segmentation data and mass-marketing its limited capacity. Thus, it is important to provide appropriate service at every interaction based upon intelligent segmentation.

6. *Help Your Employees Help Your Guests*. All employees, at all properties, should have the training and up-to-date information that allows them to provide seamless, consistent, personalized service to the customer. According to Jens Thraenhart, director Internet strategy, Fairmont Hotels and Resorts, "A successful CRM and customer retention strategy in the hotel industry is dependent on the implementation at the property level. It is important to train front line employees to capture information from many offline touch points, in combination with online data capture. Training is vital to ensure consistency and cleanliness of guest information." This information should be immediately available to front desk receptionists, call center agents, pit bosses, concierge and housekeeping staff, and so on, and should be served up at the right time.
7. *Strong internal partnerships around the CRM strategy*. We said earlier that CRM is a way of doing business that touches all areas of your organization. This means that you and your management peers need to form strong internal partnerships around CRM. If you and your organization are early on the road to CRM implementation, now is the time to bring your CRM needs to the table, and to be open to listening to the CRM needs of other areas. You may find that you have requirements that are, at least potentially, in conflict. Resist the temptation to go to war for what you need. If your organization has gone off the partnership road with CRM, then now is the time to come back together and rebuild partnership with the area that is currently championing CRM. Let them know that you appreciate what they have done. Let them know what data you have to offer and help them understand how you plan to use the data you request from them.
8. *Employees at all levels and all areas accurately collect information for the CRM system*. Employees are most likely to comply appropriately with your CRM system when they understand what information is to be captured and why it is important. They are also more likely to trust and use CRM data when they know how and why it was collected.
9. *CRM tools are customer- and employee-friendly*. CRM tools should be integrated into your systems as seamlessly as possible, making them

a natural part of the customer service interaction. A major manufacturer of specialty pet foods redesigned the pop-up screens for its toll-free consumer phone line. In the original design, the final pop-up screen prompted the representative to ask the caller's name and address. Yet, representatives had found that it was easier and felt more natural to ask, "What's your name?" and "Where are you calling from?" and "What's your pet's name?" at the start of the call.

10. *Report out only the data you use, and use the data you report.* Just because your CRM tool can run a report doesn't mean it should. Refer back to your CRM strategy, and then run the data you will actually use. And share that data with your team.
11. *Don't go high-tech when low-tech will do.* At Harley- Davidson outside of Milwaukee, WI, during the summer they often leave open the big metal doors to the manufacturing facility to let in any breeze and the cooler evening air. Unfortunately, open doors occasionally let in other things, including skunks. A team met to consider the problem and possible solutions. After discussing the pros and cons of screens, half-doors, or keeping the doors shut, they came upon the ideal solution. When a skunk wanders in, just leave it alone and wait till it wanders back out. Skunks may be Harley fans, but they never stay long. Organizations that successfully implement CRM look for the simplest solution when implementing their CRM strategy.

A low-tech solution that works for the people who actually use it is more effective than a high tech solution that is cumbersome, costly and apt to be discarded or inconsistently implemented.When aggregate customer information is strategically collected and segmented, you can target new customer prospects. When customer preference information is easily accessible, you can craft superior service experiences-be they face-to-face, via telephone, or over the Internet. And when information about changing or additional customer needs is captured, you can expand the depth of the customer relationship. CRM is the strongest weapon you have to create, maintain, and expand customer relationships and it's here to stay. This is where the true test of CRM solutions takes place. There is nothing worse for your relationships than raising expectations and then failing to meet them.

— Does the call center know about the e-mail campaign that marketing just sent out?

— Does the front desk recognize that the repeat guest standing before them remembers the way to the elevator and doesn't need a 60-second refresher course complete with maps?

— Does the reservations agent realize that the potential guest on the telephone has used the onsite spa the past three times she has been at the property, and might just want to get services booked in advance?

Truly successful CRM implementations anticipate these kinds of issues and build the requisite business processes, employee training and integrated systems necessary to meet or even exceed growing expectations.

Technology certainly plays an important role in the implementation of a successful CRM project. However, it is not a silver bullet that will solve all problems or open all doors. It is important to remember that all technology decisions are only relevant in a business context. All the technology in the world is cool, but if your business processes aren't set up to effectively utilize these resources, your company will be added to the statistics of failed CRM implementations.

Data-ownership Dilemma

CRM's success is predicated on the ability to collect, analyse, and disseminate large amounts of timely and relevant information for customer-service operatives to act on to improve the experience at each point of customer contact. Thus, a CRM initiative cannot be successful without commitment among a critical mass of properties. Hotel chains cannot provide a consistently high level of personal service unless customer data can be garnered from most, if not all, of the affiliated properties, organized and synthesised in one central location, and subsequently redistributed to each property on an as-needed basis. However, we propose that (technological constraints aside) this apparently simple theoretical proposition is difficult to realise in the lodging industry due to an inherent data-ownership conflict between the major industry stakeholders. In the following sections we present the main issues facing the brand, the management company, and the owner.

Brand

For brands, the development of an effective CRM initiative is deemed an important competitive move as it would facilitate the development of a deep understanding of customer needs and preferences, potentially resulting in a high level of personalisation, thus helping to improve service levels across the brand as a whole. As a result guests would have a strong incentive to remain loyal to the brand and patronise affiliated properties, thus increasing the value proposition for owners and operators through improvements in financial performance.

For the promised benefits of CRM to materialise, standardised information systems must be implemented throughout the franchise network to allow data to be obtained from all branded properties—a problem in the past, becoming less important as a result of recent technology improvements. Furthermore, the brand must be willing to share the customer knowledge generated by the consolidation of customer data chain-wide with the individuals that can take action based on it at each point of customer contact. Such data sharing presents the first dilemma. In some cases, the brand may be reticent to disseminate customer knowledge back to the property for fear that owners or operators might use it to poach high-value customers and divert them to competing brands within their own portfolios.

For example, imagine a management company that operates a hotel flying one flag (Brand A) in a particular market, and a competing flag (Brand B) in others. This company might be tempted to steer highvalue customers toward its Brand B hotels in markets where it does not operate Brand A hotels. Thus, Brand A is faced with a decision —either share the data it collects companywide to reap the benefits of large-scale CRM and risk the poaching of high-value customers by some of its partner management companies operating individual properties; or protect its customer knowledge from the interests of multi-flag owners and operators, thus forgoing the full benefits of CRM.

The Management Company. Management companies do not appear to have strong incentives to develop a CRM initiative for themselves. Such companies tend to operate a varied portfolio of properties, each flying different flags, on behalf of different owners. By definition a CRM initiative developed across flags is unlikely to generate brand loyalty and thus is of limited interest to most management companies.

The question arises, however, as to whether management companies should actively cooperate with the collection of operational guest data by brand-level CRM initiatives. As most companies operate a varied portfolio of flags, if the management company participates in a brand-based CRM initiative, it will stand to gain only in those properties that carry that particular brand. Conversely, participation will result in a competitive disadvantage in markets where it competes against the brand. As a result, management companies have little incentive to support brand-level CRM initiatives by contributing data about customers that stay at its properties. In fact, by doing so, they would in effect be undermining their own operations in markets where the brand operating the CRM initiative is a competitor rather than an ally.

Moreover, while the management company may not be interested in detailed customer data for branding purposes, it certainly finds value in customer data that allows it to create customer-value models and better target high-value prospects, particularly with respect to group business. Consequently, management companies have in effect an incentive to limit data disclosure and not cooperate with brand-level CRM initiatives.

Owner

While owners, like operators, typically have many flags in their portfolio of properties, they have a different focus in terms of profitability. Many primarily view hotel ownership as a real-estate investment, and have a marginal interest in the question, "Who owns the data?"Where their properties fly the flag of a successful CRM initiative, they may have an advantage over other competing properties; where their properties fly competing flags, they may be at a disadvantage. Thus, the same dilemma facing the management company seems to affect the owners—whether to participate in brandlevel CRM initiatives, or to refuse to cooperate with the collection and consolidation of customer data. The owners may also have interests that go beyond the use of the data strictly for operational purposes. Customer data may be used by the other entities (the brand and the management company) for marketing purposes and analyses that run counter to the owner's own interests (e.g., studying the feasibility of building new properties in the same geographical area).

CRM strategies appear most applicable at the brand level, but their success is dependent on the active cooperation of both the operator and the owner of each property. For CRM to succeed at the brand level, operators must supply the brand with in-depth customer data—a requirement with which operators in particular, and owners to a lesser extent, have little incentive to comply. Brands also face challenges in terms of maintaining control over the resulting customer knowledge and preventing its spread outside the brand network.

Because of this conflict, we believe that CRM in the lodging industry may never progress beyond its current, relatively limited, level of sophistication. While database-marketing techniques will continue to be used, we propose that few hotel companies will successfully implement large-scale, chain-wide, CRM initiatives. Only if significant change occurs in the structure or methods of operation of the sector are the full benefits of a CRM approach likely to be realised. In closing, we speculate as to what changes will have to occur for successful implementation of CRM initiatives. We see three possible scenarios: there will be a fundamental change in the way in which hotel brands are organized; a change in the nature of franchise agreements and management contracts; or there will be more cooperation among brands to take advantage of CRM's promised benefits.

The first scenario is that the need for adoption of a CRM approach will induce changes in the ownership and management structure of the lodging sector. If CRM truly provides compelling benefits, the large brands should begin to pressure the management companies and franchisees within their network to provide the data needed for successful CRM operations. Those brands that manage a relatively large number of their own hotels will be in a good position to take advantage of these initiatives quickly, should face little resistance as a result of the dataownership dilemma, and shoud be able to easily reap the benefits of CRM.

Wyndham International's ByRequest initiative demonstrates that highly integrated lodging brands are moving quickly to embrace CRM. If these pioneers are successful in their effort and are able to attract and retain high-value customers, competing brands will have to follow suit and develop similar CRM capabilities. Such companies would have to resolve the data-ownership dilemma either by "integrating down" or by restricting the number of flags that the companies operating their hotels can fly. Integrating down implies that brands would move aggressively to take over the operational management of their branded properties. Such integrated companies should be able to standardise the IT infrastructure needed to support CRM, mandate the collection and consolidation of customer data, and provide each property with dynamic access to the central knowledge repository. Since all operations would effectively be managed by the brand, there would be no conflicts of interest and no danger of high-value customers being poached, freeing the brand to take full advantage of the CRM initiative.

Obviously, taking over operational control of their unit properties would be a dramatic and high-risk strategy. Thus, brands, particularly in the short term, may instead concentrate on restructuring their management and franchise agreements to minimise the barriers to success discussed earlier. Redevelopment should focus on two main areas —data collection and data use. While many franchise agreements require properties to feed its customer-folio data back to the central level, few specifically mention any other data collected about the guest.

As CRM is dependent on building up a holistic picture of the guest's needs and behavior, this oversight may force brands to restructure contracts to force greater compliance with data needs. Such restructured contracts could spec-ify that all customer data generated at the property level be extracted and loaded to the brand's central data repository. Management contracts also need to be rewritten to offer protection to the brand as it disseminates customer knowledge back to the property level. Both of these measures mean that ties between brands and operators would be strengthened, which may ultimately result in further industry consolidation as owners and operators feel pressure to fly a limited number of flags. In an extreme scenario, each operator would effectively become aligned with one brand and fly only one flag.

The final potential scenario we envision is the emergence of an industry consortium that both develops and maintains the CRM infrastructure and standardises customer-data collection and distribution. As it has happened historically with hotel e-commerce systems such as THISCo (The Hotel Industry Switching Company), HDS (Hotel Distribution Systems) and Avendra (an e-procurement marketplace), competing brands could cooperate to develop the standards and the infrastructure necessary to capture, store, organize, and distribute customer information.

Such a scenario is attractive as joint development would mean that the infrastructure could be delivered and operated at a fraction of the cost of proprietary initiatives. Thereafter, rather than being used as a basis of competition, customer data would be shared and companies would compete on the analysis, interpretation, and use of such data. For example, competing brands could use the same data to market to their chosen customer bases. Competitive advantage would come from how well they could use the data to identify, target, and build a relationship with each individual.

Role of ICTs in Implementing CRM Strategies

Information and Communication Technologies (ICT) crucially impact on travellers' knowledge, attitudes and behaviours. The increased online price and product transparency and the new business models (e.g. online auctions) enhance tourists' power, who are becoming more price sensitive, less brand loyal and more sophisticated. The hotel industry is also experiencing increased globalization, competition, higher customer turnover, growing customer acquisition costs and rising customer expectations, meaning that hotels' performance and competitiveness is significantly dependent on their ability to satisfy customers efficiently and effectively. To enhance profitability and guest loyalty, hotels must focus on developing Customer Relationship Management (CRM) that aims to seek, gather and store the right information, validate and share it throughout the entire organization and then use it throughout all organizational levels for creating personalised, unique guests experiences.

ICT has been recognised as one of the major catalyst factors for developing one-to-one experiences and implementing CRM strategies. However, CRM in the hospitality industry has been defined by the myriad of ICT suppliers that are overstating the role of ICT. However, CRM is not a technology problem but a business problem that requires ICT tools and functionality to be aligned, designed and effectively co-ordinated along with business operations and strategy.

CRM has its roots in relationship marketing inaugurated by the influential work by Berry and Christopher, Payne and Ballantyne . Relationship's marketing rational is to enhance long term profitability by moving from transaction-based marketing and its prominence in attracting new customers, to customer retention by means of effective management of customer relationships. Literature on CRM highlights the diffusion of relationship marketing practices for identifying, knowing and customising services to individual customers into organization wide operations and customer touch points. Kalakota and Robinson defined CRM as an integrated sales, marketing and service strategy that prevents "lone showmanship" and relies on coordinated actions, while Couldwell defined CRM as a combination of business processes and technology.

Overall, CRM implementation entails the following tactical steps: creation and data mining of a database of customer activity; given the analysis, decisions about which customers to target, how to target, contact and build relationships with them; development of personalised customer experiences; channel management for enabling efficient share of guest knowledge across the organization, so that guests can get personalised and consistent service at anytime, anyplace, anywhere, any platform; management of privacy issues; and metrics for measuring the success of CRM.

To achieve these, businesses may need to undertake major organizational changes and transformations at a higher level, whose identification has generated wide interest and debates. Wells, William and Choobineh identified four key elements for CRM implementation: business process analysis; integration and redesign of customer data; ICT enabled customer interaction; accessibility/transmission of organizational information. Hart highlighted the importance of building a great organizational and operational flexibility and a process technology that will enable product/service customisation as well as the need of a marketing department that would support the identification and analysis of customer needs. To achieve this, Gronroos emphasised that businesses should be managed from a process rather than a functionalistic perspective. Mok, Stutts and Wong stressed the importance of ICT. However, participants in a Tourism Society's seminar on CRM concluded that CRM refers to a strategy that gets together a combination of ICT tools, processes and services, e.g. automated call centre, customer data warehouses and data mining, customised content, targeted banner advertising and targeted e-mail delivery. Stone's findings also revealed that people, customer management and detailed measurement are the most critical elements for successful CRM, while ICT was found to act as an enabler only when the previous elements were in place. Loftness highlighted the development of measurement processes and organizational culture around of customer satisfaction. Tiwana's comprehensive process for implementing knowledge based CRM strategies also stresses the complementary role of ICT, while also integrating many of the previous identified key elements of CRM implementation. Overall, Tiwana's CRM model debates the co-ordinated management and alignment of: strategic and operational (e)-business, ICT, leadership, change, cultural and measurement strategies.

An Integrated Model for CRM Implementation

Although a huge debate has been initiated regarding the identification and the importance of different elements of CRM, there is still no agreed framework as to how CRM can be best applied and adopted within organizations. However, previous debates have clearly identified the major issues for implementing CRM, which coupled with more arguments as identified in the following literature review, lead to the development of an integrated model for CRM implementation. The proposed model has both a strategic and operational value, as: a) it identifies the major managerial areas whereby strategy development and/or organizational change are required; and b) it depicts the tactical actions that the development of a strategy in each managerial area might entail.

Knowledge Management

The success of relationship marketing heavily depends on the collection and analysis of customer information for developing highly-personalised offerings. Buttle pointed out that marketing problems are by nature information handling problems. However, information should not be confused with knowledge. Knowledge is produced when information is analysed and used to enable and leverage strategic actions. Sigala argued that this confusion has led several businesses to make huge investments on ICT projects which have yielded marginal results. To overcome the ICT productivity paradox, hotel management needs to embed ICT generated information into decision-making processes. The latter involves three broad phases that run in parallel: acquisition; sharing; utilisation. Development and creation of insights, skills, and relationships (knowledge acquisition), when disseminated and shared (knowledge sharing) are followed by integration of learning, insights and experiential knowledge and bringing it to bear upon current decisions (knowledge utilisation).

Davenport and Prusak identified the critical success factors for knowledge management: ICT and organizational infrastructure; knowledge friendly culture; change in motivational practices for encouraging and rewarding staff when information is collected, shared and used; knowledge management culture; and open organizational structure. Malhotra stressed the link between ICT and knowledge management: *"...ICT embodies organizational processes that seek synergistic combination of data and information processing capacity of information technologies, and the creative and innovative capacity of human beings"*. Several other authors have also highlighted the importance of a customer knowledge management strategy and the crucial leadership role that visionary knowledge officers should play for bringing together all CRM stakeholders to share a common platform of beliefs, expectations and commitment. Tiwana also stressed that a knowledge based CRM strategy requires the development of boundary spanning communities of practice whose members are empowered and inspired by a culture of trust that in turn fosters cross-functional collaboration, sharing of expertise and creation of new knowledge. Indeed, building trust and driving out fear of knowledge management are crucial issues, as it means that an employee is confident that taking risks based on new information, customer insights and knowledge will be rewarded, not penalised. This is because cultures that do not drive out fear have two side effects: they force employees to focus on short term at the cost of long-term performance; they encourage employees to focus on the individual rather than the collective organization.

However, Dev and Olsen reported that although hotels capture considerable amount of customer data, those data are rarely assembled to create useful knowledge about customers. Cline and Warner also found that the collection and use of customer information are frequently intermittent, delayed and fragmented. Lack of ICT applications integration and legacy systems designed along functional lines that create fragmented guests' profile have been reported as the major reason of duplication, inconsistencies, incompleteness and inaccuracies of customer data in hotels. Thus, knowledge based CRM requires:

- a hotel culture whereby every customer interaction is perceived as a learning experience and each customer contact as a knowledge-building opportunity and a chance to collect new information about hotels' guest;
- incentives and rewards to staff's efforts to capture, use and share knowledge for personalising customer interactions/experiences;
- redesign of customer data across the organization and customer-centric ICT integration and infrastructure;
- understanding of guests' value drivers and requirements as well as of the ways in which hotels contribute or fail to create customer value.

Relationship Marketing (Internal and External)

Within this new paradigm, interacting with customers and satisfying customer needs are vital important. Relationships with the customers are not built and sustained with direct (e)-mail themselves but rather the types of programmes that are available for which e-mail may be a delivery mechanism. Winer argued that a comprehensive CRM is a collection of integrated components such as customer service, frequency, loyalty and reward programmes, customisation and community building. The aim of these integrated customer communication channels is to support the customer cycle by identifying profitable customers, differentiating the services/ products offered to different markets of ones, interact with individual customers in a integrated way across channels and customise/personalise customers' experiences.

CRM also largely depends on staff attitudes, commitment and performance and so, success on the external marketplace requires initial success internally in motivating and getting employees' commitment. Apart from developing the four Ps of the marketing mix, a host of other resources and activities are also needed. Although most of the people involved in such activities are not part of the marketing department, their attitudes towards customers and their ways of executing their tasks are imperative. According to Gummesson , these employees must be trained to become part-time marketers.

While the idea of maximising transactions is nothing new, what is different is that this style of guest interaction will demand substantial conceptual skills from every employee. Because it might be impossible to create ideal guest experiences solely through expert systems, organizations might have to create intelligent-response teams comprising of employees with broad knowledge bases that cut across traditional organizations functions. For dealing with guests' experience-related desires, employees will be required to have advanced social skills such as understanding of role conflict, role theory, communications and personality identification. Employees will need to be content experts who do not only know how to work with and exploit technology, but also can manage the information exchange and match guests to experiences. Moreover, as such knowledge-based work may take place electronically, staff should be able and know how to work collaborative and electronically irrespective of their spatial, time and cultural differences.

ICT Management

Data warehouses and data mining are the most popular and highly needed systems for providing CRM capabilities or else for defining, developing and managing "the segment of one". This is because they are necessary and valuable tools for trying to determine customer demographics, buying patterns, market segments, contribution margins, customer lifetime etc., as they help to wade through volumes of information and decipher meaning, patterns and relationships from many seemingly unrelated bits of data. ICT is also instrumental for gathering and storing customer data, providing ways for one-to-one interactions, e.g. website, call centre, kiosks etc, as well as identifying ways for disseminating and accessing information across the organization. However, to achieve the latter, a new ICT infrastructure is required that would enable the creation of consolidated customer databases and overcome limitations created by functional "field-doms".

The supporting role of ICT for fostering business process reengineering and restructuring processes around the customer is widely argued and does not stop at the organizational boundaries. The alignment of ICT and organizational infrastructure is critical so that the numerous systems at the customer touch points do not become "islands" of useless information. Within the hotel sector, Sigala et al. argued the need to integrate yield management, customer databases, corporate and distribution systems for implementing yield management on a one-to-one, distribution channel or hotel location basis. Wells et al. described how electronic networks allow the distribution and share of guest databases across Ritz-Carlton hotel properties allowing staff to accommodate and treat individual customers based on preferences from previous visits.

REFERENCES

Dahl, Crete M. *Housekeeping management & organization for hotels & institutions.* Stamford, Conn.: The Dahls, 1945.

Eckert, Fred William and Howard L. Dayton. *The hotel lease; a study of the business elements and principles involved in making leases that are equitable to both lessee and lessor.* Chicago: Hotel Monthly Press, 1947.

Gill, Winifred Ethel. *Business affairs for institutional management.* London: Evan.

Hamilton, W. I. *Promoting new hotels: when does it pay?* New York: Harper, 1930.

Heldenbrand, Howard Van Woert. *Front office psychology.* Chicago: The Hotel monthly press, 1930.

Salmen, John PS, *Accommodating All Guests: The Americans with Disabilities Act and the Lodging Industry,* Washington, DC: The American Hotel & Motel Association, 1992.

6

Importance of Effective Communication in Hotel Operations

Communication is a very vital element in the operations of any accommodation establishment. Without communication, operations will suffer resulting to disastrous experience for the hotel guests and ultimately, the loss of future room sales due to bad hotel ratings. If there is communication between housekeeping department and front office department, the front office staff will not accidentally assign guests to dirty rooms. With communication between the front office and the sales department, the sales team will not keep on accepting group room reservations related to conferences and seminars that could result to overbooking wherein the hotel exceeds its capacity to accept guests. When communication is constant between the finance department and the front office, room sales will be recorded properly and account receivables will be collected on time. Constant communication among hotel departments is a must for successful business operations.

Importance of Good Communication

No one has yet found a theory or method or set of communications principles guaranteed to be 100-percent effective. Experts know a lot about why people fail in communicating, and they can explain the ingredients for success, but there is no formula that will work everywhere, every time, for everybody. Nevertheless, understanding how communication takes place, why it fails, and what can be done to improve it will increase enormously the chances for success.As a manager in a hospitality enterprise, you will be communicating constantly. You will be both a sender and a receiver of messages, and both roles will be very important. You must understand what comes down to you from the top so that you can carry out your supervisor's instructions and the policies of the company. You must communicate clearly with other supervisors to coordinate your work with theirs. You must communicate effectively with customers. Most important of all, you must communicate successfully with the people you supervise so you will have the power to get things done. You cannot manage effectively if you cannot communicate effectively.

Communications is the general term that sums up the sending and receiving of messages. The way employees communicate can make or break a company. Think of the difference between courteous and surly employees and the messages they convey to guests. We want to do business with people who can communicate the company philosophy to guests and give outstanding service. This all takes communication, which is the lifeblood of companies. It is critical that the front-line associates know the company mission and goals and how they are going to meet them. This information is a formal communication and is given in via meetings, personal correspondence, e-mail, notice boards, and so on. Supervisors are vitally important as they are the ones who explain the mission, goals, and company policy to their associates.

A communication may be a word-of-mouth message such as a verbal instruction given on the job or an announcement at a meeting. Or it may be a written communication: a letter, a memo, a production sheet, a housekeeper's report, or a recipe. A message may go from one person to another, as when the sous chef tells the soup cook what soups to prepare for lunch; when the housekeeper tells a maid what rooms she is to make up; or when one person says to another, "It's nice to have you back, we missed you." This is known as interpersonal communication. A message may go down the corporate ladder from the president of the company to the general manager to the food and beverage director to the executive chef to the sous chef to the station cooks to the cooks' helpers. Such a message is likely to be a policy directive or some other matter affecting the organization as a whole. This is an example of organizational communication.

This type of message is likely to be reworded at each level, and there is little chance that much of the original meaning will survive the journey.

One study of 100 companies showed that workers at the bottom of a five-rung ladder typically received only 20 percent of the information coming down from the top. The chances of messages going up the ladder from workers to top management are even less likely, unless it is bad news. When messages move freely back and forth from one person to another, or up the ladder as well as down, we say that we have good two-way communication or open communication. Such communication contributes to a positive work climate and high productivity.

In addition to interpersonal communication and organizational communication, there are other forms of communication that a supervisor may be involved in.

1. Interviewing is often defined as a conversation with a purpose. Supervisors use interviewing skills not only to screen job applicants but also to get needed information from workers and their own supervisors.
2. In small-group communication, three or more group members communicate in order to influence one another. Meetings are examples of small-group communication.
3. Mass communication refers to messages sent out to many people through newspapers, magazines, books, radio, television, and other media. Hospitality organizations often use mass communication to advertise for customers as well as job applicants. A restaurant newsletter is another example.

Although each context is different, they all have in common the process of creating a meaning between two or more people.

Obstacles to Good Communication

How the communicators affect the message

Both sender and receiver can obscure or distort messages without being aware of it. Differences in background, education, past experience, and intelligence can often cause communication difficulties. Big words, long sentences, and formal delivery may not get through to all people. Today's slang may not reach someone older than you. Kitchen jargon may not be intelligible to a new employee. As a sender of messages, you need to adjust to such differences. You must be aware of where you are and where the other person is so that you can make your messages understandable to that person.

People also differ in attitudes, opinions, and values, and these differences can inhibit communication or garble messages. You may like to swear and tell off-color jokes as an informal and comfortable way of communicating, but some of your people may find such speech obscure, offensive, and shocking and may therefore miss your message entirely. Something that is important to you may mean nothing to your workers if it does not affect them. You care a lot about food costs and waste, but you have trouble getting that message through to your kitchen staff because they don't care-it's not their money going into the garbage can.

Prejudices can distort communication; this includes not only the obvious and, unfortunately, frequent biases, like those against women or ethnic groups but some intangible thing from your past that makes you sure that all men with beards or all tall women who wear thick glasses are not to be trusted. Prejudice can turn up in the words you choose in communicating or in your tone of voice, or it can make you leave something out of the message or forget to send it at all. If you let prejudice creep into something you say, it is likely to stir up anger and cause the message to be misinterpreted or rejected.

Sender and receiver may have different perceptions about the subject of a communication. Nobody can perceive reality directly; it is conveyed to us through our five senses, and its meaning is filtered through our minds and our emotions. Since we are all different, we do not always agree on what reality is. We do not see and hear things the same way. We do not agree on big and small, mild and hot, loud and soft, sooner and later. How many is several? How much is a lot? What does "season to taste" mean?

Everyone perceives things selectively and subjectively. If you are trying to calm down a couple of people who are having a fight, you will get two entirely different versions of the incident, because each perceives and experiences it in his or her own way. They are not lying; they are telling you the truth as they see it. As you give your people instructions and information, they all see and hear you subjectively, and they all tend to magnify what is pleasing to them in what you are saying and to play down what they do not want to hear or know about.

Many times your message will be exaggerated out of all proportion to the point where you would not recognise what you said if they repeated it back to you. Often, the sender and receiver of an instruction do not have the same perception of its importance. The supervisor may say, "Will you get this done for me?" and the worker may reply, "Yes, I will," and the supervisor may mean by noon today, whereas the worker is thinking in terms of the day after tomorrow or next week. They are focusing differently; each perceives things according to his or her own needs of the moment.

Assumptions and expectations distort communications. We assume that our listeners know what we are talking about, but sometimes they don't, and the entire message goes over their heads. We assume that our message has been received and we are angry with people when they don't do what we tell them to do. One supervisor told a cook, "Cook the chicken." What he meant was to cook the usual number of portions for a Thursday night dinner, and he assumed the cook would prepare about 20 pounds of chicken. In the cook's mind the message registered, "Cook all the chicken that was delivered today."When we make assumptions, we often jump to conclusions. If you see a bellperson sitting with his or her feet propped on a table and eyes closed, you assume that the bellperson is goofing off. If you see the director of marketing in the same pose, you assume that he or she is thinking. Your conclusions may be wrong; you do not know in either case what is really going on.

Often, we think we know what people are going to say, so that is what we hear, even when someone says something entirely different. Sometimes we even finish their sentences for them. Often in listening we extend the speaker's meaning far beyond what was said, and we answer inappropriately, as when the customer says, "My steak is tough," and you say, "I'll get you another one," and what the customer really wants is your attention to his or her feelings.

We make many assumptions about how people think and feel, what interests them, and what they value. If you assume that all people are lazy, are interested only in their paychecks, and have to be ordered around to get any work out of them (Theory X), you have probably closed the door to all meaningful communication and you will never find out what they are truly capable of.

One of the biggest troublemakers in communicating is the emotions of the people who are sending and receiving the messages. If you say something in anger, it is the anger that comes across, not the message, no matter what words you use. It always triggers emotions in the receiver: anger, hate, and fear. The message is buried under the emotions, and the emotions become the message. The receiver is likely to hear things that were not said, and the sender is likely to say things that were not intended. Communication becomes hopelessly snarled.

Sometimes underlying emotions color all communications between the supervisor and the people supervised. If there is contempt and suspicion on the part of the supervisor, there will be hatred, anger, and fear among the workers. The communi-cations climate is thoroughly polluted, and messages are taken in the wrong way, or are rearranged according to suspected hidden motives, or are totally rejected. The only healthy climate for communication is an atmosphere of trust. If your people do not trust you, they will not be receptive to anything you have to say. Only if they trust you will they receive your messages willingly, understand them correctly, carry out your instructions, and feel free to send you messages of their own.

The verbal skills of the sender will have a lot to do with the clarity of messages sent. Some people have the knack of saying things clearly and simply; others leave things out, or choose the wrong words, or tangle up the thought in long, strung-out sentences. Sometimes they mumble or speak too softly, or they write illegibly, and the receiver is not interested enough to ask the sender to translate or is afraid to ask. On the receiving end, accurate reception depends in part on the listening or reading skills or sometimes even the hearing ability of the receiver. People who cannot read or hear and people who do not listen are not going to get the message.

Symbols obscure the meaning

Since we can't transmit messages directly by telepathy, we use various symbols to express our meaning. Usually, the symbols are words, either spoken or written. Sometimes we use abbreviations (symbols of symbols). Sometimes we use pictures: diagrams showing how to operate equipment, posters dramatising safety messages, movies or filmstrips demonstrating techniques or procedures. Graffiti in appropriate places are often used to send anonymous messages of anger or contempt.

Many words have several meanings. The 500 most often used words in English have an average of 28 different meanings apiece; the word round has 73 meanings. Many words and the abbreviations are unfamiliar to inexperienced workers. Many words and phrases are vague (they, that stuff, things, the other part, and so on). Many words mean different things to people from different backgrounds. Slang expressions from yesterday may mean nothing to the teenager of today. You have to choose words that will carry your meaning to the people you want the message to reach.

If you have workers who do not speak English, you will have to speak in their language or use sign language, gestures, or pictures. Such situations require the sender of the message to watch carefully for signs of the receiver's comprehension. Actually, this is a good idea in all oral communication. Written words have the advantage that you can read them over to see if they express your meaning clearly. On the other hand, you have no feedback from the receiver unless you ask for a reply.

People also communicate without using words; this is generally referred to as nonverbal communication. They can deliberately use signs, gestures, and body language to convey specific meanings. Nodding one's head indicates, "I agree with you" or "I hear you." A smile says "I want to be friendly" and invites a return smile. Amorous glances extend invitations. Shaking one's fist means, "I'm dead serious and don't you dare provoke me any further." A listener pays as much, if not more, attention to nonverbal as to verbal communication.

People also convey feelings and attitudes unconsciously, through facial expression, tone of voice, intonation, gestures, and body language. Receivers often perceive them almost intuitively rather than consciously and respond with feelings and attitudes of their own. Sometimes nonverbal messages run counter to the sender's words, and a mixed message is sent out. A speaker may tell new employees the company has their welfare at heart while frowning and shaking a fist at them about the rules they must follow. Usually, the action speaks louder than words in mixed message, especially if the nonverbal message is a negative one. The receiver responds to the attitude or the emotion expressed nonverbally rather than to the spoken words.

Problems in sending the message

The simple mechanics of sending a message can often stop it in its tracks. If you send it at the wrong time, to the wrong people, by the wrong means, it may never reach its destination. Timing is important. For a message to get through, you have to consider the receiver's situation. The wrong time may be too soon or too late or a time when the receiver cannot receive it or cannot do anything in response to it. If you send it too soon, it may not sink in or it may be forgotten. If you send it too late, there is no time for action.

The sales manager, for example, must be able to tell the chef and beverage manager about the convention in time for them to order the food and liquor and hire the extra help and alert the station cooks. Some people are more receptive at certain times of day. Their body clocks run fast in the morning and slow at night or the other way around. Give an early bird messages in the morning and a night person messages at night.

Sometimes the message is not received because you do not have the receiver's attention. There is no point in telling people anything when they are right in the middle of something else. A switchboard operator is not going to hear his boss tell him to postpone his lunch hour when he is handling 17 calls at once. A bartender is not going to remember what her boss said right after she dropped a jug of wine on her big toe and broke both the toe and the bottle.

To get a message through, you need to send it to the right person. Give it to the person directly; do not ask someone else to relay it. The "right person" always means everyone concerned. Leaving someone out can fail in two ways: He or she does not get the message and therefore does not carry out the instruction, and he or she then feels left out, put down, unimportant, neglected. Don't let yourself be embarrassed by an employee saying "No one told me."

To get a message through, you must choose the right means of sending it.

— If you announce it in a meeting, a few people will hear it correctly. Some people will hear it but will not understand it. Some people will hear you say something you did not say. Some people will not hear it at all.

— If you send the message in a memo, a few people will read it correctly, some will not understand it, some will misread it, some will read it two weeks later, some will not read it at all, and some will not even get the memo.

— If you post it on the bulletin board, no one will read it. Some people won't even know that you have a bulletin board.

— If you tell people individually, you may get your message through to most people.

But some of them will be angry because they were the last to know. You can't win. Your best shot is to tell each person individually, one to one, which is how most communication takes place at this level in this industry. Most hospitality and foodservice people are better at seeing and hearing than they are at reading, and individual contact reinforces the impact of the message.

Sometimes, messages are never sent at all. Sometimes, supervisors assume that communication is not needed. They assume that people know things: If they bused tables in another restaurant, they don't need to be told how to do it in my restaurant. They don't need to be told how to put paper napkins in napkin dispensers-even a 5-year-old can do that-but on the other hand, it is their fault when customers can't get the napkins out.

There are other reasons why messages do not get sent. Sometimes the sender simply forgets to send the message. Sometimes he or she is unwilling, unable, or afraid to send the message because of the way the receiver might react. Supervisors who are uneasy in their relationships with their people may avoid telling them things they know people will not like, even though the people need to know. This does no one any good. A supervisor may be unwilling to send a message when he doesn't want people to know as much as he does.

In other words, he feels threatened. At other times, a supervisor may not send a message because he isn't really sure of the message himself. Sometimes, people do not communicate with the boss because they are unable, unwilling, or afraid or because they think the boss will not pay any attention. This also does no one any good.

Problems in receving the meaning

When the receiver hears or reads a message, there may still be problems in understanding or accepting it. The meaning may be obscured by the way it is phrased or by something left out, assumptions, and so on. Sometimes the wrong message comes through; sometimes it is meaningless; sometimes nothing comes through at all.

Sometimes the receiver is preoccupied with something else or may not be interested enough to listen carefully. If you want people to listen actively and open themselves to receiving a message, there has to be something in it for them. It may be information necessary to doing their job, or it may relate to changes that affect them. It does not have to be pleasant; it just has to be important to them. If they think it does not affect them, they will not pay attention, or they will half listen and then forget.

Sometimes a message or the way it is delivered will trigger emotions that make it unacceptable, and people will either tune it out or will react negatively. If a supervisor talks down to them, or talks over their heads, or makes threatening or scornful remarks, or speaks in a condescending tone of voice, or tells them to do something they do not consider part of their job, they are not going to accept the message as it was intended. They will misinterpret the instructions inadvertently or on purpose, or they may find other ways to withhold good performance sometimes out of hostility, sometimes out of inertia. If people do not like the way they are being treated, it is quite literally hard for them to do a good job.

Removing Obstacles to Communication

To summarise, let's list the many ways of removing obstacles to communication that have been mentioned in this section.

1. Build a climate of trust and respect in which communication is encouraged and messages are communicated with respect. Communicate to employees the way you would like them to communicate to you.
2. Send your messages clearly and explicitly, use language the receiver can understand, don't assume that the receiver knows anything, and take into account the receiver's ability to hear, read, and listen.
3. Send your message at the best time, and make sure that you have the receiver's attention.
4. Send your message to the right person(s): in other words, to everyone concerned.
5. Choose the best means of sending your message.
6. Check that your message has been understood, accepted, and acted upon.
7. Listen, listen, listen. This is discussed in detail next.
8. Be as objective as possible when communicating. Don't let any of your own stereotypes or prejudices shape what you say or how you send your message.
9. Avoid using slang names such as “Honey,” “Babe,” “Sweetheart,” 'Dear, “Guy,” “Fella.” They are disrespectful and annoying. Also, don't tell jokes that poke fun at anybody.
10. Never communicate with someone when you are angry. Cool off first.

TYPES OF ORGANIZATIONAL COMMUNICATION

Communication is the flow of messages from communicator to receiver. In a very tall network and flat network information flows in different directions. The organization is concerned with the flow of communication. As such it may flow by words; letters, symbols or messages. The positions in the organization structure must often interact, interface, as a process of exchange of facts, ideas, opinions etc. As such messages move vertically, upward, downward, horizontally, reciprocally. They may move through formal or informal channel of communication. Thus the total communication set-up may broadly be classified as follows:

1. According to Organizational Structure and Function
   (a) Formal Communication.
   (b) Informal Communication.
2. According to Direction of flow
   (a) Downward Communication
   (b) Upward Communication
   (c) Horizontal Communication or Lateral Communication or Cross-Wise
3. According to Way of Expression
   (a) Oral or Verbal communication
   (b) Written Communication or Black and White communication.

Formal Communication

An official communication having official backing and sanction. A precise communication channel following a fixed pattern rather than occurring without control. Under formal system of communication the message flows according to a fixed and prescribed way.

Communication is both oral and written, but mostly black and white. They originate from the formal organizational structure. They are related to the position in the organization. As such they are linked to all sorts of formalities, rules, procedures etc, Opposed to grape wine or informal communication. When information is transmitted by virtue of one's status, placement in the organization it is termed as formal communication. It flows through officially prescribed route.

The routes are located officially recognised position. For instance, when an executive instructs his subordinate by virtue of his superior position to do a particular work it is a formal communication. Formal channel of communication recognises superior and subordinate positions and relationships. In a way it is a two-way communication. It directs in a prescribed manner the employees to understand what the management intend to do.

The written formal communication is generally expressed in organizational manuals, handbooks, bulletins, annual reports, handouts etc. With these media management deliberately seeks to control the flow of communication in the organization. The objective of formal communication is to make it circulate properly and in an orderly way towards organization efficiency.

In all official communications we come across the words through proper channel. It means communication transmitted according to position in the organizational structure. It may be-single for multiple channels. In a single channel there is only one party of communication. The structure determines official relations and locations of officially recognised positions. It also determines the roles and rules, which are made and applied accordingly which results in formal flow of information.

Causes for Formulating Formal Rules

Rules are framed and enforced, in formal system. There are a number of causes for formulating formal rules and formal channels of communication. According to Myers and Myers formal rules and systems of communications exist in an organization at least for the following reasons:

1. To control and measure outputs and to articulate the rules them selves.
2. To coordinate complex activities in the system and relate the subsystems to each other and to the organization.
3. To regulate responses to other systems outside to the environment, and to competing systems so a high level of predictable behaviour may be maintained and consistency encouraged.
4. To coordinate resource allocation of people money and things.
5. To create a climate within which the organization can adjust its outputs as it receives and process. Feedback.

In an organization where there are large number of individuals the more difficult is the communication. So management frames communication rules and message transmitting ways. The rules will be mote when there are more groups and activities carrying repetitive and non-repetitive activities. Sometimes formal rules would be more rigid for effective communication. There would be many rules of communication if there were heavy inter-dependence, inter -relationship between individuals groups and between groups sub-groups and groups. To facilitate easy communication to be smooth and orderly, the management prepares communication policy manuals, procedures, rules and regulations for their implementation.

Advantages of Formal Communication

1. *Correct Information*: There is no place in formal communication to spread incorrect information as well as rumours. The dangers, which arise on account of incorrect information, would not take place in formal communication. By definition formal indicates sustentative evidence or facts. It may not be damaging when circulated and acted upon it.
2. *Official Banking*: The formal communication is always an official communication having official support and sanction. This method may not lead to distracted information because there is official sanction and may not even turn into gossip and rumours.
3. *Existence of Authority*: Formal communication through channels and commands promotes respect by subordinates to their superiors. In other words it maintains authority of the line officers - subordinates. Under this system there is officially recognised and fixed positions associated with duties and responsibilities. The deliberately created communication rules help in exercising control over subordinates. The superiors can command subordinates to get the things done.
4. *Message Handling*: Through the management recognises and gives importance to the grapevine, it cannot handle the overload of work. Formal channel of communication is adequate for handling all categories of messages expediously with clear understanding. Formal communication can shoulder any communication load.
5. *Absence of Leader*: In formal communication there is no place to any one person as key person or communication leader to spread message like in grapevine. The characters of trustworthy or credibility or not

necessary to the communicator because every one has to follow fixed rules and procedures. There is no place for bias. That is the reason why formal communication is always orderly and systematic.

6. *Efficient Communication*: Prompt and accurate flow of information is the function of sound communication. this can be achieved under formal communication method. It is sound and proper method of channelising information. There is always direct contract between the parties and relationship is always formal and official.
7. *Support form Top*: There is always official support and backing for formal communication. Management endeavours that modified regulations are implemented and enforced. And hence formal messages would always succeed.
8. *Uniformity in Transmission*: In a formal communication each position transmits the message to another in the order of line. The process continues. There is no place for wrong interpretations, misunderstanding. Bias etc. It ensures uniformity or unity in the transmission of message and understanding.
9. *Organizational Efficiency*: Organizational efficiency is indispensable to accomplish organizational goals. The formal communication is inbuilt, inherent and is the part and parcel of organizational process. Management can take suitable steps and actions to achieve organizational efficiency.
10. *No Grapevine*: In a formal communication there is always only organizational relationship. Though information communication exists, formal communication endeavours to see that positive and constructive information is circulated for healthy growth of organization.
11. *Other Advantages*: Besides, the above merits of formal communication there are many advantages emerge from formal communication. It identifies that communication is a tool of management. Executives get things done through people with effective formal transmission of common desired goals etc.

Disadvantages of Formal Communication

Delay: The formal network of communication takes more time to pass information. Thus formal channel is not a spontaneous and flexible and hence it. Would take more time in transmitting information.

Internal Means Only: Formal Communication represents natural desire of the management in the organization to interact and communicate witJ1 each other. In this superior directs the sub9rdinates. So it is an effective written internal media of communication. And hence not suitable for external communication.

Information Overload: Information overload represents overload of work with heavy information. In a complex business organization there is always many series of messages and information to be tackled. It ultimately leads to work load on executive. Delay, or illusion, imperfection and half-execution of information are the evils of information overload.

Absence of Outside Interface: Interface with other sources of information about the organization external to the organization also usually taking place in the real world situation. In a formal communication there is no interface with the outside in any way. Formal communication is transmitted only by virtue of one's position in the organization structure. It is concerned between superior-subordinate relationships arising out of officially recognised positions.

Lack of Quick Response: Formal communication is known for delay to get response from information transmitted. Response as to acceptance or rejection from formal communication cannot be interacted immediately. Immediate response for either of above two reactions is necessary in the communicator in the process of decision-making. It is particularly true in case of formal written communication. The advantage of immediate response can be obtained from informal communication.

Downward Channel: Formal communication is mostly for downward communication and communication through chains of command is not suitable vertically upward. Executives overlook subordinates and may not take active interest in the matters of subordinates.

Lack of General Interest: The formal channel of communication is also not useful for transmitting certain information which in the general interest of the. organization is necessary. Official channels cannot effectively be used in certain important, urgent matter& but which can be satisfactorily transmitted through informal channel.

Absence of Feedback: Feedback is necessarily to, understand immediate: reaction which would help in a great way hi, the decision making process. The formal channel would not serve, as an effective feedback system. Similarly it cannot be used as a testing device. Listening to the feedback response is the good principle of effective communication.

No Public Relations: In modern complex business organization, Social responsibility of business to the society, and interdependence of society and industry, the importance of public relations, cannot be over emphasised. Format communication does not promote public relations. Interface with the outside organization is equally necessary to accomplish both social and organization goals. For this formal channel is not effective.

Informal Communication

Informal communication is also called as grapevine. This type of communication arises on account of Informal relationship between the persons. Informal communication grows up spontaneously from personal and group interest. In, such circumstances communication is said to be only informal. Informal communication is characterised and may be conveyed by a simple glance, nod, smile, gesture and even mere silence. Informal channel is the most effective one and transmits information with considerable speed. It can pass both correct information as well as rumours. It all. depends upon group leader and his honesty and, credibility and trustworthiness. Informal communication network is formed to transmit, messages quickly.

Small informal groups are formed based on work and social relationship. In this there is no formal organizational hierarchies of superior and subordinates. They are not formed based on positions and lines of authority. In this type of communication there are no formalities, procedures, rules etc.

It represents the absence of official backing and there is no authority and control. It is called grapevine because which denotes informal means of circulating information or gossip. Management can utilise this channel for, effective and speedy communication. Certain messages are not suitable to calculate by formal means.

Basically informal relationship arises out of personal friendship, relationship, same group and membership of the same club, hailing from same place, common studies and other social factors. It creates situation where small groups like workers and other groups communicate with each other hours together working side-by-side. The executives have to informally deal with subordinates personally to maintain relations to get the things done through. There are two activities known is programmed activities, and non-programmed activities.

Informal communication is a situation by which people carry on their non-programmed activities within the formal bounding, of the system. As such communications are very fast; spontaneous the -management it is a very active channel of communication. Management can beneficially utilise the communication leader turn, management may create its own grapevine composed of Communication leaders. L brown remarked that "In using the grapevine, management must be able to pinpoint the leaders, and work through them, must feed in factual information, listen to the feedback response, and be discerning in not over loading, the system and using it inappropriately.

It is important that management be sure to follow up grapevine messages with official written messages and statement that will verify the accuracy of data obtained from the grapevine. This also helps in building a mutual trust based on open communication followed throughout the organization or business. Informal communication takes place in the organization were people work closely together. It also occurs in cases where the work force interfaces with the outsiders from whom they get information about the organization.

Advantages of Informal Communication

1. *Morale Uniting Force*: Grapevine acts as a driving force to unite the work force in cases of common matters. The grapevine serves as a morale uniting force when there are high interest in new policies, innovations in procedures or personnel, and sufficient data about the organization without any value judgement.
2. *Save Time*: The informal communication helps to save time in circulating information. Grapevine is spontaneous and flexible; it would not take more time in circulating message.
3. *Speed*: Informal channel of communication operates with much greater speed. Grapevine is a spontaneous growth and can transmit information with considerate speed. Formal communication network sometimes is not suitable to send message quickly.
4. *Immediate Response*: Response from informal communication can be interacted immediately; immediate response from given information transmitted to the receiver is necessary to the management to take

decisions. The advantage of immediate response can be obtained from informal communication.

5. *Public Relations*: Public Relations is another wing of the management function. Informal relations are essential for effective public relations. Public relations fail because lack of informal relations and informal communications. Thus informal communication is the key to the successful public relations.
6. *Feedback*: Feedback is necessary in all group activities irrespective of the type of organization. The informal communication also helps as feedback system. So the management can use grapevine as a testing tool. In a feedback immediate response and reaction can be gained which is more useful in the process of decision-making. Listening to the feedback response is the good principle of communication.
7. *Creation of Ideas*: Informal communication generates ideas and offer appropriate suggestions that are proved more helpful. This advantage is not available in case of formal communication. in a formal set up interactions must take place according to prescribed rules, procedures line and authority.
8. *Tool of Management*: Informal communication is a tool of management. Because it influences the behaviour and attitudes of other. Communication is not just for communication but to make others to respond to decisions. It is only with relation with others to achieve a desired goal. It is because of this communication is considered as a valuable tool of management. It is the responsibility of management to create informal environment conducive for effective communication.
9. *Accurate Information*: Informal communication transmits fast & accurate information. The communication leader is in a position to know the correct data and when to pass, where to pass and what to pass the message. He knows confidential matters and factual information. The accurate information is fed into the grapevine to provide quick, easy access to message that needs to be known.
10. *Avoids Misunderstanding*: There can be no mutual understanding without an informal relation is the core of effective communication. There are few problems in real-life-situation that formal communication cannot resolve. It produces results. In relationships, informal communication produces harmony, resolves problems and dissolves feelings of separateness.

It indicates the pulses of the work force. The message circulated is closely and collectively interacted and understood. Informal communication may supplement formal communication, grapevines are nor static but dynamic and non-stable. Grapevine communication is less heavily loaded with task information-how to do the job than with information about people attitudes, relationships, interpretations, prediction, values, norms and needs. Leland Brown has given the following merits of grapevine. Advantages to management include expediency-it saves time, gets immediate response; provides useful feedback for decision-making; generates ideas and suggestions that may prove helpful; disseminates accurate, factual information that needs to be relayed.

Disadvantages of Informal Communication

The informal communication is not free from limitations or shortcomings. it has the following disadvantages too:

— *Rumours*: Informal communication sometimes spreads incorrect information as well as rumours. As such it create serious repercussions. So it is desirable to use grapevine with certain safeguards. It is really a basic drawback to the system. Koontz and Donnell rightly remarked that this channel is unreliable: "The dysfunctional nature of the grapevine is in fostering rumours spreading them. Because rumour, by definition, lacks substantive evidence or fact, it may be damaging when circulated and acted on. Usually full of prejudice emotion bias self-serving issues and partial truths, rumours arise in situations where (1) There is great ambiguity or uncertainty and (2) Issues of high interest to group members arise suddenly Rumour passers either support the rumour coll tent, add to it, or suggest a counter rumour."

— *Distorts*: Grapevine distorts information. It is without any official sanction. So it is dangerous to the organization. It may even lead to gossip and rumour.

— *Inadequate*: Though the management cannot ignore and eliminate the grapevine this channel is inadequate for handling all categories of messages expeditiously and with understanding. Informal communication cannot shoulder the entire communication load. Only certain matters can be fed into grapevine to circulate.

— *Communication Leaders*: The success of informal communication is greatly dependent on communication leader in each group who circulates information basically. As such the key persons or communication leaders most be trustworthy and have credibility. But great problem in the organization today stems from the lack of trust within the organization arid lack of effective in format communication.

— *No Authority*: The informal communication does not help in maintenance of authority of the line. It is based on free mix up with others and rely upon the informal relationship. There is no place for respect to the superiors by the subordinates. Thus in this way it does not help to exercise effective control over subordinates. Sometimes it may fail to enforce the responsibilities fixed and assigned to individuals in respect of tasks to be carried on by the individuals in the organization.

— *Improper Communication*: Prompt and accurate flow of information is the function of sound communication. Informal communication is unsound and improper method of channelising information. Sometimes in informal group it is evident, the absence of superiors mingling with subordinates. There is no direct contact and relationship in informal communication. In a format face-to-face communication understanding the attitudes, reactions, levels of intelligent and acceptance and rejection of message are possible.

— *No Overload of Work*: Message load is less fn informal communication. In a complex organization structure and complicated correspondence network there is always heavy load of work messages to be communicated. Many messages should be transmitted only through formal media of communication. As such informal channel is not suitable to cope up with the message load.

— *Overlooking Superiors*: Communication through informal channel leads to overlooking the superiors, sometimes overlook by line officers. Grapevine is also not suitable for upward direct communication.

— *Interpretation Changes*: In a grapevine the key person tells the message to each person in a particular group. The members of this group in turn relay the message to someone else in another group. The process continues. This results in wrong interpretations, change of meaning, ideas, and half-truth. Thus by keeping an issue thrown open in an informal group or groups leads to dilution of the actual information on any given issue.

— *Other Drawbacks*: A number of communication barriers like linguistic barriers, managerial barriers that act as hurdles on a successful operation of informal communication.

Downward Communication

Another type of communication is according to direction of flow. The direction of flow may be downward communication or upward communication. The communication is said to be downward when it flows from the, top to the bottom. In the levels of management from top to bottom means flow of communication from the superiors to subordinates. When information comes from higher level to a lower level in the organization structure it is termed as downward communication.

The information passes through written orders, reports, rules, instructions, manuals, policy directives, etc. Downward communication may be circulated either-by oral media or written media. Oral media include grapevine, interviews, public address system, conferences, meetings, mechanical devices like, telephone, face-to-face conversation, house journal, union activities etc. Written downward communication may take the form of handouts, folders, manuals, periodical reports, bulletins, posters, letters, memos, instructions, clarifications, orders, etc.

In this way downward communication, which is in the nature of directives, is the most common feature in all organizations. In downward communication management transmits information, the broad objectives of the organization and policies to be accomplished. Thus it flows from the topmost or upper most levels of management towards lowest level or to the operating level. The directive nature of information moves through the organization structure stage by stage.

The executives put the decisions in the channel for their downward movement at appropriate time. Not only time but other factors should also be taken into consideration before circulating information. It is up to the managers to decide when, what and where communication to be transmitted. It is more appropriate to quote Koontz and Donnell that, "Timing, scope and means are all involved in the flow of information downward in the decision process. Selecting the correct time and communicating a decision are the prerogatives of the manager.

Most decisions flow through the organization structure level by level In downward communication the written media is mostly followed and is in common use. By this management can effectively transmit objectives and goals to be accomplished and enforced for implementation. It has official support and backing from the topmost authority. Downward message is not meant for acceptance or ratification from lower levels. It is imposition for implementation. However, there is a scope for better inter action, improving, the quality of their response.

Objectives of Downward Communication

To achieve certain objectives downward communication is imposed. Thus there are five basic purposes for sending messages from superior to subordinate. According to Katz and Kahn the following are the five basic purposes:

— To provide specific task directives or instructions on how to do the job. To provide information which produces an understanding of the task and its relationship to other organizational tasks and therefore, gives a rationale or reasons for the job.

— To provide information about organizational policies, procedure, and practices.

— To provide feedback on performance to the subordinate.

— To provide philosophical information regarding the organizations mission or orientation towards goals of the organization.

Downward communication is needed:

— To get the things done.

— To prepare for changes.

— To discourage misinformation and suspicion.

— To let the people feel the pride of being relatively well informed.

Usually downward channel is used by the management for transmiting generally written communication by way or notices, orders, objectives, policies, instructions and through other media to the. employees at lower levels in the organization. There are five reasons why managers use downward communication which may be summarised as follows:

— Job instructions

— Job rationale

— Procedures and policies

— Feedback
— Indoctrination

Advantages

— Downward system helps to inform the objectives and policies to be achieved.
— Implementation process has official backing and support. Both verbal and written media can be adopted. But mostly written media are used in downward system.
— It facilitates to improve the quality of response.
— Communication through channel of command keeps everybody in the organization informed about the matter.
— It facilitates the subject to read and re-read and filling for future reference. .

Disadvantages

1. The basic disadvantage of downward communication is delay.
2. It is a time consuming process to circulate information downward.
3. Another disadvantage is that it provides no scope for feedback. Feedback is necessary for successful implementation of downward information. .
4. It is only one-way communication system. Two-way system facilitates correction of flaws in the process. Clarifications, explanation can be sought.
5. In a tall network of organizational structure downward communication must be flexible but in reality it is very rigid.
6. It overlooks superiors sometimes by sending information direct to the concerned subordinates to avoid delay. It creates communication gap.
7. Following the above disadvantage the flat network of executives in the organizational structure has no or less message load from upward.
8. The system will not consider viewpoints from bottom before information is circulated.

Precautions

The following factors on which precautions should be taken to develop available downward communication system:

- Need to keep certain types of information confidential The timing of a situation.
- amount of information to be sent.
- The relationship between sources and receivers; and
- The workers acceptance of the tasks and goals; which the message promotes.

Downward Channel

Downward channel is a formal communication route. The objectives, broad policies, guidelines arid other, directions necessarily have to flow downward. Both written and oral media are used to transmit messages to subordinates. Reports, manuals, procedures and other guidelines come from the top level to the lower level. However, the following are the various media generally used in downward communication.

- *Written Orders*: Superiors issue written orders asking them to do a particular work or assigning tasks to be performed. Orders are issued by persons in higher authority to lower level people. Directing of what somebody must do. It is a command or instruction.
- *Bulletin Boards*: Bulletin board is the most common medium in all types of organizations It is a notice board on which, are displaced subject matters or messages relating to all the people or section of the people or sometimes relating to an individual. Bulletin: Bulletin may be distinguished from bulletin board. Bulletin includes both verbal and written but generally not displaced on bulletin boards. Bulletin is an official verbal report of news. It is a statement of printed information sheet or newspaper.
- *Posters*: Poster is either handwritten or printed for sticking on a wall at prominent places. Many employees give attention to such posters but a poster is useful as a supplementary device. All the people may not see and do not take care to see and ignore them. But a poster serves as a round the dock reminder media. Poster has a quality to attract to catch the eyes but also concise in its message. It is a large notice or advertisement for sticking on a wall. People see posters advertising or modifying messages.
- *House Journal*: Most of the big companies publish house journals containing good deal of information. It if a direct medium and meets

the needs of both the company and its employees. It covers useful, meaningful information. Management endeavours to spread message though house journals. Information about the policies, products can be disseminated through this medium.

— *Letters*: A written medium to have direct mail contact with the other person. Matters of special interest or personal matters are sent by letters. For instance, letters of appointment, letters of suspension, letters of termination, punishment etc. It is directed personally to an individual. Messages of common interest may sometime be communicated by letters.

— *Pay Inserts*: Pay insert is also a form of direct contact. Letters are usually directed to the employee's home address. Whereas the use of pay envelope inserts at least ensures exposure to every employee.

— *Organizational Guides*: Organizations issue reference guides useful to all the employees. Guides cover the procedures forms pension plan, insurance plan, profit sharing, hospitalisation, welfare and educational facilities etc.

— *Booklets, Pamphlets, Handbooks etc*: These media are used by the management when new people are joining the organization. They are issued welcoming them. They are prepared sometimes specifically for training or orientation programme as an introduction about the organization. They are often prepared to facilitate understanding organizational set-up and acceptance.

— *Message Racks*: Information racks also supply a great deal of information. Racks contain paperback literature containing about company's management techniques, production process, financial results etc.

— *Public Address System*: Loudspeaker system is adapted by the management to disseminate certain matters relating to the organization which all the employees are expected to know. Gathering of employees of any kind can be informed mechanically to project human voice before a large number of employees for making announcements, sending greetings, emergency events to be communicated.

— *Grapevine*: It is informal means of communication. Though it is not a formal and official communication media but the management should not ignore the existence of grapevine for providing factual information to counter rumours. It is a powerful medium for sending message quickly:

— *Annual Reports*: The companies should prepare annual reports as a statutory requirement; they contain lot of information about the company, its policies, employees etc. Management disseminates information as a part being written for the benefit of the employees.

— *Union Publication*: Union publications contain the voice of union. They also include the voice of the management to persuade the employees. Union plays an important role in communicating certain matters to the company employees.

— *E lectric and Electronic Media*: Telecommunication services and electronic media are now emerging as important media of management. Visual media, audio visual media, other media like video, video asset's, disc recording, video tape etc., are most commonly used to flow communication downwards.

Other Media: In addition to the above media there are many other media that arc used everyday by the management or superiors in attempting to communicate downward with the subordinates. Other media include personal instructions, lectures, conferences, meetings, interviews, counselling, orders etc.

All media usually may not be useful and may not be adopted by all the organizations. Depending upon the need, requirement and purpose different managements may adopt different media. Middle level managers may need a quite different media to communicate with subordinates internally. They may adapt different media for external communication using external means like telephone, press, radio and television to inform the employees as well as the general public. The availability of multi media imposes responsibility en the part of management to select appropriate media with the combination of various useful media.

Upward Communication

It is opposed to downward communication. A communication is said to be upward when it moves from the bottom to the top. In the organizational structure from bottom to too means flow of communication from subordinates to superiors. Whenever information moves from lower level to higher level in the organization it is termed as upward communication.

The upward communication may be transmitted either by oral media or written media. Oral media consist of face-to-face conversation, informal communication, social groups, union channel of representation etc. Upward written communication may take the form of grapevine, complaints and suggestions, personal letters, explanations and clarifications reply to memos etc.

So in upward communication, which is in the nature of suggestive and advisory is the common feature in all organizations. Upward communication is adopted to submit reports suggestions, complaints and grievances. Though upward communication is common but in practice the top management less favours it. But still upward communication is a definite chain and formal.

But in modern business organization and complex organization behaviour upward communication is considered to be important to achieve organizational goals. It acts as a main source of motivation to employees and to get the things done through them easily. Upward flow also facilitates the management to know the acceptance or rejection and the extent to which accepted or rejected and acted upon. Similarly executives must in turn know the activities and progress achieved by their subordinates. This is possible only through upward communication. For example, a general manager asks his assistant manager to do a certain task. The general manager at the same time may be interested to know how effectively he has performed.

Upward communication has many advantages such as:

— It meets two-way communication.
— Feedback on information is possible.
— It acts as a check for individual achievements.
— Flat networks have sufficient message from bottom for onward communication upward.

Upward communication is needed:

— To create receptiveness of communication.
— To create a feeling of belongingness through participation.
— To evaluate communication.
— To demonstrate a concern for the ideas of each individual.

Upward communication has to do with what the organization members say:

— About themselves, their performance, and their problems.
— About others and their problems.
— About organizational practices and policies.
— About what needs to be done and haw to do it.
— Reluctance to Communicate Upward

Upward communication moves from bottom to top. Though channel is there, upward communication is not effective. But effective upward channel is necessary to achieve two-way process. Feedback is possible only when there is upward communication to know the response or me receiver. The measurement of effectiveness of communication is not possible without upward communication. Communication, however, does not simply mean always downward from superior to subordinates. It involves both transmission and reception.

So upward channel occupies a pivotal role in the process of communication. But in actual practice upward communication is not effective and successful. The main reason is that subordinates are reluctant to communicate upward. The managers generally do not wish to know reactions and responses from the subordinates. Subordinates have to take initiative in upward communication. Subordinates are reluctant to take initiative. There are several circumstances in which subordinate is reluctant to communicate upward or even manipulates what he tells his boss, as remarked by Harris. The following are the circumstances:

Reasons For Reluctance

The subordinate will be hesitant to send upward any messages that may result in negative, punitive actions toward the subordinate by his superiors. The subordinate feels his bass will not be happy about messages and will tend to suppress or slaw down. The subordinate will be tempted to distort or rearrange negative information about himself to reduce the probabilities of negative action toward himself. If a subordinate believes that disclosure of his feelings opinions, ordifficulties may lead a superior to block or hinder the attainment of a personal goal, he will conceal or distort it.

The subordinate who feels that his superior is autocratic, unsympathetic, and taskoriented will develop distrust for his superior that may cause him to withhold useful information. The more trust and confidence the subordinate has in his superior, an the other hand the more likely he will be to give the bass messages freely and openly. The subordinate who feels that his jab is of little importance and the information he possesses is probably non-vital will not be likely to communicate messages to his superior. There appears to be a direct relationship between one's feeling of importance and responsibility and one's willingness to communicate upward.

Subordinates keep their superiors better informed when the subordinates know what will be done with their work, when they share common references with their superiors and when the superior is easily available to the subordinate. The subordinate's perception of his boss's attitude toward him the amount of interest the boss has in him etc. And the open-mindedness of the boss will affect upward communication. If the superior regularly shows desire for messages from his subordinates, practices an open door policy, and provides feedback on information received upward communication will be enhanced.

Encouraging Upward Communication

Superiors should also know reactions and responses from the receiver on their message. The message of the sender is of his own initiative. At his end downward communication moves as a direction or command but upward communication is not like that. The supervisor should encourage upward communication for effective feedback. O. J. Harris suggested the foll owing six duties on supervisor to encourage upward communication.

1. The supervisor must make known his need for messages from his subordinates and his interest in hearing from them.
2. The supervisor should reward his subordinates for their upward communication efforts when this is possible.
3. The supervisor should cultivate a relationship of mutual understanding and. respect between himself and his subordinates. Through his own actions, he .can gain the trust and respect that will also encourage more open communication.
4. Superiors should emphasise to subordinates the positive uses made of their messages as well as the negative uses.
5. Supervisors can delegate authority and encourage subordinates to feel responsible for specific action performances. The importance of upward communication will normally be felt under these conditions.
6. If upward communication is still below desired levels, other steps may be necessary in order to gain needed information. Formal

questionnaires, reports and other information sources may be called for.

Media of Upward Communication

1. *Suggestions*: Suggestions by subordinates to superiors ensure two-way communication. The employees can offer suggestions to the executives or seniors on all matters relating to work for improvement or to rectify errors. Written or verbal media can be adopted to offer suggestions.
2. *Complaints*: In addition to suggestions, employees are also entitled to lodge complaints. An, efficient organization generally encourages all types of complaints. It is. a upward media to transmit messages relating to one's displease, dissatisfaction to someone, particularly to superiors or top management about the matter. Employee complaints of working conditions welfare conditions and general matters of the organization. Complaint-boxes may be established into which an employee can place a written complaint which' the management may receive and look into the matter.
3. *Grievance Procedure*: A common and best media of upward communication is grievance procedure. It is a window through which messages can be transmitted towards upward. The workers may present a list of their grievances to the directors or executives. Messages go upward on a number of causes like illness, quarrel, and dissatisfaction relating to working conditions and on matters of unfair, unjust or inequitable treatment.
4. *Counselling*: It is a verbal upward communication medium. It is a process of giving advice. Executives are expected to give advice on the problems faced by the subordinates. It is the responsibility of the superiors to take up counselling periodically. It ensures a two-way communication. In this employees have every liberty to express their opinions, facts, feelings etc. Sometimes counselling with subordinates may fail. Special staff counsellors may be provided to whom employees can have interaction to solve the problem.
5. *Opinion Survey*: Management sometimes may conduct opinion survey to solicit opinions or feelings on a particular matter. Questionnaires may be circulated among the respondents.
6. *Open door Policy*: The superiors must have open door attitude towards subordinates. The open door policy is highly commanded but it has a

number of limitations. The policy is workable only in small organization. The frontline superior may bypass. The management cannot get adequate clues to assess a superior's skill.

7. *Exit Interview*: A type of interview, which is basically a verbal communication. The interview is convened when an employee is leaving the organization. It is an opportunity to meet the employee leaving the organization to have interaction and faceto-face conversation to ascertain employee's opinions, feelings and views about the organization and knowing the reasons for leaving the organization. The interview also may sometime follow filling a questionnaire to solicit information on certain matters. At the time of leaving the organization he may not give true and full information.
8. *Grapevine*: The management cannot ignore the existence of informal communication: It will survive in spite of many limitations. Informal communication or grapevine is the best channel to transmit messages upward. Management has to listen to it always. Grapevine arises spontaneously out of social relationship and which is always flexible. Through this, management can know the opinions, attitudes, feelings and facts about the organization from the employees.
9. *Meetings*: Participatory communication system achieves two-way process and sending message upward. Meetings ensure employees to represent their viewpoints. Periodical meetings with the employees are the best way to achieve natural course of upward communication. It improves communication process.
10. *Union Activities*: Labour unions facilitate to ventilate the voice of the union to the management. The office bearers of the labour unions on behalf of the employees convey to management the feelings, attitudes and demands of employees.
11. *Participation in Management*: Subordinate's participation in managerial decision-making is yet another usual medium of upward communication. It facilitates interaction with superiors.
12. *Collective Bargaining*: Collective bargaining also represents a medium of communication, which promotes employer-employee relationship.

Horizontal and Lateral Communication

Under the third category of communication horizontal communication is one channel. It is known by other names like sideways communication, lateral communication or crosswise communication. A communication is said to be horizontal when it takes place between two subordinates of the same superior. It is mainly an informal and is reflected in meetings, conferences, seminars etc. It occurs between two or more persons who are subordinates of the same person.

Crosswise communication is between functional executives, among section officers of department working under one top superior, the meeting of general managers of various units of the company, communications between various territorial sales managers are the examples of crosswise communication. It takes place between two or more persons who are linked to each other by equal status or equality of relationship.

In a way crosswise communication creates some confusion and difficulty. Sometimes unity of command is affected. In a tall network there is gangplank or bridge. According to Fayol: "Gangplank" gives an opportunity to the equal ranks to communicate directly without resorting vertical or up and down the organization. This refers to informal system. The informal system is generally used when the formal network fails to provide the needed information. The horizontal or lateral communication encourages comparing inter-departmental activities, performance in the organization.

Myers and Myers state on lateral communication in the words that: when two subsystems choose to communicate horizontally, then, it is altogether possible that they will create a whole set, of new messages up both 'legs' of the 'high crotch' system just to tell their bosses what they communicate about. Care taking by superiors of the subsystem coalitions, we believe, may in some instances grid measurably to the message load in the total system. Oral media for crosswise communication may be grapevine, gossip, rumour, meeting, lecture, conference, committee, telephone and its various types, union activities, interviews, face-to-face conversation etc. The written media used in horizontal communication are memos, notes, reports, house organs, posters, bulletin boards, handouts, manuals, periodical reports, union publications etc.The objectives of this communication are:

1. To bring about task of coordination among peers.
2. To furnish emotional and social support to the individual on the principle that people in the same boat share the same problems

3. Crosswise relationships exist between personnel in one division and personnel of equal, lower, or superior status in other divisions.
4. All the enterprises not, only permit but also insist on voluntary crosswise or horizontal channels of communications at-all levels, to speed information and improve understanding.

Functions of Lateral or Horizontal Communication

The following are the important functions of lateral communication:

— Department coordination is possible by meetings between heads and departments. They can instruct their respective departments in the methods of working in concert. This way productivity increases.

— Problem solving is possible. Employees generally carry their problems to their superiors, who become overloaded with employees' problems. Lateral communication makes possible solving of problems without the intervention of executives. Employees also become more self reliant, through involvement in the problem solving process.

Lateral communication enables sharing of information among department. This contributes to making the departments effective. Intra-departmental and inter-departmental disputes can be settled without the intervention of the executives. The interaction among organization peers gives emotional and social support to the worker. But if there are no problems to he solved or if there is no need for coordination among departments, lateral communication may give rise to useless and ideal gossip and rumouring. Hence if communication forms are irrelevant they should not be employed as they arc destructive of organization. Lateral communication may serve as a substitute for upward and downward communication.

Verbal or Oral Communication

Oral communication is one of the earliest as well as widely practiced medium of communication. It is through oral words or words of mouth. Oral communication has advantage of speed, correct and complete interaction. The communicator and recipient are the parties. In oral communication, process is a face-to-face conversation. In oral or verbal communication mechanical devices can also be used like telecommunication network.

The media of oral communication are telephone, dictaphone, record, radio, meeting, conference, interview, public address system, grapevine etc. In a face-to-face conversation doubts, clarifications, explanations and questions can be asked and answered at once. Effective oral communication calls for certain principles for effective communication such as clarity, brevity, precision, conviction, logical sequence, good vocabulary, completeness, clear, concrete, correct, courteous; message etc.

Written Communication

In a written communication every message is in black and white. It is the best method when the communicator and the recipient are beyond oral communication media. This media ensure exchange of facts, ideas, opinions through a written instrument but which the individual or organization comes in touch with each other and share meaning and understanding with another. In this type of communication the words get in touch with others. The process involves sending message by written words.

Formal communication is usually in writing such as rules, orders, manuals, etc. There are several media of written communication. Such as letters, circulars, notes, explanations, memoranda, leaflets, handbills, reports, forms, questionnaires, handouts; union publications, catalogue, bulletins, magazines, newspapers, posters, brochures, office orders etc.

Diagonal Communication

Diagonal communication provides a line or route for conveying information in the organization among various levels. The communication route under this takes the line from one-department individuals to different levels. It goes across the organization. Diagonal, communication, travels from subordinate to superiors and between persons, a different levels. It takes place among department or employees or different levels hierarchy. The functional authorities usually use diagonal communication. It occurs not only among individuals, but it also, travels, among, departments. To be effective the diagonal communication it is not necessary that the individuals be on the same hierarchical level.

The word crosswise communication includes both horizontal and diagonal communication. This is what Koontz, Donnell and Weihrich suggest. According to them, the purpose of crosswise communication is to speed information flow, to improve understanding and to coordinate efforts for the accomplishment of common goals of the organization. So diagonal communication takes place among individuals or departments who are not on the same level of the hierarchy. Crosswise communication exists between personnel in one department, and individual of equal, lower or superior status in other departments.

This type of communication there is no need to make a message to follow a fixed route or the chain of command. Diagonal communication does not follow the officially designated organization structure, which fixes hierarchical, level. So it is across the chain of command. Diagonal communication may be verbal and written. Verbal communication has several media like telephone, conference, meeting, oral report, lunch and tea hour meeting etc. Written, media include newspaper, magazines bulletins, handouts, manuals and reports.

One-way Communication

Two types of communication way are available to the communicator. They are one-way communication and another is two-way communication. in this part it is proposed to discuss about the nature of one-way communication. In another name it is called as one-way traffic. One-way communication is associated with formal communication. The main characteristic feature of formal communication is one-way communication. It travels simply downward from superior to subordinates. One-way implies only transmission part of the communication. It does not recognise the message from the recipient's point of view.

In the early days of communication management, the concept of communication was considered merely to, the issuing of orders, memos, directions, instructions, circulars etc. At that time the practice was to give directions, or to tell the subordinates do a particular work. The executives, under one-way communication do not bother about the subordinates who received the message, whether they understood the message or not, their responses and reactions. In one sense in one-way communication there is no provision for feedback, interaction etc.

One-way communication routes are those established by the organizations; structure. Through proper channel, going. Through channels provide a simple example of what is meant by the expression one-way communication one way is meant to convey directives from superior to subordinates or from top to middle and from middle to operating level. In this manner one way communication emerged which implies giving side of information. As generally used it means giving of information by the management. It travels with message load of orders and instructions downward from the top management through middle level manager. The absence of upward movement of reports, ideas and comments from operating level to top management through intermediary level is the case of one-way communication. One-way communication provides superiors with a route for conveying information to their subordinates. The main purposes of one-way traffic are to give specific job instructions, to understand organization structure, inter-relationship; to provide procedures and policies etc. The written formal communication is generally expressed in organizational manuals, handbooks, reports etc. The formal rules and policies of communication exist in an organization to achieve some objects like to exercise effective control, coordinate activity and to regulate reactions.

Two-way Communication

Two-way communication implies two way traffic. The process of communication is not complete by transmitting downwards. In other words it does not mean simply downward movement from the superiors to subordinates. In the earlier days it was considered communication merely to issue orders, instructions etc. Effective Communication calls for both transmission and reception. It is not sufficient just to give orders or direct subordinates to do and not to reason why but to follow and to do it. Though message is transmitted and received by subordinate he may not understand it, he may not take decision and may react immediately. It is a case of failure of-communication because in such a case it cannot produce results. The superior when conveying any information should also know its responses, reactions, acceptance or rejection of the message.

It is here the importance of two-way communication emerges. A manager directs, informs, orders but should also initiate feedback. He must listen, answer, interpret, carry corrections, accept errors and introduce amendment etc. In this way, communication involves two-way traffic or process from manager to employees and from employees to manager. It is more appropriate to quote George Terry the sender must get through tile receiver if the communication is to be complete and satisfactory. It is great mistake on the part of superior or management to assume that the job of communication is just to transmit message. Thus it is not complete and effective communication. The tactical middle management and operative lower level should have an opportunity to participate in communication to question as to the rationale of issued directions and orders, offer suggestions, rectify errors, and defend causes for amendment and all this help in a greater way in the smooth functioning of the organization. In this way two-way communication is an important element in a communication process. Two-way traffic calls for both, transmission of subject matter and reception. It implies giving and receiving, reciprocal of information.

At it has been rightly remarked "As generally use two way communication meant giving and receiving of information by both manage meant and workers; passing information orders and instructions downward from the top management through the intermediate management to the workers and funnelling reports and ideas upward from lower organizational levels to higher levels. It includes communication, which originates at any intermediate level as well as worker or top management level because communication is indeed needed by all who work together.

The feedback on the behaviour of or behavioural effects of superior communication is extremely important. Two hierarchical level or sometimes three hierarchical levels are always interested to understand what is the effect of communication transaction. In this triangle system communication flows between the communicator and the recipient in a chain of command. Two-way communication permits subordinates to speak or express openly and freely.

The executives must see themselves for accurate upward movement of information; however, it can't be ruled out the possibilities of prevailing some supervisors who do not like to hear reports from downward, which are not favourable to them. On the contrary some subordinates do not disclose opinions - freely and frankly. Some tactful middle level managers invite accurate reporting both favourable as well as good information. In such a case the upward communication can become a reality and effective. But the successful managers should always remember that they should not get flustered and angry on receiving or hearing unfavourable reports or news. If they loose their temper and balance the subordinates will once again begin to screen their comments of unfavourable nature.

Impact of New Technologies in Communications

Technology and, in particular, information technology, has totally changed the way supervisors communicate in the hospitality industry. Today, vital information can be communicated to and by supervisors about the sales and record-keeping far more quickly than previously. Examples include: a chain of restaurants' daily sales and other relevant data may be automatically sent to the corporate office rather than being typed up, faxed, and then entered into the computer system; schedules can be updated with a few clicks of a mouse; and training programs are now available via CD-ROMs; policy and procedures manuals can be checked online instead of printing and distributing copies.

Networked computer systems link corporate and independent hospitality businesses to one another, the supply chain, and various information sources via the World Wide Web. For instance, if you wanted to find some new recipes its easy to surf the Web to find several to choose from for any dish.

E-mail is a quick and convenient way for supervisors and employees to share information and to communicate to one or several people. Some progressive companies use instant messaging (IM), which is interactive real-time communication that takes place among computer users who are logged onto the computer network at the same time. With IM, there is no waiting for someone to read the e-mail, but users must be logged on at the same time.

Voice-mail allows information to be digitally stored and retrieved later. Voice-mail is also very useful in the hospitality industry because much of a supervisor's time is spent away from their desks, and messages can be checked periodically and from other locations. However for fast-paced operations it is necessary to have immediate voice communications, which improve guest service and satisfaction. For example, when guests check out of a New York hotel and need a cab, they don't have to wait around outside in the winter cold. The front desk agent or the bellperson can speak into a microphone to ask the door person to hail a cab. Fax machines permit the transmission of text or graphics over telephone lines. The "sending" fax machine scans and digitises the document and the "receiving" machine reads the scanned information and reproduces it on paper.

Intranets are private, organization-wide networks, similar to web sites, to which only people in the organization have access. Intranets are being increasingly used in the hospitality industry especially now with wireless fidelity, more commonly known as Wi-Fi. Wi-Fis provide Internet connections through wireless frequencies that are run through routers, enabling wireless connectivity within a specific range of the routers. This allows associates to make and receive calls on the same wireless broadband network that the company uses for Internet access. Wi-Fis are good for making employees available no matter where they are on property. Resorts, amusement parks, conference centers, sports complexes, hospitals, and cruise ships all cover huge areas and yet with Wi-Fi, everyone is easily and almost instantaneously accessible. An extranet is the same as an intranet, except that it allows access to specific people outside the company, such as guests or suppliers.

Business Writing

As a supervisor you are involved in all types of writing: job descriptions, policies and procedures, memos to employees and managers, performance appraisals, disciplinary action notices. It is crucial for you to be able to express yourself effectively in these different types of written documents as well as write in a clear, organized manner. Let's first take a look at some common problems, or pitfalls, in business writing:

— Too long, too wordy
— Too vague
— Too much jargon, too many hard-to-understand words
— Poorly organized
— Purpose not clear
— Sloppy, misspelled words; incorrect grammar and punctuation
— Too negative
— Indirect, beats around the bush

You have surely read letters, memos, and policies with some, or even most, of these problems.

Following are 10 tips for better business writing:

1. Pay attention to who the reader will be and write from his or her perspective.
2. Organize your thoughts so that your writing is then better organized and better able to communicate.
3. Use simple words to communicate your message. Stay away from jargon, slang, and big words, as they only clutter up your message and the reader may not understand them.
4. Get to the point quickly. Use only as many words as you need to get your point across. Trim all unnecessary words. Be specific about what

you want to communicate. Avoid vague terms and expressions such as somewhat, sort of, rather.

5. Be positive and upbeat. Even when you have to give bad news, provide some good news.
6. Write as though you were talking. Be natural.
7. Write clearly. Proofread your writing for clarity.
8. Show how the reader will benefit from reading your written communication.
9. Keep the document as short as possible.
10. Always check your document for correct grammar, spelling, punctuation, and neatness.

Meetings

Mention the word meeting to a group of supervisors, and you might hear a few groans and comments such as "What a waste of time!" Meetings appear to have a bad reputation. Surveys help tell us why. Surveys show that meetings often have problems such as people getting off the subject, no goals or agenda is set, they last too long, people are not well prepared, and important issues are not resolved. Some things you can do to make meetings effective are as follows:

1. Be prepared for all meetings. If you are calling the meeting, plan out exactly what you want to accomplish, and formalise your list of topics to be covered in an agenda, a written statement of topics to be discussed.
2. Start on time, and first review the agenda.
3. Summarise at appropriate points and move on.
4. When the conversation goes off in a different direction, bring it back to the matter at hand.
5. Make sure that meeting minutes are kept and followed up.
6. Have some rules of order so that everyone has a fair chance of speaking.
7. Handle differences of opinions with respect.

Need of Excellent Hospitality Communication

Hospitality communication in the workplace is always an important issue which is constantly addressed by employers and staff alike. Excellent communication is a vital issue, because customers are paying not only for the product - the food, the room or the facilities - they are also paying for the service. And service is just as much about communication as it is about skill.

Hospitality communication covers two important areas: customer service, and 'behind the scenes' staff and management interaction. Good communication in both areas is essential for the high standards of operation everyone expects in the industry.

Hospitality Communication in the Customer Service Level

A client may have a bad day, or be in a bad mood, but a genuine smile from the receptionist and a warm welcome from all the staff might just change their outlook for the rest of that day and the days to come. The same applies for the waitperson at the restaurant, the housekeeping or maintenance staff, or any other employee that comes in contact with the guests. A caring, positive atmosphere makes the difference between just a place you pass through and a place your guests will remember.

Employees in the hospitality industry must remember that "service with a smile" is not just a logo - it's what clients expect. It requires a positive attitude 100% of the time, even if you are having a bad day or you are tired - the customer is paying for your smile, not your frown. It requires patience when dealing with customers from overseas who have a hard time making themselves understood in English. It requires 'putting up' with grumpy people or ones who's manners are not always impeccable - because, up to a certain point, 'the customer is always right'. These are situations that staff learn to deal with and they take pride in the professional manner in which they handle 'difficult customers'.

Other important aspect of hospitality communication with customers is providing clear and useful information when asked by customers. Restaurant staff should know the menu inside out, understand special dietary requirements, know about the source of the ingredients they are serving, etc. Reception staff at the hotel should be up-to-date not only with the facilities and services that the hotel offers, but also with all the other information travellers need: activities, transport, eating and entertainment, and opening hours of shops and agencies. It is part of the service, and guests appreciate well-informed and courteous staff - it can make a difference between "just another day" and a memorable day.

Hospitality Communication between Staff and Management

Employers should take the time to explain and train their employees to always maintain a warm, welcoming and professional environment in the workplace, not only where customers are concerned, but also among the staff themselves. An employer can do a lot to promote a positive atmosphere for the staff; a nice staff room with facilities for workers to relax during their breaks will let them know they are valued, that the boss cares about them. This small investment will pay off by having loyal staff who are willing to give a little extra because they feel it is appreciated. Good communication between management and staff will be passed down the line in the form of good communication between staff and guests. Making sure that staff has all the 'tools of their trade' to do their job to the highest standards is a two-way thing - employees have to communicate clearly and on time what they need, and management should listen and make sure they are well informed of all their staff's requirements and needs.

Smiling, happy staff is one of management's most important assets in the hospitality industry. Therefore, people who are looking at a career in this sector should know that the skills required include 'people skills' - understanding, patience, the ability to perform well as a team, and, above all, a positive disposition. Bad tempered people have no place in the hospitality industry - it's a place where people come to relax and enjoy themselves.

Role of Interdepartmental Communications

Role of the Front Office in Interdepartmental Communications

The front office plays a pivotal role in delivering hospitality to guests. It sets the stage for a pleasant or an unpleasant visit. Guests, often in an unfamiliar setting and anxious to proceed with their business or vacation plans, are eager to learn the who, what, when, where, and how of their new environment. These employees are believed to have their manager on the pulse of the organization and the community. Their responses to the guests' requests for information on public transportation, location of hotel facilities, special events in the community, and the like indicate how well the hotel has prepared the front office staff for this important role. Front office managers must take an active role in gathering information that will be of interest to guests. They must also be active in developing procedures for the front office to disburse this information. The relationships the front office manager develops with the other department directors and their employees are vital to gathering information for guests. Developing positive personal relationships is part of the communication process, but it cannot be relied on to ensure that accurate and current information has been relayed. How does the front office manager encourage effective interdepartmental communication (communication between departments)? This chapter provides some background for you as you begin your professional career. It is also important to note that intradepartmental communication (communication inside a department) is applicable to this discussion.

The front office is at the center of this diagram to illustrate the many interdepartmental lines of communication that exist. These lines are based on the direction each department has been given to provide hospitality in the form of clean rooms, properly operating equipment, safe environment, well-prepared food and beverages, efficient table service, professional organization and delivery of service for a scheduled function as well as accurate accounting of guest charges, and the like. These general objectives help department directors organize their operations and meet the overall goal of delivering professional hospitality. However, in reality, it requires constant effort to manage the details of employees, materials, procedures, and communication skills to produce acceptable products and services.

Front Office Interaction with Other Departments in the Hotel

The front office staff interacts with all departments of the hotel, including marketing and sales, housekeeping, food and beverage, banquet, controller, maintenance, security, and human resources. These departments view the front office as a communication liaison in providing guest services. Each of the departments has a unique communication link with the front office staff.

Marketing and Sales Department

The marketing and sales department relies on the front office to provide data on guest histories, details concerning each guest's visit. Some of the information gathered is based on zip code, frequency of visits, corporate affiliation, special needs, and reservations for sleeping rooms. It is also the front office's job to make a good .impression on the public, to relay messages, and to meet the requests of guests who are using the hotel for meetings, seminars, and banquets. The guest history is a valuable resource for marketing and sales, which use the guest registration information to target marketing campaigns, develop promotions, prepare mailing labels, and select appropriate advertising media. The front office staff must make every effort to keep this database current and accurate. The process of completing the booking of a special function (such as a wedding reception, convention, or seminar) depends on the availability of sleeping rooms for guests. The marketing and sales executives may have to check the lists of available rooms three, six, or even twelve months in the future to be sure the hotel can accommodate the expected number of guests. A database of available rooms is maintained in the property management system by the front office. A guest contact with the marketing and sales department is usually through the hotel's switchboard. A competent switchboard operator who is friendly and knowledgeable about hotel operations and personnel will make a good impression, conveying to the prospective client that this hotel is competent. When the guest finally arrives for the function and contact with the hotel is usually through the front office staff. The front office manager who makes the effort to determine which banquet supervisor is in charge and communicates that information to the desk clerk on duty demonstrates to the public that this hotel is dedicated to providing hospitality.

Effective Interdepartmental Communications

Messages for the marketing and sales department must be relayed completely, accurately, and quickly. The switchboard operator is a vital link in the communication between the prospective client and a salesperson in the marketing and sales department. The front of.ce manager should instruct all new personnel in the front office about the staff in the marketing and sales department and what each person's job entails. Front office employees should know how to pronounce the names of all marketing and sales employees. To help front office staff become familiar with all these people, managers should show new employees pictures of the department directors and supervisors. Requests for service at meetings, seminars, banquets, and the like are often made at the front office. The banquet manager, a person who is responsible for full filling the details of service for a banquet or special event, or sales associate, a person who books the guest's requirements for banquets and other special events, might be busy with another function.

If a guest needs an extension cord or an electrical outlet malfunctions, the front desk staff must be ready to meet the guest's needs. The front office manager should establish standard operating procedures for the front office employees to contact maintenance, housekeeping, marketing and sales, or the food and beverage department to meet other common requests. Knowing how to use a small tool kit, adapters, adhesive materials, extra table covers, or window cleaner will help the guest and will save the time involved in tracking down the salesperson in charge.

Housekeeping Department

Housekeeping and the front office communicate with each other about housekeeping room status, the report on the availability of the rooms for immediate guest occupancy. Housekeeping room status can be described in the following communication terms:

- Available Clean, or Ready—room is ready to be occupied
- Occupied—guest or guests are already occupying a room
- Stay over—guest will not be checking out of a room on the current day
- Dirty or On-Change—guest has checked out of the room, but the housekeeping staff has not released the room for occupancy
- Out-of-Order—room is not available for occupancy because of a mechanical malfunction Housekeeping and the front office also communicate on the details of potential house keeping count (a report of the number of guests registered in the hotel), security concerns, and requests for amenities (personal toiletry items such as shampoo, toothpaste, mouthwash, and electrical equipment). These issues are of immediate concern to the guest as well as to supervisors in the hotel.

Reporting of room status is handled on a face-to-face basis in a hotel that does not use a property management system (PMS). The bihourly or hourly visits of the house- keeper to the front desk clerk are a familiar scene in such a hotel. The official reporting of room status at the end of the day is accomplished with a housekeeper's room report—a report prepared by the housekeeper that lists the guest room occupancy status as vacant, occupied, or out-of-order. Sometimes even regular reporting of room status is not adequate, as guests may be anxiously awaiting the opportunity to occupy a room. On these occasions, the front desk clerk will have to telephone the floor supervisor to determine when the servicing of a room will be completed. The housekeeper relies on the room sales projections—a weekly report prepared and distributed by the front office manager that indicates the number of departures, arrivals, walk-ins, stopovers, and no-shows—to schedule employees. Timely distribution of the room sales projections assists the executive housekeeper in planning employee personal leaves and vacation days.

The front desk also relies on housekeeping personnel to report any unusual circumstances that may indicate a violation of security for the guests. For example, if a maid or houseman notices obviously no registered guests on a floor, a .re exit that has been propped open, or sounds of a domestic disturbance in a guest room, he or she must report these potential security violations to the front office. The front office staff, in turn, will relay the problem to the proper in-house or civil authority. The front office manager may want to direct the front desk clerks and switchboard operators to call floor supervisors on a regular basis to check activity on the guest doors.

Guest requests for additional or special amenities and guest room supplies may be initiated at the front desk. The prompt relay of requests for extra blankets, towels, soap, and shampoo to housekeeping is essential. This is hospitality at its best.

References

Beck, C. E. *Managerial communication: bridging theory and practice,* Upper Saddle River, NJ: Prentice Hall, 1999.

Bovee, C. L. & Thill, J. V., *Business communication today,* 5th ed., Upper Saddle River, NJ: Prentice Hall, 1998.

Clark, Mona. *Interpersonal Skills for Hospitality Managers.* London: Chapman Hill, 1995.

Dietsch, R., Ericson "Hotel Communication System", Review No. 1, pp. 51-58. Dec., 1984.

Krizan, A. C. Merrier, P., Jones, C. L., & Harcourt, J., *Business communication,* Cincinnati: South-Western,

Locker, K. 0., *Business and administrative communication,* 3rd ed. Chicago: Irwin, 1995.

7

Financial Management in Hotels

All hoteliers will need to have a good grasp of the financial aspects of running a hotel. Not many people enjoy bookkeeping, form filling and dealing with complicated numbers. So for the new hotelier the first step is to meet with your accountant as soon as possible after you begin your new hotel business. You will need to ensure that any data you are collecting on a regular basis is the correct data and is collected efficiently (so that your accountancy bill remains reasonable). The more complicated your financial situation at the end of the fiscal year that more work your accountant will have to do and the higher his charge will be. Therefore by putting in place practical financial controls from day one you will have a good understanding throughout the year regarding your cash flow, profitability and tax liabilities. It's common sense to get your accountants to also do your personal tax return (as this return will be heavily linked to your financial accounts and bookkeeping records). For instance any drawings from petty cash must be accounted for, while any income drawn must be highlighted in the profit and loss account and included in your personal tax calculation. Using just one accountant will have the added advantage of minimising your overall tax burden as your accountant will be up to view the bigger picture with all the information to hand. Using two accountancy firms or two separate individuals creates unnecessary duplication, confusion, uncertainty and doubt which will inevitably lead to a higher accountancy bill at the end of the year. So it's essential you get off on the right foot and seek professional tax advice and practical advice on what you need to be doing throughout the year.

Most hotel businesses will have to deal with Value Added Tax once their turnover reaches £61,000. This threshold may change at the end of each year during the budget (according to government policy). Once your hotel business becomes VAT registered your bookkeeping must be completely accurate and up-to-date as you may be liable for financial penalties for failing to declare your VAT return at the end of each quarter. The basic formula for calculating VAT is relatively straightforward to calculate. The output tax is that which is received from your paying hotel guests. The input tax is monies linked to paying out operating expenses (such as trade hotel suppliers). The difference between the two (where your output tax exceeds your input tax) is the amount of VAT paid at the end of the period. Likewise if the input tax is greater than the output tax you can claim back the difference from the VAT man. Be aware that there are different rates of VAT for different product groups and there are also different rules which applied to different geographic areas of the world. You should consult the Inland Revenue and your accountant regarding your bookkeeping process to ensure that all of your invoices and receipts have legally identifiable amounts associated with them.

The main measure of profitability at the end of the year is your profit and loss account. Normally this is generated by your accountant based on all of the bookkeeping activities and receipts. Either you have organized these papers or alternatively you have employed your accountant to do your bookkeeping for you. Your accountant will compare your bank statements for the hotel with all of your bookkeeping records and VAT returns and quiz you on any unidentifiable items of revenue or expense. In simple terms the profit and loss account will formally show the amount of hotel guest revenue received during your annual fiscal period minus all of your allowable expenses to calculate a gross profit figure. Any banking interest is then deducted along with a calculation of corporation tax based on the amount of gross profit to get to a final net profit (out of which shareholder dividends may be allocated). The rates of corporation tax may change every year in line with budget announcements.

By classifying the huge range of expenses into logical categories your piles of receipts and bank statements suddenly become meaningful. Only by organizing a set of accounts can sales and costs become understood and therefore controlled in the future. When running a hotel there are huge range of expense items including advertising, repairs and maintenance, cleaning supplies, hotel insurance, heat and light, food, wages, items, telephone, and stationery. It is recommended that you have a formal system to record all expenses in your hotel business such as a computer software programme (such as Quickbooks, Dosh and Clearly business), ledger system or just a simple accounts book for smaller hotels or bed and breakfasts. Hotels are obviously busy places with lots of cash purchases of sometimes incremental amounts as well as credit card bookings from guests. Time should be allocated in the evening to document all of the day's takings into your system of record keeping. Failure to keep accurate records will inevitably lead to human error, (as receipts get mislaid of not entered) which would provide a nasty surprise to your end of year profit forecast.

Every penny of guests spending must be accounted for no matter how large or small. By entering all items of revenue and expense on a daily basis into some type of system it provides a central record upon which your bank statement can be reconciled. These receipts and records must be stored for at least seven years in case the Inland Revenue decides to undertake an audit to check on the reliability of previous tax returns and current accounting processes.

Your profit and loss account will also become a useful management tool as it will provide a comparative analysis to see how efficiently you are controlling your cost base. Likewise it can be used to check if you are doing a good job of marketing your hotel to attract guests to maximise your occupancy rate. For instance you may agree with your accountant to separate out sales by rooms, food sales, alcoholic beverages sales and room extras. This will help identify areas where margins are under pressure or where opportunities exist to cut costs. Your accountant will also be able to help you break down the average profitability per room and also per person. It is common to use percentages to identify each expense line-item against others to help identify trends over years. Your profit and loss account will also show your break even point once you have understood more fully your fixed and variable operating expenses. Most hoteliers will have an understanding of the occupancy rate required to break even and the rates at which those rooms must be charged out over a given period. Given that many hotels are highly seasonal, plotting cash flow over a 12 month period also becomes critical.

To account for any petty cash withdrawals from your hotel business, a simple petty cash record log book should be completed at the end of each day outlining the date, the supplier, the amount and the outstanding decreasing balance withdrawn. In other words payment of small suppliers for nominal amounts deducted from the overall petty cash withdrawn. Receipts will need to kept to prove the expense was wholly incurred by the business and is allowable under tax rules.

The balance sheet is the other main statutory document that needs to be submitted in your annual return. It summarises all of your assets and liabilities of your hotel business at a given point in time and is ordinarily produced by your accountant. Hotel investors will look closely at your balance sheet to understand any outstanding liabilities (such any outstanding business loans, supplier trade creditors and any liquid assets which could be sold off in the event of a resale or liquidation). One area of confusion most hotel owners experience is how to account for depreciation of assets. Your accountant will explain the latest Inland Revenue guidelines regarding the amount which fixed assets can be depreciated (such as kitchen machinery, computers and so on). Depreciation has the impact of reducing profitability and hence corporation tax liability. However large investments in new plant and machinery clearly involves obtaining business loans or utilising the greater investment during the hotel purchase process. The other area of confusion is the value of goodwill. Goodwill is an intangible asset and it does not appear on the balance sheet. Yet if you ever decide to sell your hotel business you'll overall hotel reputation as quality provider of hotel accommodation in a local area is paramount in charging a premium for your business.

Another important aspect of running a hotel finances is proper budgeting and forecasting. A sales forecast should be both realistic and achievable. While your and operating expense forecast should not degrade the high quality of service you aim to provide your guests via planned excessive cost cutting. Ideally your budget should be calculated on a week by week basis in order to identify guest spending and seasonal trend patterns as actual figures accumulate. For instance your sales forecast budget should identify a number of rooms you have by their respective room rates by week. A simple spreadsheet would allow adjustments based on best and worst case scenarios of occupancy levels throughout the year. By looking at previous years, the actual room occupancy rates are a good basis for future budgeting. On top of a line item for room revenues you should add on sales from dinners and drinks. You will soon understand from your actual figures the proportion of guests that will also order dinner and drinks. By analysing seasonal trends you can identify where you need to improve your sales figures. Consequently by offering promotional deals in your hotel marketing literature you can hope to plug the gap.

There are specific types of bank charges for various types of transactions which you need to be aware of the hotel owner. These may include charges every time a cheque is paid in, cash is paid out, supplier direct debits, written cheques, automatic paying ins and an authorised and unauthorised overdrafts. Keep a close eye on the volume and types of transactions your hotel has to process in order to build up a picture of the overall bank charges.

Hotel Revenue Management

In today's environment revenue management is most often recognized as the central place for the practices and processes of hotel operations. It is such an integral part of a hotel, that in many cases it dictates the processes, procedures, interactions and responsibilities that support the maximization of hotel revenues. Most hotel companies today have one or more resources dedicated to the management of hotel revenues. These resources often include regional and corporate revenue directors and/or an assistant to the revenue director on the local level.

Today's practice of revenue management is commonly focused on day-to-day responsibilities which include the fundamentals of revenue management – forecasting, unconstrained demand assessment, inventory management, displacement analysis and distribution strategies such as channel management. Hotels commonly take a narrow view of revenue management that includes one point in time and focuses mainly on room revenue.

In the past, customer relationship management (CRM) and revenue management were not considered to be a good mix. That perspective is beginning to change as hoteliers now understand the benefits of looking at all the revenue earned throughout the guest's entire stay and including all outlets; not just room revenue. Many of the traditional pricing models are no longer relevant in the marketplace. Many of those models were based on setting an artificial "ceiling" on how high the rate could go.

Today, distribution and revenue management must incorporate strategies and elements of each into the other. However, it is often the case that revenue directors do not know all costs associated with distribution or how to calculate these costs. Worse yet, the focus is often on the cost of the channel and gives no consideration to the yields through each channel, such as guest spend on ancillary service offerings that flow through that channel.

Furthermore, hotels do not always have a plan for how they will maximize their desired segmentation via selling in the appropriate distribution channels. Hoteliers are recognizing that market segments as they are currently defined are becoming less and less meaningful due to the blurring lines of segmentation. Perhaps the time has come for the industry to redefine the rules of segmentation to allow for better classification of guests?

One thought is to segment by booking conditions. For example, someone booking through an opaque channel may be traveling for business or for leisure. But their willingness to accept the strict booking terms makes them a unique group of guests compared to other guests who do not want to make any prepayment and want a last minute change-and-cancellation option.

Moving forward revenue management is well positioned to expand and make innovative contributions in several areas.

One area that is gaining popularity is the concept of one-to-one revenue management. A future vision of revenue management is to attempt to identify the guest or client that would bring in the most revenue.

Hoteliers have been collecting information on customers for years in hopes of improving customer relationship management. A better understanding of our customers will allow us to better segment our customers. Customer segmentation will contribute to getting us closer to the ability to do one-on-one marketing and revenue management. This information allows input into consumer choice models, which will in turn allow prices to be set based on estimates of demand elasticity and buying propensity by customer segment.

For the resort, gaming and ultra-luxury market, the focus on the total revenue a guest can contribute has been the desired measurement for many years. In those environments, often the focus is not on room revenue but rather on other sources of revenue such as casino, spa, food and beverage, golf and other services the hotel offers.

The future of revenue management will include a focus on the revenue per available guest (RevPAG) and CRM. Perhaps the next generation of revenue management systems will create an offer based on the value of each individual customer. This is in contrast with today's singular focus on the room-only biased measure of RevPAR.

Function room yielding is another area that will see more focus in the future. Today, most of the processes to analyze the best group fit and catering opportunities are considered antiquated. A majority of hotels are still using a "big function book" or some variation of an automated function book, to look up the space availability and are maximizing the space, based on the manual rules within the department. The future will ideally offer a sophisticated revenue management system that maximizes the group fit and catering opportunities in much more detail and with a higher level of sophistication.

Displacement has been a very challenging exercise for function room analysis. It is challenging to determine what to negotiate when considering booking a group with a significant lead time, because when compression does hit, it is possible that more money could have been made by waiting and taking the last-minute groups that are willing to pay higher prices. But that requires hotels taking significant risks and gambles.

Because there are fewer statistical data points, it is more difficult to revenue manage function space. Thus the science is more challenging to replicate in a system. Much development is currently being focused in this area by both large hotel companies and revenue management system vendors. It is expected that much improvement will be seen during the next five years.

Analysis of channel cost is yet another area that will become more of a focus. Due to the differing costs for each distribution channel and the difference in buying behaviors of their customers, different revenue streams do not net the same profit. The process will soon shift from revenue management to a more advanced concept of optimizing profits and managing higher yield demand. Furthermore, the cost of acquisition, including sales overhead, will be included more often in the cost of a booking.

Some hotel companies are tracking profit per available room (ProfPAR) for their hotels and others are willing to sacrifice average daily rate (ADR) share (as defined by Smith Travel Research) if the group opportunity generates additional profit through ancillary spend. Therefore, the future of market share reports will need to include ProfPAR measures in order to determine if a property is effective in generating their share of profit.

Additionally, it is predicted that employee reward models will be changed. It is important that the manner in which hotels reward employees be based on the right measurements and that employees be rewarded appropriately. Anyone who has an impact on revenues should be rewarded based on profit optimization. More incentive should be given for need times versus non-need days.

There is room in the future of revenue management for more sophisticated revenue management capabilities as mentioned. However, the industry needs to recognize that there is a gap between the advancement of these opportunities and the technology that exists to support them. The wider the gap, the slower the adoption rate. As the demands in this area continue to grow and evolve, it becomes more apparent that it is not feasible to handle revenue management via human assessment alone. At some point, a computer system needs to be part of the equation. But revenue management will always be both an art and a science – requiring both expert human resource and advanced technological systems to maximize profit.

Evaluatng Revenue Management Systems

In anticipation of implementing a new system or upgrading an existing one, some criteria should be established in order to evaluate the potential ROI of individual Revenue Management Systems and their suitability for the objectives of one hotel or a hotel company. Many companies do this by assembling a team of key staff members from the corporate office and managers of different departments from selected properties. Their mission is to develop a framework for identifying the key functionalities expected from a Revenue Management System and a blueprint for implementing it. This gives each property and department a role in defining the objectives and expectations of the system and so should encourage buy-in from all of those that the system will impact. Some of those evaluation criteria are:

— *Who needs to know what and why?* In other words, what does each department want to see in terms of reports and other pertinent data in order to make decisions? What is the minimum required by each department and what is the optimal requirement?

— *The Current Revenue Management System.* If you currently have a revenue management system, why are you considering replacing it? Is it all of the system that you want replaced or are there certain functionalities that you would like to "add" to it? Is it more cost effective to start from "ground zero" or to purchase "add ons?"

— *Channel Management.* Most systems do this adequately. How sophisticated a system you require is dependent upon the complexity of your business mix. Will the system allow you to evaluate different channels revenue streams or are all of them dropped into the same basket?

— *Managing Multiple Revenue Sources.* How well does the system manage and evaluate revenue from unique revenue sources? For example, a property with a water park in addition to the usual hotel revenue sources needs to be able to manage the park's revenues effectively and evaluate business that maximizes revenue to all departments. A property with a popular spa needs to evaluate how the revenues of both are interrelated and manage both the inventory of rooms and spa services.

— *Analyzing and Predicting Customer Behavior.* How will the system incorporate customer behavior into its forecasts? Can it provide reports of customers' decision making timelines by market segment so that Marketing can use it to target campaigns? Will the data enable Customer Relationship Management to catch the repeat guest at the right time with the right offer at the right price?

— *What are the Benefits for Smaller Properties?* Is the system under consideration "scalable" — can some parts of the system be implemented without purchasing more functionality than necessary? Will the benefits deliver an appropriate ROI on the investment? Will the modules of a new system interface with those of the system already in place?

— *Will the Corporate Office Have Access to the Individual Hotels' Systems?* In many companies, the situation exists where the skill sets of the property Revenue Managers vary from hotel to hotel. Will a system "level the playing field" allowing the corporate revenue manager to support those properties whose managers are less proficient?

— *How Will the System Evaluate Group Business?* Many sales people complain that they have been relegated to booking groups only on the weekends and the revenue managers conversely complain that sales only wants to sell "cheap" rooms. How will the system enable the sales department to make good group bookings that satisfy the requirements of the hotel's revenue management strategy and the sales persons' desires to meet their goals? How finely can the system "drill down" the data to enable the decision making process in RFPs and contracts?

— *Can the System Manage Demand within a Geographic "Cluster?"* Some hotel companies have multiple properties within close geographic proximity to each other. Can a revenue management system assist in the redistribution of demand so that all of them can maximize their revenue based on geographic demand?

Integration of Revenue Drivers

Revenue drivers are defined as all areas of revenue generation within the organization. This includes central reservations, property-level reservations, the sales department, the electronic distribution channels and the web site. While franchised properties have a higher level of consistency through the GDS, it still requires monitoring and management at the company or property levels.

At a recent sales seminar, participants expressed frustration that they are largely unaware of, nor are they consulted about the rates that are posted on the electronic distribution channels. One result is a very high attrition rate in meetings and conventions as attendees book their hotel at these lower rates and "fall" off the group block. Another consequence is when the rate posted is lower than what has been negotiated with third-party suppliers such as wholesalers.

A coaching client of mine expressed frustration over his lack of consultation in the development of the new property web site and the rates that are being quoted through the site. First of all, the content was skewed to a specific market segment that was not representative of the core business segment and secondly, the copy changes disrupted the optimization strategy.

Secondly, the rates that were quoted were not at all aligned with the rates being quoted at the property level or through the central reservations agent and many room descriptions were inaccurate. The end result was that not only was this hotel nowhere to be found on the key word searches in the major search engines — a potential disaster for this independent property, but fewer reservations were being made through the site.

Collaboration across all departments that generate revenue is the only way to ensure continuity. This need not be a tedious process of endless meetings. A few things put into place and adjusted periodically, based on market conditions and forecasts, are sufficient:

— *Product/Rate Positioning*: A plan for product/rate positioning is ideally developed as part of the Business/Marketing plan process and includes consideration of the product/rate positioning of the competitive set, group bookings, rate resistance input from reservations and past history. Once the strategy is developed, it then only needs to be adjusted periodically. Don't forget to monitor the franchise yield management system in light of groups or events in previous years that may not be a factor in the present year.

— *Existing and Anticipated Contracts*: These include group contracts, volume contracts with LNRs, wholesalers and any other rate commitments. Just as the sales department makes decisions based on the rate structure, so should consideration be given to any agreements made thorough sales. It is one thing to adjust rates on the web site or distribution channels to drive volume at a slow time but if it undermines the agreements above, it is counter productive.

— *Web Site Presence and Reservations*: Many leisure customers locate the hotel through key word searches on the search engines. Others locate the hotel on the electronic distribution channels then access the hotel's proprietary web site. Still others will pick up the phone after visiting both and call reservations to see if they can cut a better deal. It is essential that the "message" of rate and offering be relatively consistent across all channels to be effective. The rates on the web site need to be adjusted in tandem with the electronic distribution channels and reservations needs to be aware of what's appearing on both.

Another consideration in web site development is the increased use of the site as a sales tool. It becomes the electronic brochure. The sales department's inclusion in its development is essential to the site's secondary role as the electronic brochure. Sales people should be accessing the site with their clients to moderate the virtual tour. If there is a special rate posted that is inconsistent with the rates sales are quoting, it blows them out of the water and appears to the client that the hotel doesn't know what it is doing.

The process of collecting the information is about communication and collaboration and can be accomplished through periodic updates from the revenue drivers to the revenue management team. This swings both ways as revenue management needs to keep the revenue drivers informed of their proposed tactics in order to solicit input and buy in.

The consequence of not doing this is to present an inconsistent message to the public who is in the position of making selections without any direct contact with the property thus depriving the hotel from any opportunity to make adjustments or explain the disconnect. In the consumer's mind, a hotel that can't get its act together to project consistent rates may have the same problem when it comes to servicing them as guests.

Revenue Management and Market Segmentation

The approach of forecasting by segment began in the airline industry - where it is common to forecast the demand for different fare products. Airline fare products are designed with specific market segments in mind. Fare products generally carry restrictions (e.g., Saturday stay over, 14-day advanced purchase) that are designed to limit eligibility to specific targeted market segments. These restrictions, also referred to as "fences," are designed to minimize "slippage" or "dilution" by members of one market segment into a lower-priced product constructed for another, more price-sensitive market segment. With the exception of one advance-purchase rate product offered by Marriott, it is uncommon in the hotel industry to have rates available to the general retail public with rules-based airline style fences.

The common array of hotel rate products includes "retail" rates and "qualified" or "entitlement" rates. Retail rates are those that are available in response to the question, "What rates are available for next Wednesday night?" Whether asked via the telephone or an online booking engine, the retail requestor is distinct from the "entitled" requestor-who is eligible for a specific rate by virtue of employment or membership in a segment, club (e.g., automobile club member), or other affiliation or qualification (e.g., senior citizen).

Advanced Market Segmentation

Rather than forecast by market segment or rate product, the best practice in yield management goes further and forecasts by the value of each rate. For example, if a hotel has five retail rate products, each with single and double occupancy rates, a system should forecast the market's willingness to pay each of those rates.

Indexing to the Competitive Environment

All hotel revenue management systems optimize based on the relationship between forecasted demand and remaining capacity. Some other industries also incorporate competitive data in their calculations. These industries, such as airlines, have reliable access to competitive pricing data. Astute hotels in our industry traditionally "shop" competitors by making telephone inquiries in the guise of reservation requests. With the advent of web-based booking engines, it is possible to "shop" competitors electronically. In some markets this works well. In other markets, web rates are not representative of rates available via other distribution channels.

Nevertheless, whether done electronically or by telephone, hotels do shop one another. Revenue management solutions should provide a mechanism for adjusting rate availability in real time based on the findings of these shopping calls. Competitor pricing can have an effect on both your hotel's demand and on the market's perception of the value of your rates. If available competitive rates for a specific stay pattern are higher than yours, some portion of competitive demand will "spill" and appear as demand for your hotel.

Indifference Rates

Every rate product has an "indifference rate" schema that may vary in large or small amounts from the corresponding quoted rates. The indifference rate is a measure of the real financial or strategic value of a particular rate. As an example, if your hotel sells a weekend rate of \$159 that includes breakfast, the indifference rate might actually be \$149 for single occupancy and \$139 for double occupancy. These indifference rates reflect the estimated cost of the breakfast at \$10 per person.

It is not uncommon for a hotel to intentionally give an indifference rate that is not based on financial calculations but has an underlying strategic justification. Suppose your hotel is located in a state capitol. The rate product associated with the government segment has a low rate that would often be closed during weekdays in peak demand seasons. Since the government segment exhibits significant demand during the lower-demand season, you decide to intentionally give the government rate product an inflated indifference rate. You justify this in hopes that providing greater availability to your rooms during times of high demand will encourage loyalty that will keep government guests coming when demand is low.

Indifference rates in a yield management system gives you the ability to customize the apparent value of particular rate products for yield management purposes. This is important both to accurately reflect the real financial value of rate products and to assign a strategic value when appropriate.

Yieldability

Yield management systems should support three states of yieldability:

Fully Yieldable: Rates are subject to rate hurdles, rate thresholds, and system generated stay controls.

Non-Yieldable: Rates are not subject to either rate hurdles or TLP-generated stay controls. If there are available rooms, non-yieldable rates can be sold.

Stay Pattern Yieldable: Rates are not subject to rate hurdles but are subject to system generated stay controls. If the top retail rate is open, then any rate designated as Stay Pattern Yieldable remains open-regardless of the prevailing rate hurdle.

The third of these three yieldability statuses allows the hotel to enter into "last room availability" contracts and still yield manage them from a stay pattern standpoint. In other words, when system optimization closes Tuesday one-day stays to allow Tuesday's remaining capacity to support longer stays, last room available rates would also be closed for a Tuesday one-day stay pattern. Therefore, rate products that fall outside the control of other yield management systems can be controlled by stay patterns.

In order to implement this yieldability feature, yield management systems should further refine the rate value forecast into separate forecasts for each rate value by yieldability status. In this way, the systems also optimizes the mix of fully yieldable and stay pattern yieldable demand.

A market segment approach to hotel yield management opens or closes entire segments or rate products at one time. One future vision of hotel revenue management goes even further. It speaks to a day when each guest is a market segment of one and the availability of rates for a requested stay would depend on a guest's past history or forecasted future with the hotel or brand. One can imagine lower room rates being available to guests with a history of dining in the hotel when compared to those that dine out. Similarly, requestors who demonstrate ongoing hotel or brand loyalty might have lower rate requirements than others without such a history.

Role of General Managers in Revenue Management

General Managers have vastly different levels of understanding the revenue management process. In this year of opportunity, what a general manager doesn't know and understand can jump up and bite him or her you know where. If you as a GM fall into the first category or anywhere close, a speedy ramp up on revenue management is critical to your property maximizing the revenue that ultimately becomes the basis for your bonus or incentive.

There is a feeling on the part of many GMs that Revenue Management is simply the old yield management concept repackaged. Yield management is part of it but it is far more complex than that and advances in the discipline are morphing at light speed.

Revenue Management is more complex than ever and changes in the discipline are morphing at light speed. RM not only manages demand during peak periods but also has a huge impact on stimulating demand in shoulder seasons. RM no longer only applies to room revenue but to managing the potential revenue for all profit centers. It enables a smart Customer Relationship Management strategy that has the potential to stimulate demand from the most valuable guests.

The position of the General Manager is one of juggling competing priorities, keeping the department heads from seriously hurting each other and at the same time trying to produce an exceptional guest experience. What's a GM to do to ramp up the Revenue Management IQ? Below are a few areas to test your RM IQ.

— *Understand the Reports.* Your Revenue Manager probably produces a plethora of reports and proudly gives them to you during the Revenue Management meeting. The reports come from various sources including the PMS, the GDS, the various channels and franchise reports. The Revenue Manager has probably designed a few of their own. Stare at them until they begin to make sense, ask for explanations and don't pretend that you understand them when you don't.

— *Daily, Weekly and Monthly Disciplines.* This is key to understanding what your Revenue Manager does all day. There is a set of activities that need to be performed at these intervals. Know what they are – how else can you measure how well the Revenue Manager is executing the RM strategy.

— *Channel Management.* We now refer to channels as all sources of reservations. If you still think this refers only to the Internet travel sites, you need to ramp up. Managing these channels is more than just turning the inventory and rate faucet on and off, it also includes merchant agreements, internet specials, GDS marketing etc, to stimulate demand. This is a critical area for your Revenue Manager.

— *Web Site.* Especially if you are managing an independent hotel or resort, you as a GM need to understand site design, optimization and Internet marketing. This is critical to the success of any independent. Your Revenue Manager should be intimately involved with the design and functionality of the reservation engine on your site.

— *Rate Strategy versus Pricing Strategy.* The rate strategy is where you position your rate structure for the year or fiscal period. The pricing strategy includes closing discounts, rates for 'hot dates' etc., in the short term or within the period covered by the rate strategy.

— *Revenue Management and Customer Relationship Management.* This tends to produce the glazed over 'deer in the headlights' look. The simple explanation is that CRM is about identifying the value of customers, individually or by market segment and then developing relationships with them in order to secure their loyalty or, put simply, repeat business. It can be this simple or much more complex but GMs need to understand what this means and the implications for the future.

The above is a short list of some of the basics that all GMs need to have a grasp of even if their Revenue Manager is supported by a Corporate Revenue Manager – remember it is your hotel's revenue for which you are ultimately responsible and compensated for.

Managing Labour Costs

Due to the magnitude of the expense, labour costs and issues have always consumed a substantial portion of the time and efforts of hotel managers. Now, with news of union contact negotiations, changes to immigration laws, and proposed legislation to increase the minimum wage, hotel managers are on edge.

Several political and economic factors are brewing that may have a strong influence on hotel labour costs.

- Union contract negotiations are under way in several major cities.
- Proposed changes to immigration laws could affect the ability of hotels to find and retain employees.
- Local and state governments are proposing legislation to increase the minimum wage.

Labour costs are comprised of two major components; salaries and wage, and employee benefits. In the past three years, the rise in employee benefits has outpaced the growth in salaries and wages. Employee benefits include items such as payroll taxes, payroll-related insurance, subsidized employee insurances and meals, and retirement plans.

Labour is considered a semi-variable cost. Base staffing levels, plus management salaries, make up the fixed component of labour costs. The majority of jobs in the typical hotel are filled by hourly rate employees, and thus their cost is a direct function of the volume of business. The payroll for these employees is the variable component.

In the hotel industry, lodging facilities are frequently defined by the level of service they provide to their guests. Due to the extensive services and amenities offered at resort and convention hotels, these property types have the highest payroll ratios as a percentage of total expenses.

While managing labour expenses is important, hotel managers are also aware that employees are an integral part of the lodging experience. The interaction between hotel guests and employees has a dramatic impact on the customer experience and the success of the business operation.

The current economic climate in our industry requires that we improve efficiencies in all segments of operations. Labour represents the largest single component of operating expenses – easily comprising up to 50% of a hotel's operations. Understanding labour costs on a daily, weekly and monthly basis would allow you to manage your labour costs and productivity indicators more effectively. However, there are very few tools designed to facilitate labour analysis, with most financial professionals relying on large, cumbersome spreadsheets, which are difficult to manage and prone to error.

priZem International Inc. (pZi) is the hospitality industry's premiere source for financial consulting and technology solutions. Using a comprehensive suite of services and hosted applications, pZi provides clients with the tools necessary to maximize revenues while minimizing costs. pZi has developed *Labour Intelligence*, a labour reporting database for management that offers financial professionals the ability to perform in-depth analysis of labour costs and needs on a daily, weekly and monthly basis. *Labour Intelligence* is a simple tool that also offers in-depth analysis of labour costs as compared to revenues on a daily, weekly and monthly basis. This easy-to-use software will help management administer labour costs as compared to forecast, budget and prior year as well as help manage employee schedules based on service volume and demand. With pZi's intuitive tool, you will be able to assess and revise labour requirements to provide hotel operators with the information they need to shift labour forces and reduce costs quickly and efficiently.

pZi is a hospitality consulting group formed in 1999 to help fill the gaps in financial and technology operations within the hospitality industry. Its *Labour Intelligence, Market Intelligence* and *Budget Intelligence* applications were designed by those same hospitality professionals who have more than 20 years experience each in Finance and Technology within the hospitality industry. By bringing their experience together, they have developed simple, cost effective tools that can help fill those crucial and often unnoticed gaps.

The primary purpose of *Labour Intelligence* is to allow management to generate useful and insightful reports. With pZi's tool, you will be able to:

— Provide corporate management with the ability to evaluate labour cost from one central location.
— Measure current key performance indicators against historical key performance indicators
— Help establish property labour standards
— Export data to any spread sheet or budget programme
— Interface to any time clock

Labour Intelligence provides detailed historical labour data that provides important information needed to:

— Remove the weak link created by the common use of manual, inefficient and error-prone spreadsheets
— Provide hotel operators with the information needed to shift labour forces and reduce costs quickly and effectively

— Allow management to properly determine how associated costs compare to forecast, budget and prior year.

Linking Staffing, Labour and Budgets

Hotel budgets are done every year and all of them address revenues, expenses and labour costs. For many companies, the budget is a one-time a year exercise that focuses on analyzing past costs and projecting future costs. Many organizations use comprehensive spreadsheet models that incorporate basic principles of flex budgeting. In the most successful processes, senior and middle management participate so that all involved understand how the budget was constructed and what the underlying assumptions are.

Once the budget is complete, actual performance is analyzed relative to budget each month. Assumptions are reviewed and questioned, and may even be revised if the results are satisfactory. Unfortunately, too many organizations settle for the annual and periodic reviews. Cost management needs to be a daily and weekly endeavor, especially where labour is concerned.

Reviewing labour costs at the end of the month does not go far enough in helping managers control costs. The process is too dependent on senior management reviewing results and asking middle management to explain what happened. For labour management to be effective, department heads need to receive regular information that helps them plan and critique information. The information system must be designed to operate at both the senior and middle level, giving all involved individuals essential information.

To accomplish this, the budget and labour management processes need to be integrated. The labour standards that drive the budget must be available for weekly planning and analysis. While this approach is common for hotel housekeepers, it's not sufficiently widespread to meet the needs of all departments. Too many labour categories are budgeted as a percent of revenue rather than in either hours per day or hours per unit (or units per hour).

Labour budgets need to be developed using standards that the manager can understand and manage to. Food staffing (kitchens, stewards, servers) should be budgeted based on covers per hour. The department manager needs to be able to manage labour based on covers per hour for the day, week and month. If staffing standards are available in covers per hour but the budget does not use the same approach, there will be discrepancies in performance. And the same is true if the budget includes covers per hour but there's no system in place to help the manager plan and analyze performance using the same measurements.

Certainly, average check (and average unit price) is of concern to all. However, shortfalls in average unit price need a different solution from problems with productivity. A budget (or a labour standard) that does not reflect the different challenges posed by managing revenue and managing costs does not help an organization manage costs effectively.

To effectively manage labour, the tools and system must make staffing standards available for short term planning and analysis. There should be an information system that allows managers to develop a Labour plan based on the forecasts and that tells them how well performance compared to standard daily and weekly. This helps them constantly critique and refine labour use. It also positions them to tell senior management how they're doing rather than, as is so often the case, waiting for senior management to review a report and ask questions.

The same standards should be incorporated into the periodic and annual budgeting. Integrating the processes ensures that middle management is properly positioned to manage performance. This creates an environment in which information is shared and used by all involved to improve performance throughout the year.

Improving Labour Costs

In today's business environment labour is both a key to driving revenue growth and the largest cost item in the operating budget. The average full-service hotel spends between 32 percent and 36 percent of revenue on direct labour. Because labour represents such a large percentage of the cost base at the property level, improving labour efficiency represents a tremendous opportunity for profit improvement. However, it would be a mistake to consider a labour project strictly as a cost reduction opportunity. A plan to manage labour costs should not be about reduction. It should be about establishing a mechanism to continually ensure an organization has the right amount of labour in place to provide the necessary level of service.

More often than not, labour is viewed purely from the cost perspective and often adjustments result in negative impacts on guests, employees and ultimately the shareholder. A more effective approach is to take a strategic view of labour costs to ensure that all aspects of labour management are taken into account. The result is a broader approach that takes into account key areas of impact:

— Guest service levels and guest satisfaction

— Internal service levels

— Employee satisfaction and retention

Understand Objectives. Make sure objectives are determined at the start of the project. These will likely focus on cost reduction expectations, integration of service standards and the impact on employee satisfaction. Organizations need to incorporate a balanced approach and not just focus on the cost aspect in order to generate results that are sustainable.

Executive Sponsorship and Support. It is imperative that executives buy into the objectives and will support the development of the plan. Support and buy-in from operations is especially crucial.

Visibility Is a Necessity. In order to continually manage the improvements made to labour management capabilities, an organization must be able to review labour cost figures on a timely basis and down to a level that is meaningful such as by property, by department, by shift and by labour classification. This will require that a process be developed to gather, analyze and distribute labour cost information in a timely manner.

Make Competition a Factor. Internal benchmarking and comparisons of each property on the basis of defined, comparable labour metrics can be very powerful. Once department heads know that their numbers will be compared with their peers and included in performance measurements, they look for every improvement opportunity available. A key to this is using a balanced set of performance metrics that encompass not only cost but also guest and employee satisfaction.

Skill Assessments and Effective Training. A very important and necessary factor in the effectiveness and efficiency of an organization's labour force will be their mastery of the required skill sets. Identify the competencies that are required for each position at each level. Evaluate employees and design and implement the needed training programmes. The cost of this effort will typically be returned many times over through labour productivity gains. While tighter labour management can be viewed as a negative by employees — it actually is quite the opposite. Employees gain by knowing what is expected of them, avoiding the frustration of performing a job they are not well trained for and by having a schedule they can count on and that suits their needs. Additionally, the better the company is doing financially the more secure the employee is and the better the opportunity to participate in the rewards.

Profits and Profit Margins

An issue developing within the lodging industry is whether or not Profit Per Available Room (ProfPAR) is a better way to measure hotel performance than the well-known Revenue Per Available Room (RevPAR) statistic. Specifically, the main question is – Does RevPAR miss some important economic phenomena that ProfPAR reveals? Arguably, the first steps in gaining insight about the ProfPAR vs. RevPAR debate are to clarify the definition and measurement of profit and to obtain a better understanding of how historical revenue and profit movements differ.

Profit may be defined in many ways to address particular business topics. Operating profit from hotels represents the operating decisions made by an owner, or in many cases the management team employed by the owner. As a result, operating profits show how successful managers have been in generating income from property operations. RevPAR however, only reflects rooms revenue, which is heavily influenced by factors managers cannot control, such as business travel and the general economy.

The following definitions of profit measures are used:

— Operating Profit = Total Revenue – Total Operating Expenses.

Total operating expenses include management fees, insurance, and property taxes, but do not include interest, rent, depreciation & amortization, and capital reserve.

— Operating Profit Margin = Operating Profit/Total Revenue.

The operating profit margin quantifies operating decisions and shows how well managers have produced income from different levels of revenue over time.

— ProfPAR = Operating Profit per Year/Daily Available Rooms per Year.

To provide historical perspective on operating profit, we use three samples from Trends in the Hotel Industry survey, which has been conducted annually for close to 70 years. We examined total revenues, total operating expenses, operating profit, and the operating profit margin for an all-hotel sample, full-service hotels, and limited-service properties. The data in the three samples reflect the average unit-level, dollars per-available room of hotels for which we have 20 years of comprehensive information.

When examining the all-hotels sample, revenues increased over time, with operating expenses logically following due to the variable nature of expenses in the hotel business. However, the gap between revenue and operating expenses is the not constant beginning in the early 1990s. This gap represents operating profit, and the larger and more sustained the gap, the more unit-level managers have controlled operating expenses regardless of total revenue. The profit margin line simply translates the operating profit dollars per available room to the percentage of total revenues that falls to operating profit.

The operating profit margin for all-hotels has trended upward since 1991, and peaked at 32.9% in 2000, meaning that almost 33% of the total revenue of a property went straight to the bottom-line. The 2002 operating profit margin is estimated to be 28.1%, which is higher than the operating profit margin generated in 14 of the 20 years studied. This indicates that while we know RevPAR has been declining at rates not seen over the past 15 years, managers have effectively handled operational expenses.

The sample of full-service hotels shows a similar pattern to that of the all-hotels sample. Revenue increases are followed closely by operating expense increases until the early 1990s, when the gap widens and operating profit increases. The operating profit margin for full-service hotels peaked in 2000 at 30.6% and registered an estimated 25.7% in 2002, one of the more operationally challenging years in the past two decades.

Limited-service hotels also show an increasing operating profit over time as the gap between total revenue and total operating expenses has widened. The operating profit margin for limited-service properties peaked in 1997 at 42.6% and registered an estimated 35.6% in 2002.

High operating profits and profit margins can mean two things: sales are increasing faster than expenses or operating costs are controlled effectively. Based on the data examined by HRG, it appears that both of these explanations apply to the average hotel in each sample. Revenue began to increase in the 1990s and expenses followed at a lower growth rate. However, this discrepancy in revenue and expense growth rates was sustained over a decade, indicating that managers have been effectively controlling costs since the early to mid-1990s.

Solutions to Yield Management

The hotelier plots daily revenues from the past several years, and searches his or her findings for any type of trends. Spikes from the statistical noise produced from seasonality and demand fluctuations are smoothed to determine stable patterns. The patterns are used as a basis for making future projections, which are expected to grow at a steady rate. By comparing the future projections with any deviation from the projections, the amount of deviation, in theory, may be tied to the system. However, this approach fails to account for the impact of new events that happened after the system was installed - new marketing campaigns or the introduction of a web site, for example - which were not done in the past. It still makes it impossible to see what revenue change is due to the system or to other factors.

A process is used to estimate what the unconstrained demand would have been or may have been. The process considers demand "on the books" and, after there is no more hotel capacity, it attempts to figure the amount of demand turned down. With this information in hand, the hotelier speculates that, if he or she accepted the best business mix after the fact, how much revenue would have the property generated. That amount is compared to the actual amount of revenues. This difference or "gap" offers a possible measure for improvement. The "gap" before the system install is weighed against the "gap" after the system installation. The difference perhaps illustrates the system's impact. Simply, this approach only teaches the hotelier how to be wiser after the event, instead of making the best decisions for future booking opportunities. If you made investment decisions, in the stock market, for example, solely after the fact, knowing how prices fluctuated, and realizing when would have been the best time to buy and sell, you still would not enjoy optimum return because the decisions did not factor future volatility and uncertainty. This approach can not separate what the system is doing and what is being affected by changing market conditions and other factors.

In an attempt to estimate the yield management system results, revenues from a period after system installation are compared to a similar period last year prior to installation. To consider the effect of extraneous factors on revenues, the comparison is tracked against any demand fluctuations from a similar hotel (without the yield management system) in the same competitive set, and/or with nearly the same demographics.

Hotels and resorts pride themselves in their uniqueness. So it is impossible to imagine two hotels that would experience identical affects from the extraneous factors, and it is highly unlikely they would share the same pricing strategies directed or the same marketing mixes.

It is vital that the system measurement is conducted in such a manner as to isolate the changes in market conditions and the business environment. One of the first places where this type of system measurement with isolation was attempted was in a controlled environment, using computer simulation.

In this case, a yield management practice with basic demand data is deployed. First, booking decisions from the yield management practice are based on simulated human decisions, which result in bookings accepted and not accepted.

Next, the booking decisions are based on yield management system decisions. Again, bookings are accepted and not accepted.

Accepted bookings from both decision scenarios translate into revenue, and the compared revenues between the two illustrate how the yield management practice may deliver results. However, how can computer simulation understand truly how the humans would have acted? Humans are not efficient at executing on "first come and first served." Even if the measurement shows benefits in a controlled environment, how can the hotelier be assured that there will be benefits in the "real" world.

If demand does increase due to marketing programmes or an improvement in economy after the yield system installation, occupancy will increase, and there will be more sold-out nights. But what if there is no increase in demand compared to last year, while an effective yield management practice is put into place? As a result of the yield management system, it is anticipated that there will be a reduction in the number of turn downs multi-night stays. And the proper overbooking of rooms leads to a decrease in the amount of empty rooms on sold-out nights.

Thus, occupancy will increase through the better yield practice. The scientific measurement approach is the tool with which it can be precisely determined whether the occupancy increased because of the yield management practice or due to marketing programmes or improved economic conditions. It begins by identifying periods where the system does not restrict the hotel or resort in accepting bookings. This starts the process by which a look at what is occurring in the marketplace and in the local economy is gained. Scientific measurement isolates the impact of the marketing programmes and economic factors from the impact of the yield management solution. It shows what room revenue increases can be attributed to the yield management solution.

Leveraging the Real Values

The hospitality industry has historically measured itself with a standard metric used worldwide - revenue-per-available-room (REVPAR). More than simply a way to quantify results, REVPAR reflects our industry's fundamental structure and value proposition based on physical assets (hotel rooms) as the driver of wealth. With the magnitude of change driven by technology, it is now essential to ask is REVPAR still the best measure of performance for a hotel organization, or does it reflect an outmoded view of a hotel's performance horizon? We submit that the latter is the case. Technology is changing every aspect of how we live, work and profit, and it should come as no surprise that technology must also change how the hospitality industry serves customers and measures itself. In short, the "end game" can no longer be REVPAR - revenue measured by the physical asset.

The most profitable hotel organizations of the future will be those that capture an increasing share of the customer's purchasing power - while they are in the hotel, at home or anywhere else in the world. What drives this change is technology, which makes it possible to serve customers in both physical place (the hotel room) and virtual space (anytime and anywhere). The historic measure of hotel performance - REVPAR - must thus give way to a metric that reflects the customer as the more fundamental driver of value in the hospitality industry. Revenue-per-available-customer (REVPAC) does just that.

Today, hotel organizations are no longer constrained by physical location in serving customers. New media and systems technologies offer extraordinary efficiencies in delivering products and services with greater speed, lower cost and improved flexibility. Furthermore, technology offers unprecedented opportunities for innovation in an industry's changing menu of products and services. What does this mean for our industry? We are witnessing a period of major change as the fundamental value proposition of our industry is overturned. Customers - not physical assets - drive wealth in all industries, and the hospitality industry is certainly no exception. Technology deployed in enterprise-wide platforms makes it possible to get closer to customers. It provides tangible benefits as it offers opportunities to increase business value, reduce operational costs and create new opportunities for growth in the industry.

Technology is fundamentally changing the banking industry and has become not merely a way to boost productivity but an important - and profitable -channel for delivering (new and additional) financial services." 'That is just as true for hospitality, as it is in other industries.At stake is technology's impact on customer equity - defined as the degree to which an industry has fully developed relationships with its customers, providing them with more products and services to meet exiting and emerging needs. REVPAC, as a measure of performance, embodies a shift in perspective from an "asset play" based on hotel properties and rooms to a focus on leveraging customer equity for shareholder wealth.

REVPAC casts a spotlight on a number of key questions for the industry on the eve of the 21st century. How can hotel organizations "talk" to customers in a way they have never been spoken to before by the industry? What must companies do to "hear" their customers in new ways, learning how to better represent them and their needs in the market? How can hospitality organizations maximize revenues by making the most of their relationships with customers? Hotel guests are not lust customers who seek room and board, and perhaps a fax machine in the room. They represent a consumer with an array of needs, whose time is Limited and who, in many cases, will respond to diverse products, improved service and convenience.

In the future, the traditional "marketplace" will be greatly expanded to incorporate the virtual environment or "marketspace" - a market context and environment rendered accessible by technology as physical location becomes irrelevant. Understanding the potential of both the marketplace and marketspace sets the stage for delivery of expanded products and services - some traditional, others less so - to customers.

Technology thus plays a key role, both in delivering products and service in virtual space, but also in enhancing the ability to listen and talk with customers in new ways. Sophisticated management information systems allow companies to identify with increasing precision the customer segments and markets that offer the greatest opportunities for growth, given the pace of change in a global economy. A technology platform must incorporate two systems, however, to support the hospitality industry's potential for improving customer equity. Customer reservations systems track *when* and *where* customers are going, and *what* they will do when they get there. Customer information systems track *who* the customers are, *what* they purchase, and *how* they live and work. Hospitality companies already use reservation systems to get customers into the hotel. Information systems generate customer profiles based on tracking consumption patterns in the process defining a diverse range of wants and needs.

This poses a number of challenges. Certainly, it will be important to integrate data generated at the property level with reservations systems and customer information in a total system solution that provides for data warehouses and networked communications. In such a system, customer information is captured from a variety of sources, and becomes the platform for the highly focused marketing and product development strategies of the future.

The hospitality in the industry will thus require two types of infrastructure to do business - real estate and technology - to support a shirt from depending on "place" to a reliance on "space" to fully meet customer needs. This follows a four-stage evolution currently taking place in industries across the board.

The hospitality industry, for example, historically focused on developing major physical assets, with an almost exclusive orientation to financing and building individual properties. At this first stage, companies achieved relatively low customer equity, providing a narrow band of products and services, traditional to the hospitality industry, at various physical locations. As the industry matured, it differentiated itself to meet more diverse customer needs with properties matched to the various market niches. In this second stage, business hotels and all-suite properties are examples of such differentiation. A third stage involves serving customers in ways that do not require a physical address at all, including telephone marketing and catalog sales. And in the fourth state - the age of electronic commerce - the "real estate" is actually owned by the consumers themselves in the form of a personal computer located on a desktop, eliminating the need for many types of businesses to own significant physical assets in order to create wealth.

At each of these stages, the potential for customer equity rises with increased access to customers, regardless of their physical location, while the costs associated with fixed-assets (real estate) declines. The evolutionary track moves from exclusive reliance on major assets to combinations of physical assets and technology in reaching customers. Indeed, new media and systems technologies can be designed to give hotel organizations greatly enhanced access to larger numbers of customers - regardless of physical location. These technology platforms also spawn rapid innovation in products and services, combined with improved speed to market. The result enhanced business valuation and higher stock prices as a company's strategic, technological and financial architectures are aligned to generate customer equity.

Hospitality companies can dramatically improve the valuation of their companies by using new technology to bring them closer to their customers. This is particularly the case with major companies that have not fully served their large customer bases and have good potential to build customer equity. In many cases these organizations are our industry's major franchisors, whose goals are typically to sign up new franchisees and improve the yields from each property. In a nutshell, these companies are using franchising as a growth vehicle and their orientation is to maximizing fee income.

For these organizations, an intermediate performance measure might be described as revenue-per-available-franchisee (REVPAF). The challenge here will be to develop ways to reach the primary customer (hotel guest) directly, rather than simply through the franchisee organizations - with the end game being improved REVPAC. The typical franchisor catches the primary customer in its reservation system, but typically doesn't "speak" to that customer again, either during the guest stay or after leaving the hotel property. Franchisors will benefit as they begin to develop the strategies and systems allowing them direct access to the primary customers, with a goal of increasing REVPAC.

Value Volatility

When we think of the term "value" of a hotel we traditionally think of "appraised or market" value. It is important to keep in mind, however, that there are different approaches to appraisal value i.e. the replacement cost, comparable sales and the capitalization of income or discounted cash flow approach to value. And in today's environment, these different approaches can potentially yield very different "values" depending upon the particular situation and certain key assumptions.

In addition to "appraised" value, there are also the concepts of "Highest and Best Use" Value ", "NAV or Net Asset Value", "Assessed Value",

"Investment Value" and "Liquidation value" that potentially need to be understood and reconciled as well.

Hotel values can fluctuate due to many factors including the following:

— Changes in the net income generated from the hotel
— changes in the value of underlying real estate
— changes in investment risk versus return expectations (cap rates / discount factors) and/or
— changes in the availability/cost of capital.

And it is very important to understand how each of these factors alone and in combination potentially impact the value of a particular hotel.

While there are potential "sellers" and clearly also potential "buyers" for hotels, during these past several months there have been very few transactions. And this is due primarily to a significant gap between what buyers are willing to pay for a hotel and what sellers are willing to sell a hotel for, or often referred to as "ask" versus "bid" terms.

Many are asking why the reluctance of sellers to sell and what is different about today versus 10 years ago when many hotels ended up selling at deeply discounted prices.

There are two circumstances in particular which have changed dramatically which are influencing today's buy and sell decisions. One is the ability of the industry to absorb cash flow shortfalls and the other is alternative investment performance.

Ability to absorb cash flow shortfalls – today the industry is much better positioned to "weather the cash flow shortfall" storm. In 1990, the worst performance year ever for the hotel industry, the industry reported a loss of $5.4 billion and it was estimated at the time that over 40% of hotels were not covering debt service and as many as 80% of all hotels were generating little or not return on investment. Many hotel owners had no choice but to sell.

Alternative investment performance – ten years ago the hotel industry was reporting negative returns and at the time an investor could potentially earn a higher return from a certificate of deposit investment with minimal or no risk.

Changes in the terms and availability of debt capital can impact the value of a hotel. And changes in cap rates also impact hotel values. In today's environment, however, it is differences in thinking between buyers and sellers about the net income stream for a hotel that appears to account for much of the disconnect in ask vs bid terms and expectations.

— *From the sellers perspective.* During recent months many potential sellers have absorbed significant financial shortfalls from the fallout of the events of September 11th and the economy.

— *And buyers.* In light of recent events are understandably reluctant to pay for or give "value" credit for projected or forecasted improvement in the cash flow performance of a hotel.

Hotels that can demonstrate that they can rebuild business will be able to restore value, hotels expected to face on-going challenges rebuilding business will most likely experience declines or erosion in value.

It is important to keep in mind that individual hotel performance can vary dramatically from the industry as a whole. And as evidenced by recent events even seemingly similar hotels have been impacted very differently depending upon a particular hotels management, location, accessibility and business mix.

Some hotels, in particular ones that have a diversified business mix and that have been able to tap into and maximize opportunities that have emerged from changing demand patters (i.e. changing fly vs drive, domestic vs international, and/or price value demand patterns etc.) have been able to rebuild business already.

The ability for other hotels, i.e. destination hotels in markets highly dependent upon air lift capacity, hotels in markets that are experiencing major declines in city wide base business, hotels that are dependent upon capturing demand and have limited ability to "induce" or generate demand etc.to rebuild business will be much more challenging. More recently and increasingly going forward, we can anticipate that hotel buyers and lenders will place much greater emphasis on the evaluation and underwriting of the underlying business mix/demand generators for a particular hotel in their investment and lending decisions.

VALUE CREATION AND PRESERVATION

A relatively low level of hotel transactions have occurred to date and few properties are available on the market. As a result, it is difficult for many hotel owners, investors or even shareholders to continue to grow their investments through external sources with accretion as a mandate. Strategies for most growth-oriented hotel companies, whether public or private, will need to emphasize income growth from internal methods.

Assess Enhancement Opportunities

Those with ownership interests in hotels must be prepared to develop and encourage their operators to create sustainable income improvement solutions from all of the real estate associated with the hotel. One beneficial tool that should be utilized in maximizing the overall value of a hotel is an exhaustive Value Creation and Preservation Strategy (VCPS). This tool identifies repositioning strategies, non-traditional revenue sources, commercial and/or retail leasing opportunities, excess land use alternatives, potential benefits of capital renovation and brand repositioning, highest-and-best-use analysis and improvements in property tax burden with the overall objective of maximizing the income output of the property.

Branding and Management

The analysis would identify alternative sources for branding and/or management and the value benefits expected from each option. Implementation of the recommendations will work to improve the asset's income producing capability from hotel operations and ultimately its value. It is important to understand that some agreements tied to a hotel could be considered an encumbrance and have an adverse effect on income and value. It is always beneficial to complete a thorough due diligence on all scenarios. This component of the analysis would also benefit the passive investor or owner by having a firm knowledgeable in-management practices monitoring performance.

Physical Evaluation

Another factor that also plays a significant role in the long-term value prospects of a hotel is its physical condition. A deteriorating property will result in lost market share and revenue as guests seek alternative accommodation. Loss of brand affiliation is also a potential detrimental effect of a deteriorating asset. The VCPS would outline the benefits of a continuous property reinvestment plan or complete renovation. It will force hotel operators to be proactive and gauge the physical condition of the competition and fully substantiate recommendations for capital improvements. The feasibility component of a VCPS would identify the potential upside to a capital renovation providing rationale for project financing.

Managing a capital renovation requires significant planning in order to minimize business disruption, reduce the potential for lost income during the renovation and deliver on time and on budget. The VCPS identifies key areas requiring planning and again rationalizes the expenditure by outlining its positive effect on income. The proper development of the renovation plan will address specific areas of expertise including architecture, engineering, legal, and construction and project management. A poorly implemented renovation can result in significant cost overruns, income erosion and destroy the desired investment returns.

Impact of New Supply

The economic life of a hotel can be adversely affected by the addition of new supply. In several cases, there have been new hotels built in markets that do not support development based on the local market operating statistics. However, some hotel developers have realized that the physical condition of the overall hotel stock within a certain market is inferior. These developers believe that a new property will steal market share from each existing hotel and on its own become successful leaving the poorest performers to suffer and possibly close or be converted to an alternative use. It is believed that this trend will continue as hotel franchisors push for brand presence in more markets. By working to develop the VCPS, a hotel owner can anticipate the effects that new supply will have on the value of their asset and devise a proactive strategy that minimizes the effect or reduces the possibility of new supply.

Hotel owners need to keep in mind that the emergence of alternative forms of competition will affect the value of their hotel investments. There has been a significant rise of indirect competition in the form of furnished apartments or condominiums in major markets across Canada. This competitor has taken market share from hotels in the fairly profitable extended stay segment. The real estate in which these businesses operate is typically residential affording these entities a significant tax advantage over hotels. This is a growing industry in many markets and is establishing structure but is not easily tracked. Owners need to monitor this and other forms of non-traditional indirect competition.

Other Components

Many hotels include other components that can have a significant impact on value but are often overlooked. An office or retail piece may be associated with a hotel property. These forms of real estate demand an understanding of local real estate trends in order to positively effect lease negotiations, vacancy rates and potential rental income. If an operator does not possess this expertise, it is difficult to constantly monitor activity in these areas. In addition, a highest-and-best use analysis may indicate that excess land or the overall site location would result in higher market value compared to its current use. The benefits of local market knowledge and real estate expertise can increase rental income and identify site potential to produce property value improvements.

Leasing out Components of the Operation

The opportunity to lease certain operating components within a hotel to a third party is an option that can improve a hotel's income. Some hotels have opted to lease out food and beverage operations, spas, golf courses and parking facilities to operators specializing in these disciplines. The benefit here is that the hotel now generates a more stable cash flow through lease income and the new operator will bring expertise that can improve service and product consistency. Property value can be enhanced with this arrangement since lease income is often more stable than income from operations.

Realty Tax Reduction

A successful property tax appeal can have a positive effect on a hotel's income. Often assessments on hospitality properties include a component of enterprise value. It is key in any assessment appeal to extract the business component from the real estate value. The value of furniture, fixtures and equipment and management skill must be extracted to reveal only the real estate value. Assessment experts will perform research and analysis to achieve the lowest possible assessed value.

This is a specialized area that is best handled by a realty company that offers professional property tax advice. A hotel operating business and its real estate components are closely interwoven. We have witnessed the negative impact that negligence or the mishandling of a hotel asset has on income and value. Regardless of whether you are preparing to refinance your asset, monetize equity, sell assets or boost cash flow it is beneficial to allow a real estate expert who understands the hotel industry develop a VCPS. This tool will address issues affecting a property with the goal of extracting maximum value while the hotel operator focuses on running a successful hotel.

COMPANY VALUATION

The purpose of company valuation is to measure the the "right value" of a business. The valuation of a business provides:

1. Review the performance of a business
2. Communicate to others (such as shareholders, investors, employees and the market) the value of firm's strategies and its results.

There are different methods of measuring the value of a Hotel business.

Equity based Method

The most basic method for a company is based solely on the values recorded in the firm's financial statements (balance sheets; profit and loss statement and cash flow management statements).

This method is based on the assumption the value of the firm is nothing but the sum of its assets, leaving aside the capacity of the company to generate values.

These methods provide for a quick evaluation of a company but presents with two major disadvantages -

— *Obsoleteness* - the information recorded in the financial statements reflects the state of the company at a given past time, thus, operations made by the company form that moment on, are not considered as providing of reducing value of the company. They do not consider company as an ongoing business.

— *Inaccurateness* - these methods are not able to take into consideration, the non-monetary value of managerial know how and company's innovation, as well as the firm's capacity to create value in the future, the required funds to maintain the company running, the market value of the assets and liabilities (as they are recorded at historic value), and the value of money in time. They can also be greatly influenced by the firms accounting policy, such as the use of last in first out (LIFO) or first in first out (FIFO) method for inventory valuation, the amortization of Goodwill, the realization of expenses, and the capitalization of cost.

Accounting-based Valuation

This kind of valuation takes into account the accounting information obtained from the company's balance sheets without performing any kind of adjustments. The value of the company is given by the difference between the total assets and total liabilities.

Corporate value = Total Assets - Total Liabilities

Adjusted Net Assets Valuation

This method tries to fix the historical evaluation method by making the following adjusts to the value of the assets by moving them toward the realization value by.

a. Reduction of non-value assets [AssetsSNV] such as accrued charges and the cost of installation.

b. The inclusion of those intangible assets [Int. assets] that provide for a value in the market, such as right to exercise a leasin

c. The revaluation of fixed assets [AssetsSRV] as was going to be sold.

The value of the firm is than taken by

Corporate value = Adjusted net assets = [AssetsSRV + Int. assets] - [AssetsSNV + Liabilities]

Liquidation-based Method

This valuation approach supposes the termination of business under two different points of view.

— A progressive sale of assets- Where the company is considered to be able to progressively sell its assets, and terminate operation in the far future. Assets are then valued at liquidation value [AssetLV]. Using this method, assets are priced at Lower value than their liquidation value, and some liquidation cost is not considered.

— A forced liquidation of the company- This method provides for the liquidation of assets at the book value, but the liabilities are adjusted to include liquidation related obligations.

Corporate Value = [AssetLV] - (Liabilities)

Intrinsic Value or Usage Value

The most basic one form the buyer's perspective, considers the amount of fund required for rebuild the "company/business" to its current state based on the replacement value of the assets.

Substantial Value

It represents the economic value for the buyer. The value of the company is computed by applying in the following rules.

— All assets are adjusted to their replacement value.

— All leased assets are included.

— All assets not required for operations are included.

Required Capital for Exploitation

This method considers the value of the company to be the value of the assets and funds required for operations. Do a proper SWOT (Strength, Weakness, Opportunity and Threats) of your business and its market and choose the right valuation method. Each method will give different result but a combined analysis of all will for sure give a good valuation result.

Best Practices in Hotel Financial Management

Sound financial management is at the core of any successful business. Of course, having a product or service in high demand, priced attractively for the target market, and delivered in an efficient, customer centric manner doesn't hurt either. But, even with all of the right market demographics, there is no guarantee of success. The most successful hotels, like any other business, rely on fundamental financial management principles to enable them to manage their property profitably.

By following basic accounting principles, hotel owners and managers have the information they need to identify trends before they can have a negative impact on the business. They can reduce expenses, readily accommodate anticipated peak business times, and scale back operations during slow periods. Rather than relying on intuition and reacting to events, successful owners have the financial facts they need on a daily basis to proactively make the right decisions at the right time.

Staying on top of the hotel financials also provides an accurate measurement of management performance in every operational area and gives owners a mechanism to see where they stand against the competition.

The keys to financial success include an annual budget, detailed financial tracking model, ongoing audits, and reporting structure that keep profit and loss information at the manager's fingertips. Financial success is also driven by accountability, making employees and managers responsible for achieving financial goals in their respective functional area. Owners must have in place the personnel capable of dissecting the financial information and acting on it in a timely and proficient manner. Without this information, it is quite possible to have an area of deficient performance that goes unrecognized and creates a drain on profits.

Create an Annual Budget

The annual budget provides the complete financial picture of the property and contains the information needed to measure financial status at any time during the year. Based on past performance and goals for the current year, the budget captures projected expenses and anticipated revenue over a 12 month period. The budget covers every operational area: administration, property expenses, taxes, energy costs, capital equipment, telecommunications, maintenance, supplies, utilities, payroll and marketing. The budget also projects revenue based on expected occupancy and rates and estimates sales quotas for each sales person. Once figures are collected and documented, the budget will tell the story as to whether financial goals can be reached and where and how adjustments can be made to achieve profitability goals.

Build an Operational Tracking Model

With budget in hand, managers need to build a mechanism to easily capture and track expenses and revenue. The financial model can be as simple as a basic spreadsheet that incorporates worksheets covering every area of operations. More sophisticated worksheets will itemize costs in greater detail. For instance, the payroll worksheet will track the hours and rate of supervisors, front desk, night audits, bell service, housekeeping, room attendants, laundry attendants, sales and marketing, and all other executive and support staff. A property maintenance worksheet tracks engineering and maintenance payroll as well as other related expenses from landscaping materials to furniture and fixtures. The energy worksheet tracks monthly expenses for utilities, water and sewer. The revenue worksheet tracks room sales and daily rates. This comprehensive financial model gives managers a complete picture of expenditures and revenue, profit and loss, and financial success.

Compare Actuals Against the Budget

The next part of the financial model is to track spending in each operational area against the budget. Managers now have the information they need to identify areas where they are exceeding expectations or have inconsistencies and areas of concern. Essentially, they have an in-depth understanding of the property's financial status at any point in time. For example, food expenditures may be inconsistent with occupancy rates over a given time frame. Revenue may not be consistent with room bookings. Housekeeping schedules may not be consistent with occupancy rates. All of these issues can have a negative effect on profitability. It is also important to track each sales person's success vs. their quota. Trends can be traced week to week, month to month, and year to year.

Create and Use Reports

From the budget and operations worksheets, standard reports can be created to give managers a high level overview of each area of operations on a daily basis. Well organized reports will tell the whole story and give managers the tools they need to optimize business operations. They can quickly spot daily irregularities, identify short term trends, and anticipate potential long term issues. Reports also provide the tools to determine whether profitability goals will be achieved. In most cases, managers can create their own specific reports customized to their property and goals. In other cases, it may be wise for owners to contract an accounting firm to create the reports. In either case, managers must be appropriately trained to understand use the reports to their advantage.

Accountability

Management needs to be held accountable for financial results, from occupancy, average room rate, rev par, and inventory control to operating expenses. Standard accounting policies, systems, procedures and checks and balances need to be in place in all functional areas. Mini audits should be implemented quarterly and any deviations in the profit and loss statement or daily financial reports need to be reconciled as quickly as possible. With sound accounting and financial systems, each manager will have the tools they need to achieve their financial objectives. New hires should be indoctrinated into this financial culture and training programs put into place where necessary. Every employee should share the values of management.

Adjust to External Variables

With a sound financial management system in place, managers will be able to readily make adjustments to changing market conditions and other external variables outside of their control. For example, rising fuel costs may have a dramatic impact on both operating expenses and revenue, and thus, profitability. With well organized cost and expense worksheets, proactive managers can address this issue and identify areas where expenses can be reduced to account for the rising fuel costs.

Leverage Accurate Financials for Successful Negotiations

It is always important for owners to know the true value of their property. With sound financials, owners can have their property accurately appraised and gain a true understanding of where they stand in the market at any point in time. Key financial information is readily available to enable the owner to explore refinancing opportunities or act upon an opportunity to sell the property. .

Use the Financial Formula to Succeed

Implementation of fundamental accounting principles can make every property a top performer. Every dollar can be accounted for, potential issues identified, and adjustments made quickly and efficiently. Sound business decisions can be made based on financial facts rather than relying on intuition, or worse yet, guesswork. Hiring a property manager with accounting experience, providing training where necessary, or engaging an accounting firm can make the difference between profit and loss with any property.

References

Dicksee, Lawrence Robert. *Hotel accounts.* London: Gee & Co., 1905.

Horwath, Ernest B. and Louis Toth. *Hotel accounting, including departmental control, food costing, and auditing.* New York: The Ronald press company, 1928.

Martyn, Charles. *The financial side of hotel keeping.* New York: The Caterer Pub. Co., 1903.

Hitz, Ralph and National Hotel Management Co. *Standard practice manuals for hotel operation.* New York: Harper, 1936.

8

Ensuring Security in Hotels

Security encompasses areas such as security of the property itself, company assets, employees' and customers' personal belongings and valuables, life security, personal security etc. In all workplaces management stipulates that it is not responsible for valuables and employees personal belongings (their handbags, items kept in the personal lockers, etc.). Yet management must take all possible measures to prevent theft among employees and of employee belongings through its hiring practices and through the implementation of effective management, human resources and operational policies, such as:

- Background checks of selected applicants
- Policies related to employees' entry to, and exit from, the workplace
- Spot checks of locker rooms and lockers
- Effective supervision and control during the work cycle
- Policies related to the discovery of criminal records and wrongdoing among, and by, employees
- Control of people entering and exiting the workplace

With regard to guest valuables, management informs guests that the hotel is not responsible for valuables left in the room, advising them to secure these in safety deposit boxes provided by the hotel. Besides taking care of security issues related to the people they employ (as outlined above), management must undertake some necessary measures, among which:

- Providing "secure" (safety) deposit boxes and areas to keep valuables

- Policies and practices to ensure the security of these boxes and areas
- Management and operational policies regarding the security of guest rooms
- Management and operational policies regarding the security of public areas
- Security policies and practices for the back-of-the-house areas
- Employment and training of security personnel
- Policies and practices to minimize the "presence" and "patronage" of "shady characters" and criminals, verification of registration and check-in personal data and documentation submitted, and curtailing free movement of unknowns on the premises, as well as direct, free flowing communication with local, national and international security authorities)
- Training of staff in guest and valuable security
- Effective supervision and control procedures.

Importance of Security System

The guest, who comes to a particular hotel, comes with an understanding that he and his belongings both will be safe and secure during his stay at the hotel. At the same time it is also quite important that the hotel staff and assets are protected and secure. Hence it is very important to have a proper security system in place to protect staff, guests and physical resources and assets such as equipment, appliances buildings, gardens of the hotel and also the belongings of the guest.

The management must take care that the security and safety systems cover the following areas:

- Guest: Protection from crimes such as murder, abduction and health hazards from outsiders, hotel staff, pests, food poisoning etc.
- Staff: Providing staff lockers, insurances, health schemes, provident funds etc. Protective clothing, shoes, fire fighting drills, supply of clean drinking water use of aqua guards, sanitized wash rooms etc.
- Guest luggage: Secure luggage store rooms and proper equipment such as luggage trolley and bell hop trolley should be provided.
- Hotel Equipments: Lifts, Boilers, Kitchen equipment, furniture fitting and building etc. must be protected and for these the security and safety

should cover up fire safety equipment, bomb threat security system, water floods security system, earthquake security system , safe vault security system etc.

- Protection of raw materials, goods, provisions and groceries etc. for this the security system should cover proper storage and pest control systems, apart from the application of total material management system.

Types of Security

In hotels, three types of security is needed:

1) Physical aspect
2) Security of persons
3) Security of systems

Physical aspect

Physical aspect is divided into two parts: a) Internal b)external

a) Internal security

— Against theft
— Fire safety
— Proper lighting
— Safeguarding assets
— Track unwanted guests

b) External Security

— Proper lighting outside the building
— Proper fencing of the building
— Fecing of pool area to avoid accidents in the night
— Manning of service gates to restrict entry
— Fixing of closed circuit TV cameras

Security aspects of persons

a) Staff

— Effective recruitment and selection
— Identification of staff

— Key control
— Red tag system
— Training
— Locker inspection

b) Guests:

— Check scanty baggage guests·
— Guests suspected of taking away hotel property should be charged according to hotel policy
— Guest room security:
— Provide wide angle door viewer, dead bolt locks, night torch, chains on doors etc
— Employees should be trained to not give any information abount in house guests to outsiders
— While issuing a card key ask for key card if in doubt of the guest.
— House keeping staff should never leave keys expose on unattended carts in corridors

Security Aspects of Systems

— Record of all losses and missing items immediately
— Inventory control should be proper
— Auditing should be done on a regular basis
— Proper system for cash disbursements should be made

The term system implies the operations of the hotel eg: all the equipment used for operation, procedures laid down for operations and policies to be followed. Systems procedures and policies if followed properly shall safeguard the assets and increase life span of equipment as well as avoid any breakdown maintenance

This would mean the following:

— Fix duties and responsibilities: Fix duties of staff members so that they don't interfere with others' work.
— Make surprise checks
— Staff who have access to liquid assets should be made to sign a bond so that in case of theft the concerned person can easily be caught

— Hiring of some independent security company to check the security system of the hotel

Safety Issues

When we take the same hotel as example, it is management's duty to ensure "safety" in several areas, such as:

- The structure itself
- Installations and fixtures (check electrical, plumbing, air-conditioning and other installations)
- Public and work areas (e.g. slippery floors, hazardous obstacles in traffic areas), safety of furniture, equipment, appliances, and utensils.

This is followed by:

- Health safety (nontoxic cleaning material and detergents used)
- Good quality air (what we breathe, dependent upon the type of equipment, installations and fixtures used, and regular repairs and maintenance)
- Food safety (a whole world in itself including sanitation, food quality, food spoilage, correct handling procedures, allowable and recommended temperatures, etc.), and checking and control procedures.

An important "preventive measure" is eliminating the possibility of communicating contagious diseases. Even if local regulations do not require it, it is recommended to send food and beverage handlers for a regular medical checkup. Another preventive measure is the formulation and implementation of policies and procedures related to employee accidents which may present a threat to food sanitation.

Culinary staff who cut themselves accidentally at work, as often happens while slicing food products, have to immediately stop handling food, and report to their Executive Chef and to the person in charge of First Aid in their company (Security or Human Resources Department) for preliminary treatment and handling. Healing and precautionary measures are taken before they are allowed back at their job.

There are also some basic "dress" requirements for staff involved in food and beverage preparations: e.g. Chefs' hats (to prevent hair and whatever hair contains to fall into the food), discreet earrings (non-dangling) or no earrings for women, and long hair neatly and securely tied in a bun at the back of the head.

Of no lesser importance is the safety of work tools and work procedures covering all areas, such as stable ladders, secure shelving, safety shoes, well-fitting work garments, clearly written and complete safety procedures and guidelines from management, safety training, and safety installations and equipment, e.g. fire fighting units, regular maintenance schedules for safety equipment and installations, wider traffic areas (to prevent accidents), adequate staffing, and last but not least, continuous effective training in work procedures. All of this necessitates comprehensive planning, the creation of clear policies and work procedures, organization, implementation, training of supervisors and employees, supervision and control.

Basic Security Elements for Hotel Industry

The basic security elements for hotel industry are: deadbolt locks, viewing devices, chain locks, doors and frames, and communication devices. In some instances, when the risks of crime are known to exist, additional security has been recognised as fundamental under the circumstances. In these cases, courts have often held that the following elements are required as a matter of law: track bars for sliding glass doors, closed circuit television, and security guard personnel.Very often hotel chains have corporate security departments consisting of only a few people. This generally happens not because the company ignores its security needs, but because the security employees are assigned as staff to various corporate facilities. So while dozens or even hundreds of people may have a full-time or part-time security function, the corporate staff is limited. Each facility staff member should have a specifically assigned role to play in the security programme.

From housekeeping and maintenance to front desk and executive management staff, everyone should be trained and encouraged to participate in security programmes. Special areas that require total participation of the staff include: general disorders and bomb threats, fire emergencies, overall surveillance, first aid response, maintenance checks, parking lot patrols, response to calls for assistance, record keeping, eyewitness testimony, and internal security. Whether security personnel are employees of the facility or are provided under a contract with a security service, or even if they are part-time off-duty law enforcement officers, among the things to be considered are the following:

— All personnel should have a copy of, and be familiar with, the security manual.

— All personnel should undergo a competent training programme emphasising those subjects that deal with the institution's security needs.

— All personnel should be readily identifiable as security officers if they are to have public contract.

— All personnel should be issued and trained in the use of appropriate equipment.

— All personnel should be regularly supervised and evaluated with a record maintained of their performance.

— All personnel should undergo a background evaluation, which can reveal suitability for employment in a hotel.

— Contract security personnel should be employed under a contract that sets specific duties and responsibilities for which they can be held accountable.

— All personnel should possess a licence necessary for their employment and for the possession and use of weapons and equipment.

All personnel should receive regular and updated training and testing on their skills and knowledge to their employment.

Thoughtful analysis should be given to the manner in which law enforcement officers are employed. Different regulations of the country govern the employment of police personnel in private security assignments. In addition, civil liberty issues and conflict of interest possibilities may also be considered in the decision to utilise off-duty police. Decisions on these issues should be made with the advice of the counsel.The hotel should employ any technology it acquires to its full capacity. The reason for this is, that by purchasing it, the hotel is both acknowledging the need for the system, and advising the guests that they are under the protection of the equipment in place. In the event of loss or injury, that might have been prevented if the installed equipment had been working to its full capacity, the hotel-owner has more claim to defend against.

Close circuit television can be an effective security tool when installed and used properly. It should be placed in areas with the greatest likelihood of effective use. Generally remote areas, such as parking lots need coverage, because other eyes and ears are not available for security purposes. Electronic door locks are useful to gain better control over room access problems. Maintaining adequate key control has long been a vexing problem.

Mini-safes have become useful because theft from guest-rooms are responsible for the greatest percentage of reported hotel-related crimes Maintaining adequate insurance against claims of negligent security is essential both to defend against claims and to pay damages if awarded.

Not utilising an investment in security equipment can be as bad or worse than not making the investment at all. The development of a clearly defined procedural manual is the backbone of the security programme. The procedures manual not only directs the security effort, but also serves as evidence that security considerations have been carefully and logically thought out. Good lighting is an important crime deterrent and prevention tool.

In an environment of increasing all-round crime, increased crime in hotel-related matters is not a matter of surprise. Hotels in particular are looked at as targets for local criminals, who see a fertile source of victims carrying cash and valuables. It is common to find criminal elements from adjacent neighbourhoods or those who are even willing to travel relatively long distances for the promise of a good haul from unsuspecting victims. Among the leading causes of hotel-related crime are:

— employee dishonesty;
— failure to recognise and respond;
— inadequate maintenance;
— absence of effective security procedures;
— lack of training;
— ignorance and carelessness;
— purchase of inferior hardware and security apparatus; and
— inadequate supervision.

Certain categories of guests require special security consideration because of behaviour-patterns, special needs, cultural differences or other characteristics that cause security problems to develop. These individuals and groups require special attention to ensure that their stays do not result in preventable losses or injuries to themselves or others. Foreign visitors are often victimised by criminals because they are tricked or misled into placing trust in dangerous individuals or bad advice.

Convention guests or large groups are frequently targeted by burglars, prostitutes and con artists because of the ease of penetrating the group and learning about patterns of movement and conduct. Convention groups should receive special reminders about security hazards, should be encouraged to practise stringent requirements concerning the use of deadbolts, chains and peepholes, and encouraged to cooperate with overall hotel rules and security personnel. Women travelling on business now represent 40 per cent of business travellers. These women often travelling alone, and have in recent years become the victims of especially brutal crimes including assault, rape and murder. Care should be given with room assignments, and every effort should be made to place women on notice of foreseeable risks. Airline flight crews, and particularly female members of these crews, have been identified by criminals as targets because the regular patterns of their stay is so easy to identify. Room thefts and personal assaults are higher than average for these crews. Student groups, especially those attending proms or other school functions, often lack adequate supervision to ensure that they conform to rules and procedures. Trade shows, especially catering to industries involved in valuables such as jewellery, furs and electronics, attract thieves from all over the world.

Group tours, because of their scheduled departures and the practice of leaving luggage and purchase in lobbies, storage rooms and unattended guest-rooms, suffer a high incidence of loss. Celebrity guests, especially entertainment groups or sports teams, regularly suffer attempts by fans, curious, and persons with criminal intent, to accost them in public spaces, on sidewalks around the hotel, and even in their rooms. Always make reservations ahead of time and secure them with your credit card. Otherwise, if area facilities are overcrowded, you may find yourself stranded in unfamiliar surroundings or in an unsafe room. If your room is not ready, ask to store your luggage in a locked room.

Many hotels have a "dry room" where you can put your luggage and freshen up. If the hotel has more than one building, request a room in or near the main building. Request a room that faces inward towards other rooms or towards the lobby. Request a room that does not have easy access to the window, such as from the roof or street. Request a room on the second floor, but not higher than the seventh floor, near a fire exit, away from stairwells, elevators, ice machines, basements or garbage/refuse rooms. A room near (but not next to) the elevator helps avoid long walks down stairways. If you have valuables or important documents, e.g., passport or airline ticket, store them in the safety deposit box at the front office and get a receipt. Use a room safe to store only items of moderate value. Large sums of jewellery or money should be placed in the safe at the front desk. If there is no room safe, put valuables in a money belt that you may wear, or bring along a "portable safe". These come in many forms: hollow books, shows with hollow heels, suitcases with hollow compartments, etc. Always use the deadbolt lock when in your room. Always use the chain lock which should be securely fastened to the wall and a solid core door. Windows should open and close easily from the inside. Use the extra lock or stick on windows, sliding or patio doors so that they do not lift out of their tracks.

If someone comes to the door, use the peep hole and ask the visitor to identify himself/herself. Call the front desk to confirm the identity of the visitors, even if they reply they are with room service, janitorial, etc. If you are expecting someone, pre-arrange an exact time of arrival, as well as some form of introduction or identification: a secret knock, business card under the door, or a phone call from the lobby. Completely close the curtains, especially in the evening or if you will be away from the room for sometime. Public announcements are a means to disseminate information about terrorist threats and other relatively short-term and/or transnational conditions posing significant risks to the security of American travellers. They are made any time there is a perceived threat and usually have Americans as a particular target group. In the past, public announcements have been issued to deal with short-term coups, bomb threats to airlines, violence by terrorists and anniversary dates of specific terrorist events.

Hotel Security Programme

Although the risks may be well understood, management lacks the necessary financial resources to implement what the prudent security professional would consider to be an adequate, reasonable security programme. There are none the less certain basic security steps that can be taken with only a modest expenditure of funds. These are:

— manage by walking around;
— screen job applicants, at least those who will be in positions of trust;
— make security a responsibility of all employees;
— work with the local law enforcement;
— communicate with neighbouring businesses; and
— patrol the premises.

Most hotels and motels are concerned with security and have measures in place to prevent crimes against patrons. At the same time, however, hotels and motels continue to be targeted by criminal elements. Security in the lodging environment presents a wide range of challenges if only because the lodging business is in operation every hour of the day, every day of the year.

Inexpensive safeguards can usually be implemented at a budget motel, but the more significant and costly safeguards tend to be put on the back burner. Unfortunately, it is the absence of the significant safeguards that leads to litigation. On the one hand, budget motel management may recognise the need to upgrade security and appreciate the attendant liability risk, but on the other hand, may lack the financial resources to do anything about it. Even with new construction or retrofitting for expansion or other non-security purposes, management may be unable to find enough capital to fund needed security improvements. With the exception of safe deposit boxes at the front desk, which limit a motel's exposure to property loss, no codes or laws require a motel to provide physical security. Courts across the nation have mandated that motels must merely take "reasonable" precautions to protect their guests from physical harm.The public has become more educated concerning personal safety. In an overbuilt lodging market with heavy competition and fewer people travelling, hotel and motel owners are responding to their customers' concerns about personal safety.

Six very fundamental security steps that involve time but little cost can be implemented at the budget motel:

— Managing by walking around (MBWA) involves getting into the trenches and seeing what's going on in the business, and getting close to customers and employees. The really small "Mom and Pop" motels practiced MBWA before Tom Peters put a label on the concept. The larger, multi-unit motel chains are often lacking in this valuable practice. MBWA is a caring attitude that is imparted to employees and guests alike. Many security professionals emphasise having a written policy and programme, and although written materials can be helpful, they cannot engender the caring attitude and genuine concern that must be projected for security to succeed.

— A background investigation that includes contacting prior employers and making criminal records checks should be conducted before employees are hired. This is the second step. This is important because applicants may falsify prior employment information in order to conceal personal defects that make them unsuitable for assignment to high-trust jobs. The value of background checking is apparent at the budget motel where only one or two employees are present in the evening hours. At stake are the care and custody of the motel and its assets, and the protection of the patrons and their valuables. These are awesome responsibilities that cannot be placed into the hands of people about whom little is known.

— Employees need to be involved in security. One way to promote involvement is to make employees aware of security risks, how the risks affect the motel, the staff and the patrons, and what the staff can do to offset risks. The American Hotel & Motel Association offers a series of training video workshops on the basics of lodging security. Workshops cover everything from awareness to handling disturbances. Another consideration is to motivate employees to carry out their security responsibilities, especially with respect to emergency response procedures. Programmes that provide rewards, such as a deserved thank-you from a supervisor, a certificate of appreciation, recognition by co-workers, a day off or a merit bonus, can go a long way to building a security programme. It is not unusual in the lodging industry for an employer to pay for performance as opposed to paying for time spent on the job. The quality and quantity of work, especially work that is central and essential to the business, is recognised as having a higher value than hours spent at the workplace.

— Having a liaison with local law enforcement is crucial to the small property operator. Without adequate police protection, the budget motel is at extreme risk. The property management can contact the local crime prevention unit to identify the criminal threats confronting the motel and to learn what the police and the management can do to improve security at the property. At a minimum, the local management needs to know the nature of the police services that are available, the manner in which those services are performed, and the officers who deliver the services.

— The motel manager needs to communicate with neighbours. The idea is to share information about crime in the neighbourhood and to look out for each other's interests with respect to spotting and reporting suspicious activity. Neighbours can also share details of their successes and failures in setting up countermeasures to local crime. These are the kinds of activities that defend against allegations that the motel management was negligent by not recognising crime risks that can impact its patrons and by not having a security programme at least equal to that of nearby competitors. The motel manager should be active in the local business organizations, especially with organizations that serve the lodging industry. The contacts and information obtained through networking can be invaluable.

— Patrolling of the premises should be done during the hours of darkness and whenever crime presents a threat to property or people. Patrolling can be handled on a proprietary basis by designating in-house employees to perform the patrol or patrolling services can be handled on a contract basis with a security guard company.

Whatever the approach, four considerations are important.

— First, screen the persons to be selected for patrolling. Ensure they are drug-free, psychologically stable, trustworthy, and possess the physical ability to meet the rigours of constant movement in an outdoor environment.

— Second, provide the selected persons with the knowledge and skill to do their jobs effectively. Teach them how to look for the indicators of crime and hazardous conditions, and how to respond when the indicators are present; make sure they understand the limits of their lawful authority; and motivate them to convey an interested and caring attitude in their dealings with people.

— Third, give them the proper tools to carry out their jobs. Distinctive uniforms, inclement weather gear, flashlights, and a means of communication are essential.

— Fourth, give them plenty of supervision and lots of positive guidance.

Unlike other security specialists, the lodging security manager operates in an environment where the protected group is nearly always changing. With the exception of the employees working on the property, the guest population changes nearly everyday. A wide spectrum of society is represented in the guest population; also represented are the problems the guests bring with them. As with any facility security programme, the security manager will develop a loss prevention plan and programme based on the results of a survey. Ideally, although seldom the case, the survey will occur prior to the facility being constructed.

The survey of a hotel is similar to that of a survey for any other facility, except possibly that more attention must be paid to the surrounding area. The foreseeability of crimes is a concept that has great significance at lodging facilities, requiring careful analysis and formulation of effective countermeasures. Lodging operators have been placed on notice by the courts that the owner/operator "may be liable for failure to warn guests and to prevent criminal assault where prior criminal activity in the area should have made the attack on the hotel guest foreseeable to the owner/ operator". Lodging industry professionals are clearly faced with a duty to act to protect guests. The security survey is an element in meeting the duty.

Zone Approach to Hotel Security

In zone approach, the facility, the land it sits on, and the surrounding neighbourhood are compartmented in four zones. Zone 1 is the neighbourhood immediately surrounding the property. Obviously, if the hotel staff is afraid to walk the sidewalk in front of the property after sunset, there is a real problem. While the hotel staff may be aware of crime in the immediate area and may in fact have developed personal strategies for dealing with it, the guests will have no awareness, no warning, and no personal defence mechanisms at hand. A good way for the security manager to begin to appreciate the crime problem is to walk the area during various times of the day and week, and determine first-hand the types of activities occurring on the fringes of the property. A next step for the security manager is to establish working relationships with officers in local, county, and state law enforcement agencies. These may be the supervisors of patrol operations in the neighbourhood, vice squad officers, and robbery and burglary detectives. The security manager can learn from them the types and frequencies of crimes, the criminal methods of operation, and the nature of the criminal threats, e.g., whether the criminals act individually, in small teams, or as large gangs.

The security manager will follow a logical progression from analysis of threat to analysis of vulnerability to formulation of countermeasures. This is also another way of describing how the security manager will construct an overall protective programme. As a small example: in a walk-through of the neighbourhood the security manager observes gang activity (threat); joggers make up a good percentage of the clientele (vulnerability); the security manager asks for increased police patrol presence along the jogging route.

Zone 2 begins at the property boundary and extends to the wall of the first building. In nearly all cases, this area will include parking areas. The swimming pool, tennis courts, and other outdoor recreational facilities might also be in this area. The zone 1 analysis will provide clues to the types of security problems that can be anticipated in zone 2. Other factors requiring consideration are: the perimeter, parking areas, exterior lighting, recreational areas, and the exterior walls of the lodging facility. The security manager should examine the boundaries of the property to determine needs for psychological deterrents and physical barriers. It may be possible to inexpensively create boundaries by linking a natural barrier, such as a stream, with a hedge row, or by installing a short fence that extends from a fence or structure on neighbouring property. Lodging facilities are often constructed amid shrubbery and trees. Although aesthetically pleasing, these offer concealment to criminals who would prey on unsuspecting guests walking on the grounds or moving to and from their vehicles in the parking areas. Parking schemes for guests vary widely in the lodging industry. There is close-in parking, in which the motel guest's vehicle is parked within a few feet of the guest's room, garage parking, valet parking, on-street parking, parking lots in walking distance, and parking lots with shuttles to the facility. Within the limitations imposed by the type and configuration of parking areas, the security manager must set up safeguards that primarily protect the guests and secondarily protect their vehicles.

Good lighting is both a deterrent to crime and an aid in detecting and apprehending criminals. Lighting is a basic security tool that can also be pleasing to the eye; for example, when it is artfully integrated with foliage and water. Security lighting in a parking area is essential. Unfortunately, a parking area is sometimes not lit properly because management wants to avoid projecting an image that the lodging facility is in a high crime area. In open general parking areas it is recommended that between 0.9 footcandles and 0.6 footcandles be maintained on the pavement. Lighting may go as low as 0.2 footcandles when there is a low level of night-time activity. In covered parking facilities, the recommended illumination levels increase to 5 footcandles for general parking and pedestrian areas; 10 footcandles for ramps and corners; and 50 footcandles at entrance areas.

The security manager must consider the routes and means of transportation utilised by guests going to and from outlying recreational areas; the times of utilisation; the types of guests; and the valuables they may be carrying with them. These considerations will aid the security manager in assessing the security risks involved. The nature of the recreational activity is also a consideration. A swimming pool, for example, may be used at all hours of the day or night when it is fenced or inside a locked building/area where entry is controlled, and where some degree of staff attention is given to the safety and security of guests while using the pool. However, if the pool is near an unfenced/unprotected perimeter, the relative security of the using guests may drop to a level that would require either closing the pool during high-risk hours or increasing the protection. Hiking, walking, jogging, and biking on unattended trails present similar risks.

The innermost line of defence in zone 2 is the exterior of the lodging facility. Passage through the walls can be made by guests and trades people at any number of entrances. The control of access through the entrances is typically by lodging staff whose training and experience permit them to discriminate between authorised persons and unwelcome visitors. During late evening hours when traffic into the lodging facility is minimal, many or all of the remote entrances can be secured, requiring persons to enter through one or a few entrances that are under the direct observation of staff. Unwelcome visitors who are able to pass through an entrance unchallenged or by subterfuge would be confronted with the safeguards of zone 3. The term unwelcome visitor is substituted for the term intruder because zones 2 and 3 are essentially public areas. It is not the movement of people through public entrances that is of greatest concern to the security manager—it is the movement of criminals through exterior doors and windows that lead directly into guest rooms or into areas containing the lodging operator's assets.

Zone 3 consists of public space that may include restaurants, lounges, shops, rest rooms, and reading areas. Guest room corridors and fire exit stairwells are technically public but from a practical standpoint the security manager will insist that the lodging staff be alert to suspicious persons in these areas. The main thrust of security with respect to zone 3 is not to keep people out but to exercise subtle controls over human activity inside the zone. Security awareness should be second nature for all employees. It means being aware of the methods that criminals use, being able to spot suspicious persons and activities, and knowing what to do when the indicators are present. An awareness technique that incorporates both courtesy and attentiveness is for staff to greet persons who are on the premises and to offer assistance when it appears they are not sure of their bearings. To the guest, the employee making the greeting is seen as a helpful person; to a criminal looking for the opportunity to commit a crime, the employee is seen as a potential adversary and witness.

Robberies at motels, motor lodges, and hotels occur more frequently than property owners care to admit. The foreseeability issue is strongly connected to robberies because of the potential for injury or death to guests and employees. Data gathered in the zone 1 analysis will indicate the probable nature of the robbery threat. Employees should not be permitted to congregate in the lobby for two reasons. First, an unprofessional image is presented to arriving guests by the appearance of too many employees. Second, the security manager will be concerned that a dishonest employee will have the opportunity to observe guests entering with expensive valuables and act upon this information or pass the information to a confederate. On the latter point, thieves who specialise in victimising lodgers will wait near the registration desk looking for a prospective victim (the "mark") as he or she checks in and hoping to overhear the registration clerk mention the assigned room number. Registration clerks should be trained to simply point to the room number on the registration card when checking guests in.

Zone 4 comprises the guest-rooms within the facility. The guest-room is the traveller's home away from home; a sanctuary from the rest of the world. The major separating point between the sanctuary and outsiders is the guest-room door. The door should be a solid wood or steel door. In most areas, local building codes and/or fire codes will specify doors with a specific fire rating. Hollow core doors should never be used at the entry point to a guest-room. The door should be equipped with at least one viewing port or peep hole. With the recent enactment of the Americans with Disabilities Act (ADA) serious consideration should be given to providing two peep holes in every door: one at a standard height and one at wheelchair level to accommodate guests in wheelchairs. These view ports or peep-holes should provide the guest with a 180-degree view of the corridor outside of the room.

The door lock is another important element. Whenever possible electronic locking systems should be employed that permit a "key/lock change" with every guest's arrival and departure. Electronic locks also make it possible to determine which key card was used to open a door at a particular time. This audit trail feature can aid investigations that involve unauthorised entries to guest rooms. It is not uncommon, however, to find smaller properties continuing to use the standard lock-in-knob arrangement, which is well known for problems associated with key control.

Even the best hardware can be defeated when a key has been stolen or duplicated. The worst thing that can happen is for a master key to be compromised. Professional thieves are always on the lookout for lodging employees who will sell or rent master keys. It is absolutely essential that mechanical locks be changed immediately whenever a key is missing. This includes keys that the guest forgets to turn in. The guest-room should not be sold to another guest until the locks have been changed. Each employee must turn in at the end of the work shift any lodging facility keys. It should be policy that only a responsible manager, such as the general manager, chief engineer, or manager of security, will be permitted to take keys off of the property.

The door should be equipped with a deadbolt with at least a one-inch throw and self-closing hinges that cause the door to swing into a closed-and-locked position. The self-closing feature must be reliable because guests will expect the doors to always and perfectly close behind them; if the feature fails, resulting in a loss or injury to the guest, the management can expect a claim for damages. The sliding glass or patio door often used in resort properties must be capable of resisting forced entry, including the technique of lifting a door panel out of its sliding track. The rule of thumb is to augment the locking capability of a sliding glass door with the use of a secondary device, such as a charley bar.Consideration must also be given to where a guest will store valuables. Nearly all states have some version of an innkeeper's law requiring the lodging operator to provide safe deposit boxes for guests. Consideration should also be given to providing a guest with an in-room safe. The survey should determine why and how often employees enter guest rooms. Entry is usually related to the need to make heating, ventilation, and air conditioning (HVAC), mechanical, and plumbing checks, but includes also the need to determine damage to or theft from rooms.

More important, these checks make it possible to discover if a guest inside a room is ill or injured. The standard practice is to conduct a check of each room in every 24-hour period. Unlike office building security, where the office population is generally stable, the lodging security approach is tailored to address the unique problems of an unstable, ever-changing guest population. In coming to grips with these unique problems, the lodging security professional must take into account the diversity and the changing nature of the clientele. The relatively young lodging guests, those in their 30's and 40's, have different values and expectations than guests who are younger or older. The security manager must be able to balance the need for security, the guest's desire for privacy, and the organization's need to reduce liability and losses.

Structure and Functions of Security Department

A typical department structure consists of the security manager, assistant manager, shift supervisors, and security officers. The structure ideally coincides with the size of the property, which usually is categorised by the number of rooms. In most hotels the department head usually will be called the director or manager. Commonly, the title "Director of Security" is used to denote multiple property responsibility or multi-job function responsibility. He or she reports to a member of senior management—either an operations manager or directly to the managing director. A "Security Manager", on the other hand, is usually responsible for a single property, or else has the primary job function of security and reports to varied levels of management depending on the company. It is very important for the department head to have an assistant who can substitute when the manager is not present and manage the department operationally on a daily basis. A security department will encounter difficulties operating effectively with just a single person in charge. There will always be some situation to which the department head cannot attend, due to the usual limitations of a regular work schedule. A hotel cannot afford to depend on the availability of a single individual. The role of the assistant security manager should be just that—to assist the director/manager by shared job tasks such as scheduling, payroll, training, hiring and firing, and coordinating department meetings. The assistant in most hotels must be capable of working flexible hours and days.

The management structure of a security department should include shift supervisors: individuals designated as being responsible for the officers working a given shift. The supervisor is the vital link between employees and security management. The supervisor represents management's needs and views to the officers and at the same time has the responsibility of representing the needs and views of the officers to management. Without a knowledgeable supervisor available, the staff are left to make decisions in haphazard ways. A lack of structure could lead to an increase in poor decisions. Even if there are no actual supervisory personnel, some system of supervision must be in place.

Little instruction material is available concerning the individual lodging security employee's role, contribution, or importance in the overall security function. It must be remembered that regardless of how knowledgeable security management may be, the line employee's performance is the ultimate measurement of success. The security officer's daily patrolling and presence have a deterrent and prevention effect that must be acknowledged. This is true both for employees and would-be criminals intending to commit a crime.

The size of a security staff required will generally be proportional not only to the number of rooms, but also to size of the facility and the number of employees on the hotel payroll. It also will depend on a number of factors that must all be considered simultaneously. In a pre-existing hotel, it is somewhat easier to determine staffing needs by reviewing the history of problems and guest-related issues addressed by security. If there are records available for review, a workload analysis can be conducted to indicate the types of calls for service and their distribution according to times and days of the week. One rule of thumb that deserves mention concerns the number of staff required to cover a single post around the clock, for three eight-hour shifts. The number is not 3, but 4½ or 5 persons, to allow for days off, vacation, sick time, training and other administrative tasks. Other important factors to be considered include the design of the property and the location of the property relative to both the neighbourhood and the type of setting.

An urban hotel in a high crime district should anticipate overflow problems from the neighbourhood, such as streetwalkers, vagrants, and trespassers. A hotel in a suburban location that is accessed only by motor vehicles and is surrounded by a residential community is less likely to experience the problems of the urban property. Crime rates, economic growth or decline, climate conditions, and the availability of public safety resources such as police, fire, and ambulance services must all be taken into account when planning staff size and distribution.

The level in an organization to which security reports will greatly affect the ability of the department to achieve desired results. Lodging security departments have been known to report to a wide variety of managers, including the managing director, general manager, operations manager, human resources manager, building superintendent, and—perhaps most commonly—the rooms division manager. Ideally, however, the security department should report to the highest level as possible; the operations manager is practical, for example. If the property is operated in such a way that the general manager is accessible to the security manager, then this is the person to whom security should report.

A general manager's schedule is often so busy that it precludes regular accessibility except to a few senior managers. The security manager needs to be able to communicate routinely with the senior manager who oversees the security department.

There are other problems caused by having security report to middle- or lower-level managers or to a manager who represents only one area of the company's operation.

— Each layer of management that security must penetrate to reach the general manager must be acutely and accurately aware of the problems. The more layers of people a manager has to communicate through, the greater the chances of misrepresentation.

— Not everyone in an organization is an advocate for the security and prevention needs of the hotel. It is clearly possible for a middle-level manager who oversees the security department to lack the enthusiasm needed to both advocate for and utilise security successfully.

— In order to maintain a global perspective, it is critical for the security manager to be aware individually of all aspects of the hotel's operation, including sales, accounting, human resources, and so forth.

Some security professionals lack a broad company-wide perspective on the role of security. Their narrow view does not take into consideration how the entire operation is affected by their department. Security solutions must be consistent with the overall operation of the hotel. Closing the general storeroom at night, for example, may reduce losses in inventory, but such a "loss prevention" decision will also have an adverse effect on other departments such as banquet and food and beverages personnel who need items immediately.

Duties of Security Personnel

The most basic function for the security personnel in any hotel is to perform regular patrols of the property, both inside and outside. There are three different types of security patrolling that have been utilised in hotels for decades, yet continue to serve the needs of guests, employees, and the property in general: random routine patrol, lobby patrol, and basic rounds. In random routine patrol, the security officer walks, or in some cases drives, around the property on a random basis to check for irregularities, suspicious circumstances, and intruders. There are two objectives achieved by this type of patrol.

First, any irregularity or suspicious circumstance hopefully will be discovered before a major problem develops. For example, there may be a leaking roof, broken pipes, dark hallways or stairways, and other unsafe conditions that may cause injury to a guest or employee.

The second objective is crime prevention. By patrolling in a randomised fashion, potential assailants or other wrongdoers can be detected or deterred from committing their acts. It is essential that this form of patrol not become too methodical or predictable. The officer should never patrol a site in a fixed schedule or pattern; however, it is critical to have key checkpoints throughout the patrol.

The second form of security patrol commonly employed in a hotel is lobby duty or surveillance. Any area of the hotel open to the general public requires a different type of patrol. The officer who is assigned to a public area, such as the lobby, must stay in one general location for extended periods of time to fulfil his or her duty. There are three benefits or purposes filled by this type of security presence: observance of undesirable persons or behaviour; assisting guests or others; and, deterring crime as a visible presence.

The third and most traditional form of security patrol is the fire watch. It differs from randomised patrol, although both may be accomplished simultaneously. On a fire watch, the officer patrols every floor and section of the building, including locked areas, in hopes of discovering any potential fire hazard, smoke, or actual fire. It is a common practice to utilise some type of watch clock, checklists, or an electronic wand to record what items or areas were checked and at what time. Caution should be taken by security managers to control the keys and discs that are imprinted from this equipment to prevent tampering and destruction. Accurate records should be maintained with the daily log books and incident reports, mostly for insurance purposes but for legal purposes also.

A contemporary version of the watch clock is an electronic device that reads barcodes similar to those used in grocery stores. The officer carries the device, which is about the size of a hand-held calculator, and passes it by a code placed on a tag at the location to be checked. At the end of the shift, the officer can insert the device into a recorder, which will read all rounds made, critical areas missed, and so on, and generate a hardcopy printout. Any of these measures is helpful to enhance the level of watchfulness necessary during late night hours. An important aspect of patrolling for all security personnel is the awareness of arson signs. Arsonists are known to use hotels as avenues for committing theft by setting fire to one location and, while everyone evacuates, stealing the guests' or hotel's property. Other arsonists like to watch people evacuate from buildings and will usually blend in with the crowd watching the scene. The typical arsonist has little concern for a facility's occupants or the firefighting personnel. Arsonists, particularly a professional "torch", will use flammable liquid in quantity. Look for liquid containers that may hold accelerants that can turn a small fire into a major fire in a short time.

One accelerant of which most people are unaware is the basic corrugated cardboard; it will burn intensely. Other items to be noted and acted upon include: dynamite charges connected with primer cord; hydrants or sprinkler valves that have been shut down or have deliberately damaged threads to prevent hose hook-ups; and unusual odours such as gasoline, kerosene, or fuel oil. Documentation is essential to the proper operation of a security department in any environment. Reports usually generated by a hotel security department include incident reports, activity or shift reports, and safety rules violations. Well-written, typed, and accurate record keeping is very important and helpful to the future planning of the hotel in general and of security specifically. A security manager should be able to review the previous year or more of reports and identify patterns of activity that will help direct available resources in the security programme.

Security reports are important as records for insurance or prosecution purposes; they should be thought of as important management tools, not locked away in a storage room or discarded. It is easier to maintain and research incident reports if they are kept chronologically. Caution should be used when storing these records; a fire file safe is recommended. Be sure to check the state statute of limitations for civil action suits and keep all records for the required time, as well as keeping records for specific pending cases until the cases are completely settled; check with your legal department.

Hotels offer a wide variety of services to guests, and like most other businesses they also maintain a lost-and- found department. The number of found items a hotel can accumulate varies with the size of the hotel and the volume of business within the hotel. Property that is turned in to security can potentially belong to a guest, patron, employee, or someone passing by the hotel. For ethical reasons as well as ensuring that all found property is secure, all lost-and- found items should be turned in to the security department daily. The property should be logged in and only given to its rightful owner on request. Lost-and-found sheets are critical, as well as a lost-and-found log book tracking the property chronologically.

References

Cote, Arthur E., *Fire Protection Handbook*, National Fire Protection Association, March 2000.

Crowe, Timothy D., *Crime Prevention Through Environmental Design,* Boston, MA: Butterworth-Heinemann, 1991.

Dalton, Dennis R., *Security Management: Business Strategies for Success,* Boston, MA: Butterworth-Heinemann, 1995.

Fischer, Robert J., *Introduction to Security,* 4th ed. Stoneham, MA: Butterworth Publishers, 1987.

Sennewald, Charles A., *Effective Security Management,* 2nd ed. Stoneham, MA: Butterworth Publishers, 1985.

Bibliography

Beale, Joseph Henry. *The law of innkeepers and hotels: including other public houses, theatres, sleeping cars.* Boston: William J. Nagel, 1906.

Beck, C. E. *Managerial communication: bridging theory and practice,* Upper Saddle River, NJ: Prentice Hall, 1999.

Boni, G. de. *Hotel organization, management and accountancy.* London: Pitman, 1939.

Boomer, Lucius Messenger. *Hotel management; principles and practice.* New York: Harper, 1931.

Bovee, C. L. & Thill, J. V., *Business communication today,* 5th ed., Upper Saddle River, NJ: Prentice Hall, 1998.

Clark, Mona. *Interpersonal Skills for Hospitality Managers.* London: Chapman Hill, 1995.

Cote, Arthur E., *Fire Protection Handbook*, National Fire Protection Association, March 2000.

Crowe, Timothy D., *Crime Prevention Through Environmental Design,* Boston, MA: Butterworth Heinemann, 1991.

Dahl, Crete M. *Housekeeping management & organization for hotels & institutions.* Stamford, Conn.: The Dahls, 1945.

Dalton, Dennis R., *Security Management: Business Strategies for Success,* Boston, MA: ButterworthHeinemann, 1995.

Dicksee, Lawrence Robert. *Hotel accounts.* London: Gee & Co., 1905.

Dietsch, R., Ericson "Hotel Communication System", Review No. 1, pp. 51-58. Dec., 1984.

Eckert, Fred William and Howard L. Dayton. *The hotel lease; a study of the business elements and principles involved in making leases that are equitable to both lessee and lessor.* Chicago: Hotel Monthly Press, 1947.

Fischer, Robert J., *Introduction to Security,* 4th ed. Stoneham, MA: But-terworth Publishers, 1987.

Fisk, Warren Wells. *Evidence of needs of hotel managers in regard to training and education.* 1947.

Gill, Winifred Ethel. *Business affairs for institutional management.* London: Evan.

Hamilton, Francis Frazee. *Hotel front desk management, a treatise on the best methods and procedures in use in small hotels.* Miami, Fla.: Francis Frazee Hamilton, 1947.

Hamilton, W. I. *Promoting new hotels: when does it pay?* New York: Harper, 1930.

Heldenbrand, Howard Van Woert. *Front office psychology.* Chicago: The Hotel monthly press, 1930.

Hitz, Ralph and National Hotel Management Co. *Standard practice manuals for hotel operation.* New York: Harper, 1936.

Holmes, F. H. *Hotel training course.* Chicago: F.H. Holmes, 1937.

Horwath, Ernest B. and Louis Toth. *Hotel accounting, including departmental control, food costing, and auditing.* New York: The Ronald press company, 1928.

Hotel Management Clipping Bureau of Good Ideas. *Hotel Management Clipping Bureau of Good Ideas.* New York: Ahrens Pub. Co., 1931.

Krizan, A. C. Merrier, P., Jones, C. L., & Harcourt, J., *Business communication,* Cincinnati: South-Western,

Locker, K. 0., *Business and administrative communication,* 3rd ed. Chicago: Irwin, 1995

March, C. A. *Building operation and maintenance.* New York: McGraw-Hill, 1950.

Martyn, Charles. *The financial side of hotel keeping.* New York: The Caterer Pub. Co., 1903.

O'Brien, Daniel J. and Charles Bennington Couchman. *Hotel administration, accounts and control.* New York: McGraw-Hill book company inc., 1927.

Rogers, R. Vashon. *The law of hotel life; or, The wrongs and rights of host and guest.* San Francisco.

Salmen, John PS, *Accommodating All Guests: The Americans with Disabil-ities Act and the Lodging Industry,* Washington, DC: The American Hotel & Motel Association, 1992.

Sennewald, Charles A., *Effective Security Management,* 2nd ed. Stone-ham, MA: Butterworth Publishers, 1985.

Tellman, John. *The practical hotel steward.* Chicago: The Hotel monthly, 1913.

Van Hoof, Hubert B. *A Host of Opportunities: An Introduction to Hospitality Management.* Chicago: Irwin, 1996.

Virts, William B. *Purchasing for Hospitality Operations.* East Lansing: Educational Institute of the American Hotel and Motel Association, 1996.

Walker, John R. *Introduction to Hospitality.* Upper Saddle River: Prentice Hall, 1996.

Woods, Robert H. *Quality Leadership and Management in the Hospitality Industry.* East Lansing: Educational Institute of the American Hotel & Motel Association, 1996.